·BROWN· SUGAR

EIGHTY YEARS OF AMERICA'S BLACK FEMALE SUPERSTARS

BROWN SUGAR

BY DONALD BOGLE

A DA CAPO PAPERBACK

Library of Congress Cataloging in Publication Data

Bogle, Donald.
  Brown sugar: eighty years of America's Black female superstars /
by Donald Bogle.
      p.   cm.—(A Da Capo paperback)
  Reprint. Originally published: 1st ed. New York: Harmony Books,
c1980.
  Includes bibliographical references (p.
  ISBN 0-306-80380-1
  1. Afro-American entertainers—Biography. 2. Women entertainers—
United States—Biography. I. Title.
[PN2286.B6   1990]
791′.092′273—dc20   89-25840
[B]   CIP

*Grateful acknowledgment is made to the following for the loan of photographs used
in the book: Lester Glassner, Frank Driggs, Museum of the City of New York, Lincoln Center
(Library of the Performing Arts), and Culver Pictures.*

*Grateful acknowledgment is made to the following for permission to reprint excerpts from
previously published material: Atheneum Publishers, Black Manhattan by James Weldon
Johnson copyright © 1930 by James Weldon Johnson; copyright renewed in 1958 by Mrs.
James Weldon Johnson; Dodd, Mead and Co., Inc.; Black and White Baby by Bobby Short
copyright © 1971 by Bobby Short; Little, Brown and Co. in association with The Atlantic
Monthly Press, Celebrating the Duke & Louis, Bessie, Billie, Bird, Carmen, Miles,
Dizzy & Other Heroes by Ralph J. Gleason copyright © 1975 by the estate of Ralph J.
Gleason, Jane R. Gleason, executrix; The New York Times © 1940/77/78 by The New
York Times; The New Yorker, a passage from "Tables for Two" by Douglas Watt in the
October 30, 1948 issue; The Viking Press, My Lord, What a Morning by Marian Anderson
copyright © 1956 by Marian Anderson; The Viking Press, Paris Was Yesterday by
Janet Flanner copyright 1925–1939 (inclusive) © 1972 by The New Yorker Magazine, Inc.,
copyright 1934, 1935, 1940, copyright © renewed 1962, 1963, 1969 by Janet Flanner.*

Book design by Joan Peckolick

This book is dedicated
to a number of very special
women in my life:
to my mother
to Jacqueline and Roslynne
to Susan and Carol
and
to Marie Dutton Brown
and
to the sensational
Marian-Etoile Watson

photo by Douglas Rossini

Donald Bogle is one of the country's leading experts on blacks in American popular culture. His recently reissued book, *Toms, Coons, Mulattoes, Mammies, & Bucks: An Interpretive History of Blacks in American Films,* won the Theatre Library Association Award as best film book of the year. He is also the author of the recently published *Blacks in American Films and Television: An Illustrated Encyclopedia. Brown Sugar: Eighty Years of America's Black Female Superstars* was turned into a four-part documentary series for PBS. Mr. Bogle wrote the scripts and was an executive producer of the series, which was named one of the best documentaries of the year by the association of American Women in Radio and Television. He lives in Manhattan.

CONTENTS

ACKNOWLEDGMENTS

I would like to extend my gratitude to various people who helped me while I was writing this book. Foremost I thank my first editor, Laura Dearborn, whose comments were always intelligent, sensitive, and encouraging. I would also like to thank my editor, Harriet Bell, as well as the following: David Jackson of the Studio Museum in Harlem; Jerald Silverhardt of Hush Productions; and, of course, the staffs at the Schomburg Collection in Harlem and at the Library of Performing Arts at Lincoln Center. My gratitude is also extended to Bettina Glasgow, Cheryll Greene, Ann Marie Cunningham, Lester Glassner, Alberta Hunter, Gloria Foster, Barney Josephson, Fredi Washington, Vivian Dandridge, Carol Scott Leonard, Susan Peterson, Bobby Short, Catherine Bogle Garcia, Jeanne Moutoussamy Ashe, Monty Arnold, Barbara Reynolds, Herma Ross, Anna Deavere Smith, Eric Poindexter, Ronald Mason, Linda Doll Tarrant, Zeffie Fowler, Robert and Toni Smith, Sarah Orrick, Robert Bogle, Brad Shiley, Frank Driggs, Sheryl Dare, and Elaine Markson. And final special thanks go to David Anthony Stewart, Marian Watson, Henry Ramdess, Arthur Rossi, and dear Sally, who insisted one evening in the mid-seventies that I take her to see Josephine Baker on a return appearance in New York. I balked at first. But, God, did I glow afterward!

D.B.

INTRODUCTION

When I was a kid, I was always fascinated by black entertainers and show business. I spent most of my Saturday afternoons at the local movie house, watching Dorothy Dandridge or Sidney Poitier whenever one of their movies was playing. Or I sat at home propped up in front of the television set watching old movies with Hattie McDaniel and Eddie "Rochester" Anderson. On those Saturdays when there wasn't anything good at the movies or on television, I settled for going with my father to his office. My father was the Advertising Director of the *Philadelphia Tribune*, one of the oldest black newspapers in America. While he was busy working, I would prowl around, almost always finding my way to the newspaper's library where I leafed through back issues of two, three, sometimes five or ten years before. One day I came across a photograph of a woman with a gardenia in her hair. I had never seen a face like hers: open, lush, romantic. The caption referred to her as Lady Day, and the headline over the article read that she had died in New York. There were other photographs tracing a career that began in the 1930s. I was puzzled because, as someone addicted to movies, I didn't know very much about entertainers outside the world of movies and television. When I asked my father who this woman was, he looked at me as if to say "Where have you been all your life?" He said little that day. And I could not understand what the newspaper fuss was all about. But later when my father let me hear a Billie Holiday record, I immediately knew that here indeed was an extraordinary woman. I still had many unanswered questions about exactly who she was and what she had done. Aside from her artistry, what intrigued me most was how a black woman could have become such a national heroine, whose every move was covered by the press. I had never read about such a figure before, and I knew I would learn more about her as time went on. In the *Tribune* library on other Saturdays, I discovered countless other black personalities: Paul Robeson, Fredi Washington, Fletcher Henderson, Ethel Waters, Marian Anderson, Duke Ellington, and Mahalia Jackson. I got caught up in their careers, the moments when they first became successful, the years they peaked as artists, and the periods afterward when they slipped into decline. The old personalities always seemed to have such a great sense of style. Often they were decked out in extravagant, elegant clothes. And the smiles on their faces led me to believe they had found the secret for enjoying life. I was also troubled and haunted by many of their personal difficulties and tragedies. Many of the names and faces I read about were no longer spoken of.

Except for scattered comments in jazz histories, there were no reference books that commented on their experiences, their careers, their images. Even then, I could not understand why no books had been written about the contributions Black Americans had made to popular culture. Perhaps more than any other part of American life, popular culture had consistently been invigorated by black achievements, not only in music but in dance, sports, and films. I knew there were stories that had not yet been told. Billie Holiday's was only one of many.

Years later, when I wrote my first book, *Toms, Coons, Mulattoes, Mammies & Bucks*, I had a chance to tell some of the stories that interested me, those of black performers working in American motion pictures. Afterward, however, I still felt that there was more to say, additional comments to make on other artists. But I was not sure on what I wanted to focus.

More than anything else, what made me decide to write about black female entertainers was an extensive series of lecture tours I began in the fall of 1975. At hundreds of college campuses around the country, I spoke on black film history. I went to all types of schools; many, all white; others, all black; most, fully integrated. During a three-year period I traveled to some forty-two different states and every major American city, as well as towns and communities I had never heard of. What always impressed and sometimes surprised me most were the great number of questions asked about black female entertainers—in movies and out. The questions were endless. How did Josephine Baker's career begin? Why had Baker never been as great a sensation in the States as she was in Europe? Why and when had she first gone abroad? What did Ethel Waters do before she became the prototypical black matriarch in films? Had she ever really been a skinny, slinky vixen called Sweet Mama Stringbean? What was Marian Anderson's People's Concert all about? Why hadn't Dorothy Dandridge made more movies? Who were Bessie Smith and Ma Rainey?

I knew the answers to many questions, but there was much I did not know. I was certain of one thing however: that a diversity of Black American female entertainers were already legendary figures about whom there was great interest. I also knew that there was no book around that told their history and their contributions. Theirs was a complex story too, because it not only involved their careers but touched also on America's attitudes about sex and race.

The college groups' curiosity sparked my own. And I finally decided I wanted to write a book that answered not only their questions but some of my own—the very kind I had privately asked myself as a kid when I first saw Billie Holiday's picture.

It would be impossible to discuss the work of every black female performer, so I decided to concentrate on the important figures—those women who captured the imagination of millions and became bona fide legends. As I worked on the book, I approached each woman individually. Sometimes information on a woman's career was not enough. In some cases (as with Billie Holiday and Dorothy Dandridge), it was important to say something about their private lives and their personalities. In other cases (as with Marian Anderson and Lena Horne), it was important to comment on their public images and personal styles. With all the women, though, I wanted to show the effect they had on the periods in which they performed—and to show, too, how they had dazzled audiences decade after decade.

All in all, the past two years of research and writing have been a hectic, invigorating, trying time, but also greatly challenging and satisfying. All the women covered in this book were off on a quest—to discover who they were through their work. They all had ups and downs. It's been exhilarating to be able to go along with them on that quest again—to see how some stumbled and fell, but how most were always able to pull themselves back up and continue on.

·1900~1920·
BEGINNINGS

In 1900 in a tiny town in Georgia, a black girl, no more than fourteen, stepped onto a stage and looked straight ahead. Her audience quickly gave her the once-over. She was short, fat, and jet black with a mop of unruly, kinky hair. And she was scared because this was her very first public performance. And in an age that judged everything by appearances, she was not even attractive. But when she opened her mouth to sing, well, everything changed for for her and her audience. The little girl grew up to be the woman and the legend that refused to die: Ma Rainey, the mother of the blues, and one of America's first black beauties of wit and style.

Ma Rainey heads a long line of talented and dynamic black women —Bessie Smith, Josephine Baker, Ethel Waters, Fredi Washington, Billie Holiday, Ivie Anderson, Lena Horne, Katherine Dunham, Eartha Kitt, Dorothy Dandridge, Aretha Franklin, Diana Ross, Cicely Tyson, and Donna Summer.

Everyone has been fascinated by these women who stood before us with an array of attitudes and a variety of colors that spanned the chocolate rainbow, everything from honey brown to dark brown to cinnamon-colored to plum purple. With a wink or a nod or a shake of their shoulders or hips, they acted out fantastic stories full of whispers and secrets. They played with myths, created legends, turned the social order topsy-turvy. In the black community these women were known as dark divas—black beauties or sepia sirens. But call them what you will— one thing is certain: From the beginnings of popular culture in twentieth-

Bessie Smith, "Empress of the Blues," the most famous black star of her day.

12

century America to the very present, an impressive lineup of striking black women have dazzled and delighted us with their energy and style. They were incandescent dark ladies who lit up the Great White Way and movie screens, and set nightclubs, cafés, and concert halls aglow with their particular brand of black magic.

We have watched these women on stage and off. And in time their images, their careers, their childhoods, their families, their marriages, their divorces, their tumultuous ups and downs, their private anxieties, and their public poses have seemed a part of our own lives. Often when the divas' troubles have overshadowed their careers, we have watched with an even greater fascination because their lives have told us something about America's attitudes on race and sex.

Almost all the divas have started in the same way.

They have risen from ghettos around the nation. Early in life, they decided to hit the road, to entertain, and to grasp hold of the American Dream itself. No matter what they encountered in their professional or personal lives, they learned early how America viewed its black women.

In the eyes of the white world, the black woman was never thought of as pretty, soft, or sweet. If anything, she was an awkward hag or nag. At best, she was considered little more than a lusty sexual object, to be used, dumped, and forgotten. Or if she were older, then she became a sexless motherly figure, miraculously endowed with certain spiritual powers and the ability to heal all wounds. To paraphrase black writer Zora Neale Hurston, *the black woman was the mule of the world.* Often, too, she represented Mystery, the Other Dark Side of Experience. But she was never accepted simply as herself.

Ada Overton Walker with George Walker (*left*) and Bert Williams.

13

"The essence of cool": Duke Ellington's description of Billie Holiday.

14

America's dark divas have seen all the misconceptions and eventually have laid those misconceptions to waste. All the divas from Josephine Baker to Diana Ross have been determined to prove that the black woman was to be taken seriously. But at the same time, the divas have exuded a cunning sense of self, which has made all of us aware that something else transpired beneath the smile and the fur; that indeed, alluring as they were, they couldn't be taken cheaply. Taking pride in themselves as black women, America's dark divas have demanded respect. And always what they have used to gain that respect—and to entertain so brilliantly and so distinctly—has been their sense of style.

Each diva has perfected a public personality uniquely hers. But as different as Baker, Ethel Waters, Bessie Smith, and Donna Summer have been, all have had uncanny similarities of style that have set them apart from conventional white goddesses.

Diva style has sometimes been part put-on, part come-on, part camp, and part a reflection of an authentic black folk tradition. Haughtiness, control, and energy seemed to govern the style. Extravagance, optimism, and humor were all part of it too. They have always lived by three distinct rules: Dazzle your audience, keep 'em hungry, and don't lose your cool, sister. Their costumes—the colors and fabrics—have sparkled and danced in the night. The repartee between songs has been spicy and naughty, yet used to keep the audience at a distance. And despite their backgrounds, not a one has ever projected the image of the poor, woebegone ghetto girl. Instead, they have been live wires. In the black communities where they grew up, they hadn't been taught to be ashamed of their bodies or of movement. Never had they been taught to fear big emotions. Nor had they been taught to be embarrassed by extravagance and elegance. So they have strolled, strutted, stomped, and sashayed like crazy, attitudinizing all over the place. They have liked showing off, speaking up for their rights, shouting out to the world that they were women born for luxury and that they had no intention of holding back. Each diva has been a champion of rebelliousness and self-assertion. That in itself may be the essential characteristic defining their appeal and the basis of their style. Often we have known a white goddess to wilt and wither on us or sigh and cry. But we have always felt America's dark divas never had time for such foolishness.

Different divas have done different things with that basic style, but all have used it to examine life, sometimes politics, not through blatantly spelled out dogma but

Ethel Waters became famous for her blues and sexy bumps and grinds.

15

through push and pizzazz. And with their style intact, the divas have made their way through various periods, saying different things to us all. In the 1920s we saw the great diva personalities, such stars as Josephine Baker, Bessie Smith, and Ethel Waters, each of whom was genuinely larger than life. In the 1930s we saw divas who were the embodiments of popular myths, such stars as Billie Holiday and Fredi Washington whose smooth, mellow styles comforted Americans during the hard years of the Depression. In the 1940s such new stars as Lena Horne and Hazel Scott emerged as social symbols for a nation torn in two by war. In the 1950s steamy stars such as Dorothy Dandridge and Eartha Kitt became sex symbols for a period hungry for sexy rebelliousness. In the 1960s when politics was very much on the minds of all Americans, Aretha Franklin arose as a transcendent, soulful political symbol. And in the relaxed atmosphere of the 1970s America's dark divas emerged as survivors. No matter what the period, the divas were able to pick up on the temper of the times, to answer the specific needs of their age, and to use their style to make personal statements to us all. That is still true today with a diva such as Donna Summer. And that was certainly true during the earliest days of the twentieth century when America's first dark diva, a country woman named Ma Rainey, decided she wanted to go on the road and sing.

MA RAINEY: OLYMPIAN BLUES GODDESS

Ma Rainey was the woman who popularized the blues in America. She was the woman who had been everywhere, done everything, and seen everybody. She drank hard, lived hard, and fought hard too. She liked her men. And sometimes she liked her women. And she didn't give a good damn what anybody had to say. Life was tough. But she wasn't ready to call it quits. Even in her day, nobody knew what was really true and what wasn't about Ma Rainey. But it was more fun to believe she was wild, tough, and unpredictable because that was the kind of woman she often sang about.

Little is known about her early life. She was born Gertrude Pridgett in 1886, the second of five children of a couple who had recently migrated from Alabama to Columbus, Georgia. She was baptized at the First African Baptist Church, and at age fourteen debuted at the Springer Opera House in a talent show. Four years later, at age eighteen, she upped and married a minstrel show

Lena Horne: the most beautiful of the divas, also the most aloof.

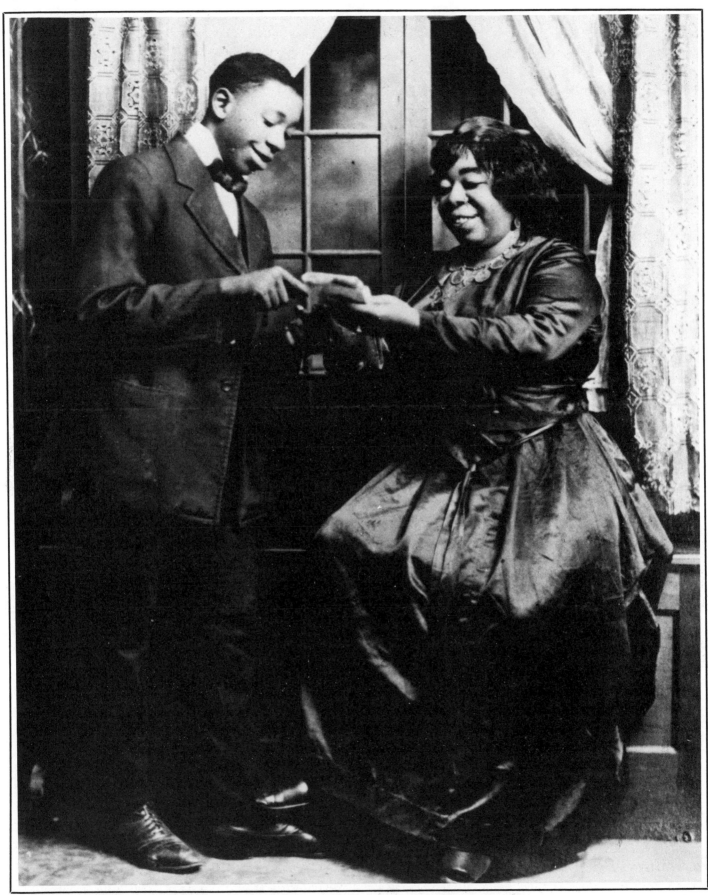

Ma Rainey, "Mother of the Blues," with a troupe member.

manager, Will "Pa" Rainey. Afterward she became the star of his road-show company, The Rabbit Foot Minstrels. Later she worked in Silas Green's Shows and Tolliver's Circus, and for a time she and Pa were billed as "Rainey and Rainey, Assassinators of the Blues."

In her day black entertainers still made their living by traveling from one town to another, appearing in tent shows, theatres, circuses, or whatever was available. They lived out of their trunks and stayed in colored boardinghouses. Sometimes they slept in the open fields. There were countless road companies, all of which were fast moving and hotly competitive. Amid the hustle and bustle, the singers and dancers had to compete not only with one another but with acrobats, jugglers, and sideshow freaks. And there were signs on the roads in small southern towns that read "Nigger! Read and Run! If you don't Read, then Run anyway!" And then there were the audiences: farmers, field hands, factory workers, day laborers, all ready for a raucous, lively down-home-style show. The show was a communal experience, and they

Audiences were suspicious of any woman who called herself an entertainer. Female entertainers were looked upon as not much better than streetwalkers.

didn't hesitate to participate, to reveal their feelings, to shout to a friend, or even eat their dinner while watching a show. "They did what they pleased while you were killing yourself onstage," Ethel Waters once said of the black audiences she encountered during the early days of her road career. But if they liked you, she added, "they were the most appreciative audiences in the world. They'd scream, stomp, and applaud until the building shook."

Usually, audiences were suspicious of any woman who called herself an entertainer because this still was, after all, a man's world. The church looked on female entertainers as not much better than streetwalkers. All the early big stars of black vaudeville and the minstrel shows were men, such as Bert Williams and George Walker. Occasionally, some women had met with success. As far back as 1851, concert performer Elizabeth Taylor Greenfield had performed with the Buffalo Musical Association. Later this gifted singer, who was known as the Black Swan, gave concerts in New York and throughout New England. Eventually, she worked her way to Europe where she was invited to sing at Buckingham Palace. Sissieretta Jones, known as Black Patti, also had made a name for herself and even had her own minstrel show,

Black Patti's Troubadours. Ada Overton Walker had become well known after she worked onstage with her husband George. But these black women were exceptions to the general rule. Ma Rainey's success, however, proved that the world of black vaudeville had to make permanent room for a female headliner.

For most, Ma Rainey best represented the black woman out to glorify herself, dressing up and stepping high, the "average" black woman emerging onstage as the sophisticated, experienced woman of color determined to live high.

She would saunter out onto the stage, loud and rowdy, flashing a wicked killer of a smile. Her very look announced that she was a queen, ready to flaunt her success in a world that had said no such thing was possible. She wore rhinestones and sequined gowns, elaborate headbands and horsehair wigs. Then there were her gold bracelets, her gold fillings in her teeth, her string upon string of necklaces, and, most of all, there were her diamonds—in her hair, on her clothes, around her neck and arms. She strolled, strutted, posed and postured, jammed and whammed, did the whole magnificent snap, crackle, and pop bit. The diamonds and gowns and the push and power of Rainey's personality—her attitudinizing—helped transform a plain Jane into a blues goddess.

Ma's blues, some of which she wrote, were usually classic in form (twelve-bar melody, three-line stanza), burning deeply into the consciousness of her audience. The songs were varied, relaying a range of feelings, gliding easily from hot to cold, heavy to light.

Often her talk was about men, the dirty critters, the lowdown no 'counts. She would caution her sisters to "Trust No Man" and set herself up as an example of what could go wrong, 'cause now here she was, she would sing, drunk as she could be just cause that no good man was tryin' "to make a fool of me."

But she did not stop there. She talked to the men too. In a sly, comic tune "Sleep Talking Blues," Ma crooned that when a papa talked in his sleep, he had better be sure his mama's not awake. Other times she sang "Bo-Weevil Blues" or "Levee Camp Moan." Or she might turn playful with a song like "Prove It on Me Blues," in which she sang of a woman who dresses like a man and then goes out for some fun with the girls. Even today on recordings, you can almost hear the strut in her voice.

And, finally, of course, there was the sad, somber Ma, who sang of the days and nights when nothing seemed to work out, when she was ready to call it quits. Take me to the basement, she sang, 'cause she was as low as she

Josephine Baker, the poor girl from the ghetto who became an international star.

BETTER THAN A CIRCUS

"Shows may come, Shows may go, but the PERPETUAL SUCCESS goes on forever."

VOELCKEL & NOL'AN'S

WORLD FAMOUS INCOMPARABLE

Black Patti
Troubadours

GREATEST COLORED SHOW ON EARTH!

Home Office, 18 East 22nd Street, New York.

R VOELCKEL

JOHN J. NOLAN

THIRTY OF THE MOST TALENTED SINGERS, DANCERS, VAUDEVILLISTS AND REFINED COLORED FUN-MAKERS UNDER THE SUN.

ALL NEW FEATURES, THE VERY INCARNATION OF MIRTH, MELODY, MUSIC AND DARKEY FUN.

BLACK PATTI.
(MME. SISSIERETTA JONES)

Whose marvelous voice and lyric triumphs are unparalleled. The most popular Prima Donna in the world with the people of all nations and all races. Countless millions in every part of civilization have been charmed by her phenomenal voice. H. M. King Edward VII, the Duke of Cambridge, and other members of the Royal Family of England have honored her with their distinguished patronage.

NEW STAR Theatre
107th St and Lexington Ave.
NEW YORK CITY.
CLOSING WEEK of the most successful trans-continental Tournee on record.

Monday Matinee and Week
— EVERY EVENING. —
AFTERNOON
MONDAY, WED. AND SAT.

JUNE 2

15c
25c
35c
50c
75c

GET IN LINE FOR THE
BIG BLACK PATTI
GOLD MEDAL
Champion
Cake Walk Contest

Concert singer Black Patti toured the country with her own troupe.

20

could be. And with a song like "Leavin' This Morning," her voice heavy and weary, she was a woman ready to clear out, fed up with the way life had treated her.

No matter what the mood or tone, Ma Rainey's blues always retained a folksy purity to them that her audience could immediately respond to. Her songs had a religious fervor to them because her audience was made up of churchgoers out for some fun on the sly. Ma could pound out a number like a pious churchgoer testifying before her congregation. In the middle of a song she might cry out, "Lord, Lord, Lord"; other times Ma hummed and ran one word into another or sometimes forgot the words. When the lyrics were brooding or melancholy, Ma would be quiet and reflective. As her recordings now reveal, her basic enthusiasm—her fundamental joy in being able to communicate—always took over during a performance. Her name, Ma (which she started using when she was eighteen), immediately set up a distinct one-on-one communication with the audience.

At the turn of the century America was connected only by the railroads, newspapers, a few telephones, and even fewer automobiles. The traveling black road shows soon became underground railroads of sorts in which information, news, and gossip were disseminated. The position of the black entertainer took on an unexpected significance because he brought messages of hope or despair. Ma Rainey never spoke directly about politics nor did she comment on the war raging in Europe where black boys were sent to fight for other people's freedom. But those audiences listening to songs such as "Leavin' This Morning," "Runaway Blues," and "Black Cat, Hoot Owl Blues" heard stories of a tight, oppressive world that offered nothing but bad luck. If one black cat did not cross her path, Ma sang, then another surely would. She had to run away, she announced; she had to leave this neighborhood. Armed with such material, black performers editorialized, satirized, sometimes prophesized too. Ma Rainey was aware that in this new world of popular entertainment where performer might be prophet, she, as the first black female blues singer anyone had ever heard of, was an oddity, a woman in a man's arena who would have to have a device that would automatically quiet the cynics, that would wipe away doubts and command prompt audience respect. Ma gave her a place in the scheme of things, setting up a clearly defined relationship between her and the audience.

Later, other divas would adopt similar maternal poses. Jackie Mabley became Moms Mabley. The young Ethel Waters was billed as Sweet Mama Stringbean. Even Sophie Tucker, influenced by Waters and Alberta Hunter, was called the Last of the Red Hot Mamas.

Ma Rainey entertained from the turn of the century to the Depression era. In time, she traveled with her own group, the Georgia Jazz Band. The stories about her were often racy, catty, and totally implausible.

Ma was sometimes called the ugliest woman in show business—but never to her face and never when she was performing. Other entertainers watched her, studied her style, and marveled at her rapport with her audience. Mary Lou Williams, who would later become a fine jazz pianist, has never forgotten her childhood excitement upon seeing the great Ma at work. And surely no one was more influenced by Rainey than Bessie Smith. For years it was rumored that Bessie was just a plump, oversized gal up from Tennessee, trying to find her way around in the tent shows and tiny theatres when Ma and Pa Rainey had been so taken with her talent that they kidnapped her.

Years after the two had met, when Bessie was a big star and when Ma's career was almost over, Bessie, arriving in

Ma Rainey found her earthy blues music replaced in popularity by jazz. By 1935 she gave up her career, ran two theatres in Rome, Georgia, and became a churchgoer.

a town where Ma was performing, slipped out to see the older woman's show. That was indeed a rarity because it was well known that Bessie Smith almost never went to see any other performer. But here was the first great link between two important black female stars, each recognizing the other's position, each giving the other her due. Later some divas, such as Waters and Baker (or even Bessie and Waters), might be fiercely competitive or suspicious of each other. But Rainey and Smith's friendship reveals their mutual respect.

As the years passed, Ma Rainey found her earthy blues music replaced in popularity by jazz. By 1935 she gave up her career entirely, ran two theatres she owned in Rome, Georgia, and became a regular churchgoer. When she died in 1939, her death certificate stated that she had been a housekeeper. Ma Rainey had clearly been a phenomenon on the entertainment scene, not only an extraordinary artist but a presence and stylist who had altered the basic nature of the minstrel/vaudeville circuit. Now there was a place for other black women headliners. No road show would be complete without a Mama singing the blues. And in the long run, she set the tone for the fast and furious twenties.

·THE 1920S· PERSONAS

After Ma Rainey had cleared the way and was jolted from her throne, there was a mad rush and scramble to see who would be the next bearer of the crown. And there were countless contenders anxious for the spotlight.

Suddenly, in the twenties, an array of black female entertainers emerged, almost all of whom sang or danced, romped or stomped, or cavorted like crazy in hopes for something they now knew was attainable—stardom.

During the twenties the great diva personas—Bessie Smith, Josephine Baker, Florence Mills, and Ethel Waters—emerged. "Up You Mighty Race," black leader Marcus Garvey announced to the black community of the time. And few seemed to understand his message as well as the divas. But they also understood something else—the basic mood of an age anxious for the daring, the bizarre, and the new. And they made the most of it.

No other period has been quite as permissive and encouraging for the divas as the twenties. The whole look and feel, tone and texture, of

American popular entertainment was undergoing a dramatic transformation. Despite President Harding's proclamation that this new era would mark a return to "normalcy," in the twenties it seemed as if everyone suddenly wanted to break loose, to pry himself from the traditional middle-class moral order of the past, to forget the fake optimism that had characterized the turn of the century, to wipe out the pain and disillusionment of the First World War. The twenties can now be seen as the dawning age of America's intense, often unfathomable, interest in the celebrity, be it Babe Ruth, Clara Bow, or Charles Lindbergh. Celebrities represented part of a golden dream of unlimited fun and adventure. Records, movies, and plays picked up on the new fun spirit. On dance floors around the country, the black bottom and the charleston (both of which originated in the black community)

In the 1926 Folies Bergère, Josephine Baker wore nothing but bananas and a smile.

caught hold of the mass imagination as no other popular dance crazes ever had. Nightclubs and speakeasies sprouted up, overcrowded with dapper hotshot young men and a new kind of young woman, the pencil-thin, flat-chested, sexually liberated flapper. Not only had corsets and long skirts gone out the window, so too had many of the inhibitions and hangups of the past.

In this period there were black flappers too. But, generally, because the nature of her existence always demanded that she be resourceful, the black woman had long been more independent than her white counterpart. What the twenties did for her, if she chose to entertain, was simply to offer her new arenas in which to shine and dazzle. So caught up was consumer-oriented America in

Light-skinned chorines popularized the charleston and the black bottom.

its own uninhibited frenzy that there was repeated demand for fresh products, new, different, offbeat items to be quickly snapped up, digested, and enjoyed. Anything was permissible as long as it was not boring. Nightclubs, theatres, movies, and in time Europe all made way for the black beauty in the twenties, so much so that there was indeed a cultural revolution going on in America. But all those fabulous twenties opportunities grew out of something old and something new: the blues and race records.

Blues singer Ethel Waters helped bring race records into vogue.

BLUES SISTERS

Perhaps more than any other art/entertainment form, the blues legitimized the black female entertainer. Even in the days before the scholars and the buffs moved in to explain the artistry of the early blues singers, black audiences responded to the power and grace of the female blues singers. What added to their popularity was the coming of the race record, which arrived in the hands of a black woman.

In 1920 black composer Perry Bradford brashly marched into the offices of OKeh, an independent, ambitious phonograph company in New York. Convinced that there was a black audience as anxious as whites for music that could be taken home and played on the Victrola, Bradford persuaded one of OKeh's white executives to record black singer Mamie Smith. When OKeh released Smith's version of "Crazy Blues," the company thought it might make a little bit of money. To OKeh's surprise, "Crazy Blues" sold 75,000 copies

24

Columbia's big stars in the twenties were Ethel Waters, Clara Smith, and Bessie Smith.

Spunky Alberta Hunter ran away from Memphis to become a star in Chicago.

within the first month and over a half million copies within the next half year in the black community. The music industry realized there was a whole new market for records. Soon the major companies were spinning out race records, music by black artists for black record buyers. Listed in special catalogs and sold in black areas, they kept a number of music companies in business.

The success of race records created a wild search for blues talent. In New York, one of the few black owned record companies, W. C. Handy and Harry Pace's Black Swan label, ambitiously and quickly signed up a singer who showed great promise, Ethel Waters. At the same time Black Swan rejected another singer named Bessie Smith. Out of Chicago, Paramount released records by the very popular Ida Cox and a newcomer named Alberta Hunter, who also wrote blues songs, one of which, "Down Hearted Blues," became a hit for Bessie Smith. Paramount also launched a search for the most legendary of blues singers, Ma Rainey. (Louis Armstrong was sometimes one of her backup musicians.) Trixie Smith, Clara Smith, Edith Wilson, Rosa Henderson, Bertha "Chippie" Hill, Victoria Spivey, Maggie Jones, Gertrude Saunders, Martha Copeland, Lucille Hegamin, and Sara Martin all recorded race records. Not all were blues singers in the classic sense. Some were vaudeville entertainers more at home with pop tunes.

With so many blues singers, each was eventually given a nickname to distinguish her from the other singers for the record buyers. Ma Rainey was billed as the "Mother of the Blues." Mamie Smith was known as "the first blues singer on records." Clara Smith, who did occasional duets with Bessie, was "Queen of the Moaners." Sippie Wallace was the "Texas Nightingale." Lucille Hegamin was called the "Chicago Cyclone." And Ida Cox was touted as the "Uncrowned Queen of the Blues."

With her blues and her nickname, each woman created a distinct persona. Alberta Hunter developed the persona of the tough little cookie who could take care of herself. Hunter was a small woman with a quick mischievous smile. In 1907, at age twelve, she ran away from her home in Memphis and hopped a train to Chicago. She had heard girls there were paid ten dollars a week to sing. Hunter performed and worked with such entertainers as Bricktop, Florence Mills, Cora Green, and the legendary King Oliver Band. She came to know many of the important music figures of her day: Louis Armstrong, Fletcher Henderson, Fats Waller, Lil Hardin, Sidney Bechet, and Bessie Smith. Eubie Blake said that when she sang "you felt so sorry for her you would want to kill the guy she was singing about." Hunter and the other blues sisters used their material to act out dramas and to examine the "issues": money, heartache, men, sometimes race problems. Sometimes they were just dishing out sex—with the bawdiest of lyrics. In one song a singer might announce that if the fellow didn't like her ocean, then he better not fish in her sea. Or she might tell him to stay out of her valley and to let her mountain be.

In time, the blues brought black women from behind the shadows. Curiously, the sisters were far bolder than some of their male counterparts (and far more popular), perhaps because as mere women they were not considered as threatening, so it did not matter what they said; perhaps also because finally, through song, women had found an outlet for articulating the things affecting them most. Here again, though, the black woman presented herself as the embodiment of restless energy, intelligence, maturity, and drive. Many became pop heroines for the black community. Ida Cox toured the country with her own revue. She had sixteen chorus girls,

A 1924 catalog promotes female headliners.

27

comics, and backup singers. She also wrote her own material and selected the musicians who accompanied her. If all this were not enough to dazzle her audience, then surely the stories of her mansion in Tennessee and her luxuriant life-style were certain to keep the fans in awe. By the mid-twenties the blues sisters had had such an extraordinary effect on popular culture that even so mainstream a publication as *Vanity Fair* ran an article by Carl Van Vechten on blues performers Ethel Waters, Bessie Smith, and Clara Smith.

The styles created by the blues singers were eventually lifted and presented in far more acceptable form by white quasi-blues/torch singers Sophie Tucker, Helen Morgan, and Ruth Etting. No matter how successful the black blues singers were, not a one ever reaped the vast rewards and acclaim generated by the white singers. Some never knew what royalties were. Others took the few dollars they earned without complaints or demands. And often after their initial success in the twenties, the course of the black blues singers' lives took sad, even tragic twists and turns. During her heyday Mamie Smith made nearly a hundred records in seven years and later appeared in movie shorts. But when she died in 1946, her money and fame were gone. Some performers such as Ida Cox, continued singing long after the blues had gone out of vogue. Her last recordings were made in 1961, and she died in 1967. Victoria Spivey got a chance to work in the movie *Hallelujah* and in later years managed her own small record company. Edith Wilson returned to the musical theatre and also posed as Aunt Jemima for the famous Quaker Oats pancake commercials. Spunky Alberta Hunter used the blues as a springboard for another kind of career. In 1928 Hunter won the role of Queenie opposite Paul Robeson in the London production of *Show Boat*. Nightly her rendition of "Can't Help Lovin' Dat Man" brought the house down. Afterward she toured Europe, replaced Josephine Baker at the Folies Bergère, and took over Paris' Chez Florence where she hobnobbed with everybody from the Prince of Wales to Cole Porter to Noel Coward, who wrote "I Travel Alone" for her. As special as Hunter was, she later left singing to become a nurse, assuming no one would ever think twice about her. For a long time she was right. Then she resurfaced in the late seventies, repopularizing the blues all over again. For the most part, the early blues singers, for all their uniqueness, often retired or disappeared or struggled on at tiny clubs and cafés, slowly fading into oblivion, never seeing their work fully appreciated. That almost happened to the woman considered to be the greatest blues singer of them all, Bessie Smith.

BESSIE SMITH: THE EMPRESS COMES TO TOWN

In the twenties Bessie Smith was *the* blues singer. Her title, The Empress, was rightly hers and hers alone. Not only was hers the big powerful voice of the era, but her very style was also the distillation of those other blues singers struggling to make themselves heard in a man's world. In many respects, it was also a dazzling tribute to the woman who influenced Bessie most, Ma Rainey. With Bessie Smith's arrival too, there came the idea of a black woman's life as a drama, a lopsided morality play with the mythic cycle of birth, life, death, rebirth. Through her records, her road tours, her inimitable high diva stage style, and her hotly discussed life-style, Bessie Smith became the most famous black woman of her age, marking the end of one tradition—the diva enclosed solely in the black community—and the beginning of another—the diva coming aboveground, openly affecting the dominant culture. Bessie Smith was a distinctive twenties diva persona so powerful that later she was transformed into social symbol, legend, myth.

Bessie was born dirt poor in Chattanooga, Tennessee, around 1894 (she was never anxious to give out her birthdate), the second of seven children of a part-time Baptist minister. Bessie was nine when her parents died and she took to singing in the streets to earn pennies.

By 1912 she had left Tennessee and was performing in a troupe with Pa and Ma Rainey. A year later, she was singing at the 81 Theatre in Atlanta. She married a young man named Earl Love who died not long after the union.

Bessie Smith at the height of her career—stepping high, caring less.

A reflective Bessie at the end of a long and flamboyant career.

Through the teens of the century, Bessie spent long, lean, tough years performing on the black vaudeville circuit, the Theatre Owners' Booking Association. She worked anywhere, in tents, carnivals, honky-tonks, performing in her street clothes, often dancing as much as she sang. By the early twenties when she settled in Philadelphia and married a former policeman, Jack Gee, her reputation was established. But her great fame came with her recordings.

Incredibly enough, three different record companies rejected her. They thought she sounded too raw, too loud, too unsophisticated, no doubt downright too *cullid* too. In 1923 Columbia's Frank Walker signed her up. Within a year her first recordings had sold one million copies, surpassing the sales of all the other female blues singers.

Records broadened her audience. She continued to tour, eventually starred in her own show and played in some of the larger cities such as Nashville, Memphis, Detroit, Chicago, Philadelphia, New York, Cleveland, Atlanta, Birmingham, Cincinnati, and Indianapolis. Soon her reputation preceded her, and for many in the tiny rural towns or the big cities, seeing Bessie Smith was a once-in-a-lifetime experience.

Bessie's stage persona in the twenties was similar to that of Ma Rainey's: the emotionally well-traveled woman, returning to relate her troubles and triumphs. Nothing was ordinary about Bessie, not even the way she looked. For she was a large woman, big-boned, massively built, and very dark. She stormed stages, circling and courting her audience, dressed in outrageous getups: short horsehair wigs, sequined gowns, ostrich plumes, furs and jewels, and outlandish hats. Her style was in keeping with the uninhibited, far-out air of the era, making her the personification of the bighearted good-time gal out for lots of fun. Her emblem was her huge, joyous smile, which, as a great artist, she knew when to turn on and off. In no time the sensual, hepped-up, partying sister could give way to the reflective, pragmatic soulful woman recording the woes of the world.

Bessie's material was varied. She sang of love and heartache, coming on as a woman who understood men, their good points and their bad. Characters in her songs needed men to complete the story of their lives. Yet, in Bessie's hands, often having a man seemed her divine right. Bessie sang of men in general, using them as a backdrop (on occasion as an explanation) for a story of weariness and pain.

At the same time her attitudes toward men were similar to those men expressed toward women. In "Do Your Duty," she sang that if she called her man three times a day to come and drive her blues away, then he should naturally come prepared to play, to do his duty. Bessie demanded from the man all the service he could supply. And in an era when the conventional flapper sought her independence, Bessie already had hers.

In her music she never feared the thing women were always cautioned never to be: self-assertive. It was precisely her self-assertion and her nontraditional role as woman that drew female followers to her. In the song "Put It Right Here (Or Keep It Out There)," she emphatically laid down the law to a man who had been playing around while living on her money. And in her bawdy songs, "Need a Little Sugar in My Bowl" (she sang that she was tired of being lonely and blue, and needed not only a little sugar in her bowl, but also a little hotdog on her roll), "I'm Wild About That Thing," and "You Gotta Give Me Some," Bessie represented the sensual woman stepping forward, expressing her needs, appetites, and fantasies.

Other Bessie Smith songs struck different moods. In

In her music she never feared the thing women were always cautioned against: self-assertiveness. Her nontraditional role drew female followers to her.

"Taint Nobody's Business If I Do," a song that was a favorite for other divas as well, she announced that if she had the notion to jump in the ocean, then it wasn't nobody's business if she did, adding that if her friend didn't have any money and that if she should say take all hers, honey, then again it wasn't nobody's business if she did. Bessie approached this song as if it was an anthem proclaiming woman's independence, her right to her own follies and idiosyncrasies. "Nobody Knows You When You're Down and Out" tells the story of a woman who once lived high and has now fallen low without money or a friend to help, and sounds as if it came straight from the hard-luck thirties. "Gimme a Pigfoot and a Bottle of Beer" remains one of her best pieces, capturing the energy of Harlem rent parties, speakeasies, and bootleg gin.

Offstage Bessie was a fascinating figure as well. In this period when the black press was still evolving, black newspapers such as the *Philadelphia Tribune* and the *Chicago Defender* (as well as the powerful black grapevine) had a field day with Bessie's offstage antics. Bessie's biographer, Chris Albertson, pointed out that in the twenties black audiences came to theatres anticipating the legend as much as the entertainer. Everyone had some

Bessie story to tell. According to Albertson, there were tales of her flights of fancy when she might desert her traveling troupe and rush off to another town for some fun and loving. There were stories about her spending sprees. In one summer alone, she and husband Jack Gee were said to have spent $16,000, and she was known to have paid cash for cars. Her drinking binges were famous. She would enter a local tavern, tell the bartender to lock the door, not to let anyone out or in, and then lay a hundred dollars on the counter, after which there were unlimited drinks for everyone as they all partied, sometimes for days. Her temper was legendary too. She hit anybody who annoyed or messed with her, man or woman. When she thought her husband was fooling around with some other woman, she would haul off and slap him. On one occasion, she even chased him down a railroad track while firing a pistol at him. Her lovers, male and female, were talked about. At one time, when a young woman buckled and withdrew after being publicly kissed by Bessie, the girl was given such a dressing down by Bessie that thereafter she was kissed where and when the Empress wanted—without a word of complaint! She was extravagant. She traveled with her own entourage and in her private railroad car, which would be detached at the local depot, after which Bessie's workers would set up tents, then roam the streets, passing out flyers that said the Empress was here in town for a performance.

Bessie was a woman no one tangled with. She was tough on any entertainer she thought might be a possible threat. During Ethel Waters' early days as a struggling young performer, she appeared on the same bill with Bessie in Atlanta. The Empress laid down the law that Waters, whom she called "long goody," could not sing any blues. When the audience cried out for Waters to sing some blues songs, she broke Bessie's rule. Backstage, a loud Bessie let it be known what she thought of those "northern bitches." And later, as Waters wrote in her autobiography, the Empress really spoke her mind. "Come here, long goody," Waters quoted Bessie as saying. "You ain't so bad. It's only that I never dreamed that anyone would be able to do this to me in my own territory and with my own people. And you damn well know you can't sing worth a ----."

Throughout the twenties Bessie's records and personal appearances were tremendously successful. On rare occasions she performed before white audiences. She also did radio shows and starred in the 1928 film *St. Louis Blues*. By the thirties some white college students started to collect her records. Even Mae West may have picked up her hands-on-hips pose from Bessie.

The high period of Bessie Smith's career came to an end by the late twenties. Blues fell out of favor. New stars, with a different kind of refined flash, came into vogue. Bessie's engagements became few. Her money was running out. She was drinking steadily. Eventually, even her husband, Gee, took off with another entertainer, Gertrude Saunders.

Then the Depression nearly wiped her out. Record producer John Hammond ran across her working as a hostess in a North Philadelphia dive, singing pornographic songs for tips. In 1933 she made her last recordings for Hammond on Columbia's label. (Three days later a youngster named Billie Holiday made her first records for the same company.)

Bessie fought to regain her stardom and went so far as to modify her flamboyant style. She wore simple elegant gowns without the wigs or the wild hats; her hair brushed back, revealing a striking middle-aged woman. Although she never made a big comeback, Bessie never stopped working in the thirties. In 1937 she set off on a tour through the South, with a new man by her side, Richard Morgan, Lionel Hampton's uncle. During the tour Bessie's car, driven by Morgan, crashed into a truck. Her right arm was nearly severed and she lay bleeding for hours on a lonely country road. Bessie Smith died at a hospital in Clarksville, Mississippi.

A massive crowd turned out for her funeral. Far from diminishing her legend, her years of decline simply intensified it. After her death the story spread that she had bled to death when refused admittance to a nearby white hospital. Although the story has been discounted, it remains part of her legend.

In 1961 Edward Albee used this legendary story of her death as the basis for his play, *The Death of Bessie Smith*, which was a denunciation of bigotry in America.

Bessie Smith was the last of a specific type, the dark diva firmly entrenched in the black community. The black beauties who followed, from Baker to Waters to Holiday, started in the black community but eventually met with great success in the white world too. And perhaps what disoriented some of the later figures was that, unlike Bessie, they were torn from their roots and found they could never really go home again. Although Bessie took the diva into the mainstream culture, she was never part of it.

Theresa Harris went from theatre to the movies playing maids.

To attract white patrons, club owners demanded that show girls be high-yellar, straight-haired beauties.

Otis Butle

CHORUS GIRLS: CAFÉ-AU-LAIT CUTIES

During this era of accelerated fun and frivolity, Bessie and the blues singers were not the only type of popular entertainment around. There were also the serious stage actresses and the show girls. In the twenties black theatre (or black-oriented theatre—plays with black characters or themes) really seemed to be taking off with new opportunities for everyone. Eugene O'Neill's *All God's Chillun Got Wings,* focusing on an interracial romance, appeared in 1924, followed by Garland Anderson's *Appearances,* then *Black Boy* with Paul Robeson, and David Belasco's spectacular *Lulu Belle,* which boasted a cast of sixty or more, three-quarters of whom were "colored." It told the shocking story of the rise (from Harlem to Paris) of a beautiful wanton colored girl!

In the world of the new black theatre, new dramatic black actresses appeared: Inez Clough (in *Earth* and *Harlem*), Abbie Mitchell, Edna Thomas, Evelyn Ellis, Georgette Harvey, Fredi Washington, and the magnetic Rose McClendon. Throughout the twenties McClendon was no doubt the most talked about dramatic black actress around. She starred opposite Charles Gilpin (and later Paul Robeson) in the 1924 production *Roseanne,* played the mother in Paul Green's Pulitzer Prize winning play *In Abraham's Bosom,* and appeared in the original 1927 production of *Porgy.* Her 1926 performance in *Deep River* was critically acclaimed by New York theatregoers. Even the *New York World*'s feisty critic Alexander Woollcott reported that when Ethel Barrymore had slipped in to see the play, she had been told by her friend Arthur Hopkins to be sure to stay until the last act just to watch McClendon descend a flight of stairs. He told her, "She can teach some of our most hoity-toity actresses distinction." Wrote Woollcott: "It was Miss Barrymore who hunted *him* after the performance to say 'She can teach them *all* distinction.'" McClendon was a tall, slender brown beauty with a regal bearing and a high sense of the dramatic. In the thirties producer John Houseman launched elaborate plans to star McClendon as the dark, *savage* queen Medea. With a white actor playing Jason, there were to be mulatto children and a stunning chorus of black women. The rest of the cast would be white. This would have been a daring piece of theatre, but McClendon fell ill, and the project was shelved. For a short time in the thirties, she and Houseman headed the Works Progress Administration's

Negro Theatre Project. After a long and painful illness, McClendon died just before the project took off. For years afterward, Rose McClendon remained one of those unsung heroines of promise whose fundamental success had proven there could be a place for black women in the legitimate theatre.

Of all the new black theatre projects, none, however, could hope to compete with the new style of black musicals. *Shuffle Along* set the tone and pace for such shows. Created by black composers Noble Sissle and Eubie Blake and the black comedy writing team of Flournoy Miller and Aubrey Lyles, *Shuffle Along* opened on Broadway in 1921, immediately winning raves from critics and public alike. This was the era of the Harlem Renaissance when black writers Langston Hughes, Claude McKay, Alain Locke, and Jean Toomer injected some black culture into the history of American arts and letters. *Shuffle Along*'s success indicated there was also a place for black Americans in popular, commercial theatre. It ushered into vogue the whole notion of the all-black Broadway show that could please whites as well as blacks, and inspired an array of other black musicals, *Runnin' Wild*, Miller and Lyles' *Rang Tang*, *Keep Shufflin'*, Lew Leslie's various editions of *Blackbirds*, and *Hot Chocolates*. Emerging from these musicals were show girls Lottie Gee, the haughty Gertrude Saunders, Valaida Snow, Elida Webb, Adelaide Hall (who, for a spell, was almost as great a European sensation as Josephine Baker), Minto Cato, Ada Ward, Marion Gant Tyler (who married Eubie Blake), Baby Cox, Florence Mills, Fredi Washington, Ethel Waters, and Baker. Even the great Paul Robeson got a break in the musicals when he replaced one of the Four Harmony Kings in a road-show version of *Shuffle Along*.

No other figure was as firmly grounded in the animated flip spirit of the flapper age as the show girl. Sharp and sassy, slick and slender, the chorus and show girls all seemed to be making a frantic bid for attention, Junior League divas struggling for self-definition (or self-escape) through movement, song, and a display of energy. In the new musicals the chorus girls set the pace and tone, often operating much like a chorus in an ancient Greek play: standing as one character, commenting through music and jokes on the action.

When they weren't working in legitimate theatres, the chorus girls found other work in the sporty new black night spots then coming into vogue—the Cotton Club, Connie's Inn, the Plantation Club, the Shuffle Club, the

A glittering Harlem chorus line and specialty act of the 1920s.

36

63rd Street Music Hall

63d ST. THEATRES, LTD., INC., Proprietors
DIRECTION OF HARRY L. CORT and JOHN J. SCHOLL
Sixty-third Street, Between Broadway and Central Park West

NOTICE: This Theatre, with every seat occupied, can be emptied in less than three minutes. Choose NOW the Exit nearest to your seat, and in case of fire walk (do not run) to that Exit.
THOMAS J. DRENNAN, Fire Commissioner.

WEEK BEGINNING MONDAY EVENING, FEBRUARY 27, 1922
Midnight Performance Wednesday at 11:30 P. M.

SHUFFLE ALONG CO., INC.
Presents
A Musical Melange

SHUFFLE ALONG

Conceived by Miller and Lyles
Music and Lyrics by Sissle and Blake
Entire Production Staged Under the Personal Supervision of
F. E. Miller
Ensembles Staged by Walter Brooks
Dances by Lawrence Deas

Cast of Characters
(As They Appear)

At the Piano..............................EUBIE BLAKE
JIM WILLIAMS, Proprietor of Jim Town Hotel....PAUL FLOYD
JESSIE WILLIAMS, His Daughter.................LOTTIE GEE
RUTH LITTLE, Her Chum.....................FLORENCE MILLS
HARRY WALTON, Candidate for Mayor........ROGER MATTHEWS
                                          RICHARD COOPER
                                          ARTHUR PORTER
                                          JAMES WOODSON
                                          SNIPPY MASON
BOARD OF ALDERMEN...........................

PROGRAM CONTINUED ON SECOND PAGE FOLLOWING

BETWEEN the ACTS
Little Cigars MILD HAVANA BLEND

They are just the thing for a short smoke when you haven't time for a Big Cigar, or when you want only a few puffs.

PROGRAM CONTINUED

GROCERY CLERK...........................
MRS. SAM PECK, Suffragette..............."ONION" JEFFREY
TOM SHARPER, Political Boss..............MATTIE WILKES
STEVE JENKINS, Candidate for Mayor.......NOBLE SISSLE
SAM PECK, Another Candidate for Mayor....F. E. MILLER
JACK PENROSE, Detective.................AUBREY LYLES
RUFUS LOOSE, War Relic...................C. WESLEY HILL
STRUTT, Jim Town Swell...................BOB LEE
MAYOR'S DOORMAN..........................W. H. HANN
UNCLE TOM...............................BILLY ANDREWS
OLD NED.................................CHARLES DAVIS
JACK JOE................................ARTHUR PORTER
SECRETARY TO MAYOR......................BOB WILLIAMS
                                        INA DUNCAN
TONY KINGS..............................I. H. BROWNING
                                        C. E. DRAYTON
                                        W. H. BERRY
                                        U. S. THOMPSON
Misses Goldie Cisco, Mildred Brown, Jennie Day,
Lillian Williams, Beatrice Williams, Evelyn
Mitchell, A. Andrews, Lydia Wess,
LADIES—Misses Marguerite Weaver, Marion Gee,
Dorothy Yarburg, Wilsa Caldwell, Evelyn Shep-
herd, Madeline Odlum.

ON SECOND PAGE FOLLOWING

Shuffle Along, the 1921 hit, introduced
Florence Mills, Josephine Baker, and Fredi Washington.

Two promising young dramatic actresses of the 1920s: Edna Thomas *(left)* and Fredi Washington.

Savoy, and later, Small's Paradise. It was during the twenties that whites first started wandering uptown to Harlem for a good time, much of which was provided by the girls performing nightly in the clubs. Some of the so-called black clubs actually were no such thing. They might have had only black entertainers, but the establishments were owned by whites and often had only white customers. A few sepia joints were even located downtown. Regardless, the colored chorines were seen. Producers Florenz Ziegfeld and George White were even said to have hired black chorus girls to teach the downtown white chorus lines the new jazz dancing.

What distinguished the black chorus line was its rhythmic, exhilarating energy level. Having grown up exposed to such popular dance forms as the cakewalk, buck dancing, and ballin' the jack, the dancers were well prepared for the fast turns, high jumps, and kicks demanded by their black choreographers. The dance numbers themselves were clever fusions of the styles of the minstrel shows and burlesque, all in all creating a large-scale carnival of activity. The high point was the sweeping, dramatic, sometimes comic strut.

The black chorus line was also distinguished by the fact that its members were almost always café-au-lait cuties: light-skinned black women with straight hair and keen features. In photographs of the old chorus lines, occasionally a brown face appears, but there is never a dark one. In the 1890s black revues such as *The Creole Show* and *Octoroon* had glorified the Afro-American Girl, who actually was nothing more than the light-bright-damn-near-white kind of black beauty. Such shows simply intensified a color caste system that had long existed in the black community. The same was true of the twenties black night spots, particularly a place like the Cotton Club, which catered exclusively to whites and had to have light-skinned women. The great irony is that the few women who rose from the chorus line to become stars were brown beauties such as Baker, Mills, and Waters.

Guitar-strumming Adelaide Hall, the star of *Blackbirds of 1928*.

Florence Mills: the pixieish girl-next-door who became an international star.

FLORENCE MILLS: MAKE WAY FOR LITTLE TWINKS

Florence Mills was one of the lucky ladies from the chorus line to emerge as a bona fide star. Mills had been in show business all her life. Born in Washington, D.C., she was known as Baby Florence when, as a child, she performed in the drawing rooms of various Washington diplomats. Later she and her sisters, Olivia and Maude, performed as the Mills Sisters. By the twenties Florence was working with her dancer husband, U.S. (Slow Kid) Thompson, on the Keith Circuit in an act called "The Tennessee Ten."

The big break came when *Shuffle Along* lost its leading lady, Gertrude Saunders. Somewhat uneasily, the producers brought Mills in as a replacement. And then with the kind of a-star-is-born magic the theatre thrives on, her rendition of the hit song "I'm Craving for That Kind of Love" made the replacement an even greater sensation than the original star. Later Mills successfully appeared at the Plantation Club, then traveled to London and Paris and other European capitals where she became a tremendously popular international star in *From Dover to Dixie* and Lew Leslie's *Blackbirds*.

Onstage, Florence Mills introduced the adorably innocent little black girl with a playful wild streak. She would don a sky-high blond Afro wig and throw herself into an exuberant charleston. Or she dressed up

Part of the $100,000 Floral Tribute at Dancer's Funeral

Thousands publicly mourned the sudden death of "Little Twinks" in 1927.

41

A dreamy concoction, Josephine Baker was part come-on, part put-on, part camp.

innocently as a hitchhiker off on the road to find love. "I'm a Little Blackbird Looking for a Bluebird," she sang, and the audience took her to its heart. She was a small woman as "delicate as Dresden china," the perfect gamin lost and alone in a cruel world. She had great spunk and vigor and was one of the few important black female stars who succeeded with the little girl bit, the kind of woman all the big guys on the block felt they had to look out for. First-hand accounts of her skill have always been glowing. Black critic James Weldon Johnson wrote:

> She was indefinable. One might best string out a list of words such as: pixy, elf, radiant, exotic, Peter Pan, wood-nymph, wistful, piquant, magnetism, witchery, madness, flame; and then despairingly exclaim: "Oh, you know what I mean." She could be whimsical, she could be almost grotesque; but she had the good taste that never allowed her to be coarse. She could be risque, she could be seductive; but it was impossible for her to be vulgar, for she possessed a naiveté that was alchemic. As a pantomimist and a singing and dancing comedienne she had no superior in any place or race.

Florence Mill's career did not last long. By the latter years of the decade, the star, sometimes affectionately known as Little Twinks, looked edgy and tense, moody and overworked. In 1927, Florence Mills died after an appendectomy. According to columnist Whitney Bolton of the *New York Morning Telegraph*, over 150,000 people lined the streets of Harlem for her funeral.

A Mills legend developed soon after her death, that of the tragic artist stricken down much too early. But later generations have remained baffled because she left behind no recordings. (Strangely enough, her life was so rushed that she simply never got around to making records.) The other important divas acquired staying power because long after their heydays had come to an abrupt end or long after their reputations had been tarnished, there were either records or films to reveal the way they had once dazzled. Bessie Smith and Ma Rainey were brought back into the cultural mainstream by the re-release of their records. Also important to a diva's longevity have been tales about the turbulence and disarray of her life, all of which could be incorporated into her myth. No such dramatic stories about Mills survive. Today all that remains are a handful of striking photographs that capture her playfulness and at times her endearing vulnerability. But perhaps another reason Mills is not well remembered now is because of Josephine Baker.

JOSEPHINE BAKER: THE WOMAN WHO GOT AWAY

Josephine Baker obliterated the reputation of just about every other show girl in sight. Her legend took hold in the twenties with a firm, tenacious grip. With various clever modifications, it held on and endured for some six decades. Ultimately, Josephine Baker stood as the personification of the rip-roaring twenties as well as the archetypal symbol of the black flapper as International Exotique. She perhaps understood her legend—her image, her career, her audiences—better than any other diva. She was a showbiz personality to her bones. And with insight and skill, she fused her public and private personalities in such a way that she witnessed the ultimate fantasy come true: the transformation of the world into her private stage.

Even before she hit the stage, Josephine Baker had steered past a hazardous course. Like Bessie Smith and the other divas of the period, Baker was born into poverty—in 1906 in the heart of the ghetto of St. Louis. Her mother was a washerwoman; her real father, so she was to say later, was a Spaniard who did not want to marry the colored girl he had impregnated. As a lanky, skinny child who stole to eat or who cleaned for whites to earn a few pennies for her family, Baker exhibited the grit and ambition that would later bring her the fame she so desperately craved. Everything about Baker suggested a woman who had to get out, to break loose, to find herself and her own notion of freedom.

So at age thirteen, she ran away from home to join a traveling road show. By the early twenties she found herself in Philadelphia. It was there that she decided to audition for *Shuffle Along*.

At first she was turned down because she was too young, too thin, too dark. The next time around she auditioned wearing the lightest face powder she could find, and was hired as a dresser for one of the show's various road productions. Baker was clever enough to prepare herself for the inevitable. She immediately learned all the songs and dances of the show because she knew at some point some chorus girl had to miss a performance. When a dancer dropped out because of a pregnancy, Baker persuaded the stage manager to let her go on.

That night lingered on in the memories of many. This unknown, skinny, young girl strutted onto the stage, crossed her eyes, made faces like crazy, and shook,

A sketch from the magazine *Vanity Fair*, proclaiming Baker "all but the dictator of Paris."

shimmied, and wiggled her backside. Taking an ordinary dance slot, she transformed it into a high-falutin', ferociously energetic theatrical event. She brought the house down and word-of-mouth spread quickly. Audiences came to the theatre hoping to see the "little cross-eyed, out-of-step girl" at the end of the chorus line. Eventually, Baker became the highest paid girl in the chorus, the most acclaimed, and, among her fellow chorines, possibly the least liked.

Fredi Washington, another black beauty who worked with Baker in *Shuffle Along* and who remained a lifelong friend, has recalled the theatrical pettiness Josephine was a victim of. She was referred to as The Monkey by the other girls, who never forgave her for stealing the show right from under their noses. They never hesitated to let her know what they thought. One evening when Washington entered the dressing room, she saw that all of Josephine's makeup had been lifted from the dressing table and dumped into the hallway. Washington found the culprits and demanded that they put everything back in place before Josephine arrived at the theatre.

Baker has also been remembered as an ambitious, tense young woman, perhaps uneasy and insecure because she was the brownest girl on the chorus line. During the early part of her career, the idea was that, as a brown woman, she could never get attention on her looks alone, the way the high-yellar (light-skinned) chorus girls did. At this time she was hardly the white or black ideal of beauty or appeal. Baker was acutely aware, however, that the one thing that could save her was her own incomparable effervescence. So she used it to provide comic relief every night at the theatre. She became known primarily as a high-steppin' clown, something of a ribald joke. But the clowning, coupled with her fierce drive and energy (and her formidable talent), enabled her to steal scenes from everyone in sight.

Josephine Baker used *Shuffle Along* to break through and establish herself—but as an important chorus girl. She was not yet a star. That was true even in 1924 when Sissle and Blake wrote special material for her in their new all-black Broadway show *Chocolate Dandies*. Baker entered wearing a clinging silk dress with a sexy slit up the side. But for the most part, she still crossed her eyes and grinned wildly as she climbed about stage in outsized shoes and a sash with a huge bow. She was still the cutup. Some of the photographs of Baker during this period are now shocking because the woman who most now think of as the symbol of European chic played a pickaninny figure. And the flagrant hot sexuality that was later to

During her Folies Bergère period, La Baker became the darling of Parisian society.

A Slinky Baker in one of her French films, *Princess Tam Tam*.

drive audiences wild was then buried under layers of grotesque makeup and unbecoming costumes.

After *Chocolate Dandies* closed, Baker appeared in the chorus of the Plantation Club, the downtown Broadway night spot that had launched Florence Mills and was then starring Ethel Waters. Baker was now developing an offstage style that made her a noticeable Harlem figure. Her bobbed hair and the insolent spit curls on her forehead gleamed. One day she walked the streets decked out in an outfit that could not help but draw attention: a blazing orange jacket, bright green shoes, a jaunty silver lame hat cocked to the side, pearl gray golf pants that clung to her firm buttocks and flared down to her ankles.

Hungry for success at the Plantation Club, she learned without any hesitation all of Ethel Waters' material, in hopes of replacing the star should she ever miss a show. When Waters took ill one night, Baker went on, winning audience approval as she sang Waters' hit "Dinah." Afterward Baker was ready to move in with her own act at the club. What she had not taken into consideration was Ethel Waters herself. Throughout her career Ethel Waters was a difficult and demanding woman, a figure suspicious of almost everyone and a formidable talent whom no other entertainer dared mess with. (Waters could be as tough as Bessie—and as evil too.) When she learned of the Baker triumph, Ethel laid down the law to the club managers—and Josephine. Baker tangled with Ethel only once and never had a second chance. Ironically, her biggest break—the chance to go to Europe with an all-black revue—came about because Waters, the producers' first choice, was unavailable. In later years this was probably a subject neither woman was anxious to discuss. Waters' attitude was always that Baker had done all right abroad—with *her* stuff.

The show was *La Revue Nègre*, which startled postwar Europeans in 1925. The company consisted of twenty-five black dancers, singers, and musicians. The rest of the cast faded into the woodwork when Baker made her sizzling appearance, considered one of the most sensational of the first half of the century. Nearly fifty years after the event, Janet Flanner, who wrote about Paris for *The New Yorker*, still had vivid memories of Baker's extraordinary presence:

> She made her entry entirely nude except for a pink flamingo feather between her limbs; she was being carried upside down and doing the split on the shoulder of a black giant. Midstage he paused, and with his long fingers holding her basketwise around the waist, swung her in a slow cartwheel to the stage floor, where she stood, like his magnificent discarded burden, in an instant of complete silence. A scream of salutation spread through the theatre.

Baker greets guests at the New York cabaret she ran briefly in the thirties.

Flanner said that within a half hour after the curtain had fallen, news of Baker's stunning appearance made its way through the cafés and haunts on the Champs-Elysées. Those who had seen the show retold its wonders time and again, never tiring of the tale, hoping through talk to recapture the spectacular moments. In no time the nineteen-year-old runaway from St. Louis found herself the most acclaimed and sought-after woman in Paris.

A year later, Baker starred in the Folies Bergère in a show that took months to rehearse, had 500 cast/crew members, and 1,200 costumes. She dazzled European audiences with her version of the charleston. Baker leaped onto the Paris stage, crossed her eyes, swung her hips, and wore nothing but a festoon of bananas and a smile.

Baker was now an international celebrity. She floated through French theatrical, literary, and intellectual circles with the greatest of ease. She met many of the most prominent European personalities of her age: Max Reinhardt, Colette, Cocteau, Le Corbusier, Marcel Pagnol, Pirandello, Albert Einstein, and writer Erich

---

She dazzled European audiences with her version of the charleston. Baker leaped onto the Paris stage wearing nothing but a festoon of bananas and a smile.

Maria Remarque, who said she brought "a whiff of jungle air and an elemental strength and beauty to the tired showplace of Western civilization." Those captivated by her onstage exoticism were anxious to see if the woman away from the footlights was just as exciting.

Wisely, Baker understood the connection between her public and private personalities. And she promoted the stories that circulated about her extravagance, her hauteur, her unconventionality. One night she might roam the dance floors with a snake wrapped around her long neck. The next day she might be spotted on the Champs-Elysées with a leopard on a leash. Fashion editor Diana Vreeland has recalled sitting in a Parisian movie house with Baker *and* Baker's pet cheetah. (Vreeland has also said that, along with Isadora Duncan and Consuelo Vanderbilt, Baker was one of America's few authentic women of style.) When the French press learned that she had a Louis XVI bedroom, they thereafter insisted she slept in Marie Antoinette's bed. She was said to have received 46,000 fan letters within two years. There were 2,000 marriage proposals and scores of suitors, one madman who pursued her throughout Europe, another young man who, enamored of her, shot himself, then fell

at her feet. Italian Count Pepito Abatino became her jealous lover/manager. Bandleader Jo Bouillon would let his own career fade when he became her husband, her consort, her housekeeper, her baby-sitter. Incredible as some of the Baker stories sound, most are true or at least have a truth at their base. Were all the stories simply the fabrications of a shrewd press agent, Baker might have been a more relaxed figure. Instead, even at this early stage, while still in her twenties, Josephine Baker seemed hell-bent on constructing an elaborate mythology that would cast her as the most glamorous and exciting woman of her time. Few people ever really knew the woman behind the extroverted personality, the figure who made the legend and crystallized the style. "Why spoil the illusion?" she said in the seventies to an eager-beaver New York reporter who she felt was trying to get too close.

Yet despite whatever confusions even Baker may have had concerning her personal identity, she was just what post-World War I Europeans were in desperate need of. For a generation that had been denied much and had been forced to take everything seriously in order to survive, here stood "La Ba-Kair" (later she would be simply "Josephine"), a towering ebony Venus to teach everybody how to relax and live again. In this period Baker's particular style and attitude—an outrageous delight in her own prettiness (something she discovered late), a delight that even then often slipped over into exhilarating self-parody—startled and invigorated audiences. Baker—with her daring (she was going topless long before it was fashionable), her imagination, her outlandish costumes, her gorgeous chocolate shoulders—was a one-woman extravaganza, the most shamelessly assertive form of self-pride any audience, black or white, had ever seen. Throughout the twenties she toured the great European capitals—Berlin, Budapest, Amsterdam, London, Madrid—and epitomized the new freedom and festivity with a hint of decadence always just beneath the surface. And so before anyone knew it, she had taken America's flapper spirit to new heights and in an unexpected direction. When people were just beginning to collect *art nègre* and the world was discovering *le jazz hot*, Josephine Baker represented the new black talent and the new black music just about to sweep through Europe. She cleared the path for scores of jazz musicians and black beauties such as Adelaide Hall, the Peters Sisters, and Florence Mills, all of whom would find European audiences much more receptive to their talents than the folks back home.

In the long run hers was probably the twenties' most compelling diva personality—and maybe its most disturb-

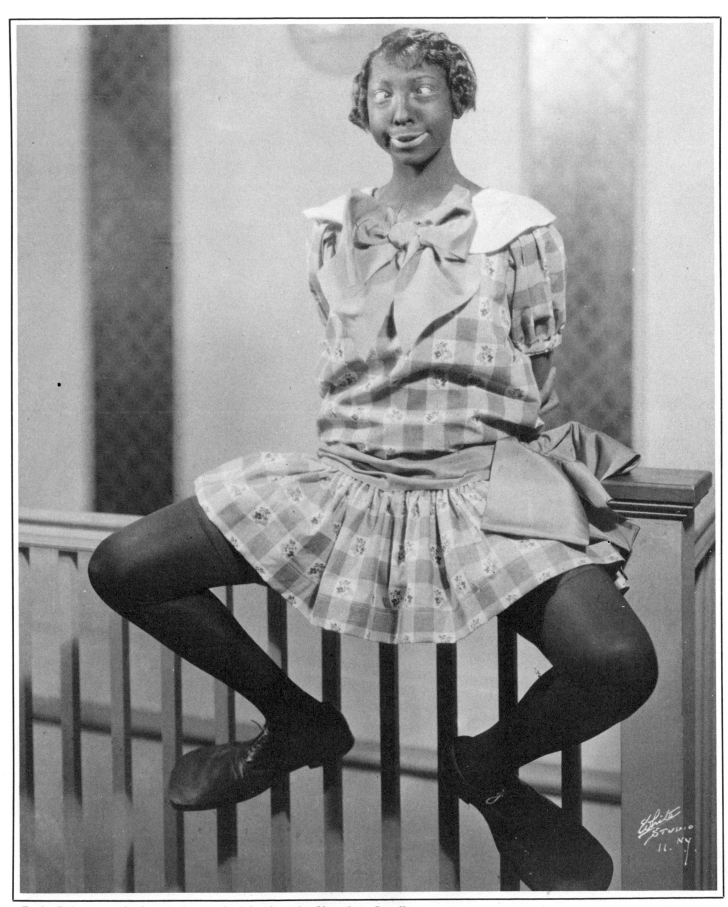

Early Baker: a grinning, cross-eyed pickaninny in *Chocolate Dandies*.

JOSÉPHINE BAKER

Famous for her exotic menagerie, Baker cuddles up to her pet leopard, Chiquita.

ing. For it has to be admitted that Baker succeeded with European audiences in part because she played on their view of the black woman as something of a supersexy noble savage. Those Europeans with disdain for aggressive, coarse Americans could contentedly pride themselves on being superior to a culturally deprived nation that had, after all, completely overlooked this Eighth Wonder of the World. She seemed the perfect object, a glittering artifact that could never fail to please. At the same time, White America never seemed at ease with this woman who would eventually speak out openly about its racism and bigotry, who would often also speak with dramatic romanticism of having had to flee the home of the brave in order to find her freedom. On those occasions when she returned to the States for appearances, even critics seemed skeptical, not wanting to fully acknowledge her talent. (Ironically, Baker's great theme song was "J'ai Deux Amours," I have two loves—my country and Paris.)

American culture has never taken to its expatriates, particularly those who fail to "repent" and return. For a black woman to behave in such a manner was unheard of.

But that hardly bothered black women in America who read of Josephine Baker's triumphs with great curiosity and pleasure. In the black community there had long been a fantasy of another world, another place and time, where the black woman would be seen for her unique brown beauty. In essence and act, Josephine Baker had escaped and lived out the fantasy for women back home. Black women reveled in her success, identified with her, and had the utmost respect. Blacks loved hearing the stories of the way Baker, when around whites, flaunted in their faces her chocolate color, her height, her big beautiful hips. "What a wonderful revenge for an ugly duckling," she said of her fame. The statement reveals Baker never forgot her early torments or her roots. In the twenties she put Harlem on the map of the world.

Offstage she delighted in the crowds and fans who followed her everywhere.

ETHEL WATERS: SWEET MAMA SHAKES HER THING

Just at the time Josephine Baker was hypnotizing Europe, Ethel Waters' career took its first upward swing in America. Waters injected the giddy flapper spirit with a new kind of social realism, introducing the ghettoized flapper, a hincty (difficult, arrogant), raunchy girl determined to make good. Hers was also the pure city girl, no longer just singing the blues but exposed to pop music. Ethel Waters fully understood her girl-from-the-school-of-hard-knocks persona because it was so close to herself.

Waters' early life had been a harrowing experience, full of city terrors. Born out of wedlock in Chester, Pennsylvania, in 1896, she had moved, as a child, from one tenement to another, quickly picking up the ways of the street. She ran errands for whores, was a lookout for pimps, and early acquired a reputation as a tough foul-mouthed girl. At thirteen she married. Two years later, the marriage was over. Afterward she took a job as a chambermaid and laundress at a Philadelphia hotel. Always a large girl, big-boned and awkward, she felt forever the outsider. The one person she stood in awe of, the one figure who showered Waters with some much needed attention, was her grandmother, Sally Anderson, who died when Waters was still young. Later her great dramatic characters of stage and film were to be modeled on this strong, tragic figure.

While young, Ethel Waters often stood in front of mirrors, bowing to imaginary crowds applauding her. But she never gave serious thought to a professional career until she performed informally one Halloween night at a Philadelphia club. The audience enthusiasm propelled her on. Soon she was traveling on the road with the Hill Sisters as part of their singing act—until she learned she was being cheated out of money, an experience she never forgot. Then she took off on her own, hitting one tiny town after another, building a large following. Before long, this lanky girl with sweet curves all over the place was packin' 'em in at Edmund's Cellar in New York where, by then, she was billed as Sweet Mama Stringbean. Although never a pure blues singer, she became the first woman to record W.C. Handy's "St. Louis Blues."

The Waters of this period was a startling far cry from the strong-as-a-rock maternal figure she would later popularize. In the twenties she was a good-natured girl with a chip on her shoulders. She was rough and knew how to handle men too. Often she talked during her numbers—about and to men, ever ready to shake them up some. Songs like "Shim Me Sha Wabble" and "I Want to Be Somebody's Baby Doll So I Can Get My Lovin' All the Time" were playful crowd favorites. But with "Brother You've Got Me Wrong" and "Go Back Where You Stayed Last Night," she set the male population straight. In the latter she commanded that the dude take it where he had had it the night before and to move away from her door, or she would call the law. Somehow she miraculously made the words door and law rhyme. But all of this kind of thing could change when she did bumps and grinds to an insolently sexy number like "Shake That Thing," in which she knowingly gave males a heady come-on, although she was sure to pull back at the crucial moment. Her attitude seemed to be: You can look, baby, but you damn well better not touch! Black men went wild over her; the greater the challenge, the better the woman.

Gradually, during this time, Waters' work took on a new sophistication, and her stage presence cooled down some to the point where this mix of ghetto raunch and rowdiness, this exotique, had become, in the words of Alberta Hunter, "a very refined performer." Her big twenties hits "Dinah" and "Sweet Georgia Brown" were smooth, easygoing pop tunes. More than any other star of the period, she legitimized the Harlem clubs. Whites were going uptown to see this woman who could sing songs by important white composers in a new *cullid* way.

In 1927 her first Broadway appearance in the short-lived, all-black revue *Africana* marked her emergence out of the clubs and onto the legitimate stage. By the end of the twenties Sweet Mama Stringbean was about to undergo some dramatic image changes, and eventually would become the first dark diva to make Broadway her domain.

Ethel Waters went from sexy flapper to blues singer to renowned dramatic actress.

Nina Mae McKinney, chorus girl turned movie star, with Paul Robeson in *Sanders of the River*.

NINA MAE MCKINNEY: COUNTRY GIRL GONE CITY GONE HOLLYWOOD

The twenties came to a fitting close with the appearance of Nina Mae McKinney, a South Carolina-born teen-ager lifted from the chorus line of Lew Leslie's *Blackbirds* and transported west where she opened the door most black women thought would be permanently closed: Hollywood. With the arrival of the Al Jolson movie *The Jazz Singer* in 1927, American motion pictures learned to talk. Afterward in 1929, the film industry released two all-talking, all-singing, all-dancing, all-colored musicals, *Hearts in Dixie* and *Hallelujah*. Of the pair, King Vidor's *Hallelujah* has remained impressive, not only because of the skill and sensitivity of his direction, but in large part because of its star—McKinney, a foot-loose, fancy-free Kewpie doll of an actress, one of the few authentic film delights of this period of transition. In *Hallelujah*, she was cast as Chick, a high-strung, high-yellar strumpet who lures a good, clean-cut colored boy (played by Daniel Haynes) away from his family and the church. Her rival is a homely, dark-skinned girl (played by blues singer Victoria Spivey), who is content to spend her days picking cotton. Spivey's sincere homebody was no match for Nina Mae's tantalizing tart.

Tremendous break that *Hallelujah* was, McKinney soon found herself up against a wall: Hollywood's rigid color fixation. Originally, Vidor had wanted Ethel Waters as the star of his film. Had Waters, a brown woman, played the leading role in this picture, the history of black women in American movies might have taken a different course. What happened in films, however, was that black women were divided into color categories. Dark black women would be cast as dowdy, frumpy, overweight mammy figures. Those black women given a chance at leading parts would have to be close to the white ideal: straight hair, keen features, light skin. They would become Hollywood's treasured mulattoes, women often doomed in their films seemingly because their blood was mixed. This tradition started with McKinney and continued with Fredi Washington, Lena Horne, and Dorothy Dandridge. Never would a black movie actress have a chance at fully developing her own persona as had Bessie Smith and Josephine Baker. It is interesting to compare the work some divas did on stage, when they were in control, and on screen, when instead of playing characters, they played against them. In the case of Dorothy Dandridge, the tension—and basic dissatisfaction with her film roles—brought out a jittery vulnerability that makes her always a fascinating film presence.

On screen McKinney was the consummate mulatto tease. For a brief spell it looked as if she would be the one sepia star in Hollywood's lily white heaven. Everyone from director Vidor to producer Irving Thalberg predicted a glorious future for her. But McKinney learned what every other black love goddess of the screen was to discover: after one great triumph, there were no significant follow-up roles. In such later films as *Safe in Hell, Sanders of the River*, and *Dark Waters*, she was generally misused, although she was always splendidly energetic.

For the most part, the later years of her career were not happy ones. At one point McKinney appeared abroad in cellars and cafes, elaborately dressed and coiffed, and billed as the Black Garbo. Then she returned to the States to do her black vamp bit in all-black shows and independently produced black movies. In the late forties she popped up, looking older, heavier, and far less energetic in a supporting role in *Pinky*. But unable to duplicate the success of *Hallelujah*, she seemed forever haunted by it. Her last years were spent in New York City, and she died in 1967.

At the close of the twenties America's dark divas remained confident and optimistic about their futures. And they took pride in their accomplishments. Few dealt explicitly with racial issues. Baker, the defiant expatriate, was the only one to openly comment on racism in America. Often enough, however, the blues singers, with their tales of two-timin' men who had cheated or mistreated them, obviously indicated that they lived within the walls of an oppressive system. Men, in general, represented the constraints and controls of society itself.

Most significantly, throughout this period, the divas were free women with a world of new opportunities opened to them, and perhaps because they still performed mostly for their own communities, they were indeed freer than they would be at any other time. They had been able to set their own stage, to call the shots, to decide what clothes to wear and what material to perform, and finally to create whatever stage personalities they themselves desired. Of course, the situation would soon change as the diva fully entered the mainstream culture.

In the trumped-up heat of the twenties and in the guise of the carefree flapper, the basic outline of high diva style, her way of dealing with the world and in looking at it, had taken its foremost evolutionary shape.

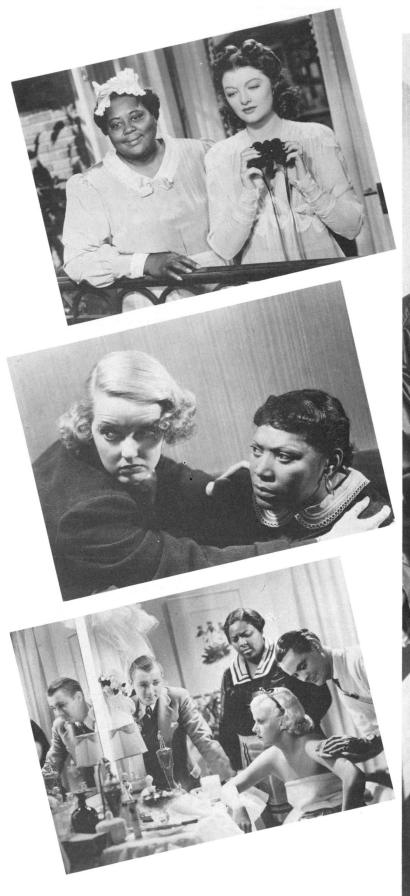

Heaven help a white star in the thirties who didn't have a loyal, cheery black maid around when times were tough. What would Myrna Loy *(top left)* have done without the ever-faithful Louise Beavers, or Bette Davis *(center)* without Libby Taylor? After Beavers had attended to Loy, she provided some counseling to Jean Harlow *(bottom left)* and then ran over to Kay Francis's pad. Mae West *(right)* contrasted her own sexuality with the dowdiness of her black maids, such as Libby Taylor.

· THE 1930s ·
POP MYTHS

Suddenly, the stock market crashed, and the diva found herself smack in the middle of the Great Depression itself. While analysts and government officials spoke of the "great slump," or "temporary setback," the diva beauty knew only two things for sure: First, it was tough to find work and second, many of the tricks of the trade—the flashy, flamboyant, overblown twenties style—would no longer do.

In the thirties American audiences determinedly searched their popular culture to find workable myths. The old-style twenties vamp or flapper was replaced by the working girl heroine, smart brassy women like Jean Harlow and Jean Arthur. Actresses Sylvia Sidney, Loretta Young, Bette Davis, Claudette Colbert, and on occasion even Marlene Dietrich and Katharine Hepburn personified the woman up against hard times. The divas also toned down their styles. They were aware of the demands of White *and* Black America.

By 1930 there were over 11 million blacks in the United States. And every day, in one form or another, this 10 percent of the nation's population was becoming increasingly more mainstream—and more politically outspoken too. In 1930 the all-black show *Green Pastures* was Broadway's hottest ticket. In 1931 the first of the Scottsboro trials (nine black youths accused of raping two white women) made headlines across the country, becoming a

Isabel Washington, the thirties diva: mellow, controlled, self-assured.

major cause célèbre. That same year the NAACP launched a full-scale attack against segregation and discrimination in North Carolina. As the era moved on, Mary McLeod Bethune came to national attention when named president of the newly formed National Council of Negro Women. And Olympic runner Jesse Owens and heavyweight champ Joe Louis emerged as black folk heroes.

What with Black America's social changes and the nation's economic upheaval, the divas intuitively understood that the new kind of personality Depression audiences craved was one whose personal control might be taken as a comment on a larger theme: the restoration of order and balance to the social system itself. New stars such as Billie Holiday, Ivie Anderson, and Fredi Washington offered a soulful mellowness that Depression audiences found reassuring. Sometimes the new stars had a wacky joyousness that provided comic relief. For the most part, because the black beauties kept their cool equilibriums intact, they seemed to tell Depression audiences that nobody could keep a good woman down.

THE GIRL-SINGERS

The first of the thirties new-style divas was a collective one, the Girl-Singers. During this era of Swing and the Big Bands, almost every orchestra, be it Duke Ellington's, Count Basie's, or Artie Shaw's, had a female vocalist. Swing was really a man's thing. Males played the instruments, worked out the arrangements, held the baton, and bought most of the records. Usually, the last thing traveling musicians wanted was a woman in the troupe, who could hardly cope with their rough-and-ready life-style. (They had short memories. For Ma, Bessie, and all those twenties blues sisters had helped make the road par-for-the-course for all musical entertainers.) But the big band managers, aware that audiences latched onto female vocalists in a way they never connected to males, came up with the idea that it never hurt to have a woman by their side. For a spell, Billie Holiday traveled with Basie. From 1938 to 1942 Helen Humes worked with the Count. She also recorded with Harry James in 1938.

Girl-singer Ella Fitzgerald, who had her own band, proved women could operate in a man's world.

Ella Fitzgerald got her big break at the Apollo's amateur night contest.

Valaida Snow appeared with Earl Hines. Not only did she sing but she also played the trumpet. Noble Sissle's orchestra employed Lena Horne, the new girl beauty of the era. Chick Webb took a chance on a plump teen-ager from Newport News, Virginia, who seemed timid but mighty anxious to please, the young Ella Fitzgerald. And Pennsylvania-born Maxine Sullivan appeared with band-leader John Kirby, whom she later married. Sometimes the girl-singer sang the hit that overshadowed the band. Sullivan not only had the popular swing version of the Scottish folk tune "Loch Lomond," but she appeared in the movies *St. Louis Blues* and *Going Places* and also worked opposite Louis Armstrong in the 1939 pop version of *A Midsummer Night's Dream* called *Swingin' the Dream*. And Fitzgerald had jukeboxes jumping to the beat of "A-Tisket A-Tasket." Once she hooked up with Webb, the two of them reigned as the King and Queen of Harlem's Savoy Ballroom. When Webb died in 1939, Fitzgerald took over management of the band and kept it going for three years. Countless other women such as June Richmond, Velma Middleton, and May Alix performed with various groups.

Closely aligned to the girl singers were the other women on the sidelines of the big bands, pianists Lil Hardin Armstrong (Louis' first wife and an important jazz artist in her own right), Vivian Smith, Irene Wilson (at one time the wife of orchestra leader Teddy Wilson and also the composer of three of Billie Holiday's favorite songs: "I'm Pulling Through," "Ghost of Yesterday," and "Some Other Spring"), and Mary Lou Williams. In Kansas City, Mary Lou Williams joined Andy Kirk's Clouds of Joy, arranging, composing, and performing as pianist from 1931 to 1942. Eventually, Williams came east where her radio performances and records won her a national following. She also wrote for Benny Goodman and had her own band for a short time in the forties.

Almost automatically, the girl-singers stood as symbols of resourceful, knowing women on the move, hip and clever enough to travel on the band's bus with the boys, to play cards with them (and win), and to swap stories.

But at night when the house lights went down, the girl-singers stood under the spotlight and took on another dimension. As they sang of loneliness or despair, of hard times or low ones, they represented woman alone, coming to grips with feelings in a way no male singer would have dared. Finally, what distinguished them was that, unlike the raucous Bessie out to shake society up, these women, even when singing of hot, wild times, had a quiet, restrained, comforting approach.

The ebullient Helen Humes sang with Count Basie's Band from 1938–42.

Ivie Anderson *(far right)* with Duke Ellington *(fifth from right)* and his orchestra.

IVIE ANDERSON: THE DUKE'S LONELY CO-ED

For many, the thirties quintessential big band girl-singer was the sleek, sometimes chummy, sometimes aloof Ivie Anderson. For audiences black and white, she represented a wholly new statement in black womanhood, her look and manner entirely different and distinct. Neither a hefty mama like Bessie nor an exuberantly high-spirited gal like McKinney, Ivie Anderson was slender, with a rich brown coloring, expressive eyes, and a long sensual face that could convey a variety of moods. She slipped onto stage often wearing white gowns that were long, silky, slinky, elegant, and very, very sexy. Often entertainers had been given to overstatement or to showy expressions of their affluence. Ivie Anderson ushered in the look and demeanor of the classy colored girl—the kind of figure she seemed to be singing about in her big hit "A Lonely Co-ed"—from a good black girls' school like Bennett or Spelman (the black Vassar and Radcliffe of the South).

Surely, what contributed to Ivie's well-mannered style was her early training. Born in Gilroy, California, in 1904, she had been reared in a convent until her early teens. Throughout the twenties this ladylike young singer worked the West and East coasts, appearing with such bands as Curtis Mosby's, Paul Howard's, Sonny Clay's, even for a brief spell with the white band of Anson Weeks. By the thirties she had joined Earl Hines at the Grand Terrace in Chicago. Here her career took a dramatic turn when Duke Ellington, anxious for a girl singer to spice up his debut at the Oriental Theatre, hired Ivie (then spelled Ivy). Originally, he had wanted May Alix, but some thought she was so light-skinned that she might be mistaken for white and that there might be problems. Finally, the Duke settled on hiring the browner Ivie but he never had any regrets because Anderson was an extraordinary presence and a singer of great skill.

During the twelve years Anderson toured throughout the States and Europe with Ellington's orchestra, she was often considered the group's high point. If anything, she may have blended in too well with the Ellington sound for she never became a major solo artist.

Onstage, she was versatile and perceptive enough, like the Duke, to instantly gauge an audience's mood. Blessed with a comic flair and an impeccable sense of showmanship, she worked up an act with drummer Sonny Greer in

By the late thirties, Ella was billed—above the band—as the First Lady of Swing.

Ivie Anderson sang with Duke Ellington's Orchestra for twelve years and retired at a young age because of poor health.

which they exchanged playful banter that had sexual innuendos flying all over the place. Anderson always kept the upper hand because she was too cool to ever be done in by a souped-up cat. With a nonchalant shrug or a toss of her head, Ivie Anderson was above everything, operating in her own magical kingdom where maintaining your cool meant more than anything, except music.

As a singer, she was versatile too. Such songs as "When My Sugar Walks Down the Street," "Truckin'," and "All God's Chillun Got Rhythm" were delivered with enthusiasm and a wonderful sense of fun. She performed the last in the Marx Brothers movie *A Day at the Races*, announcing to Depression moviegoers that troubles didn't mean a thing and that it was time to turn their frowns upside down. She also calmly mastered the song considered the battle hymn of the period, Ellington's "It Don't Mean a Thing (If It Ain't Got That Swing)." Here she captured the era's sentimental longing for a return to happy days. As Ivie sang it, the idea was: Let's have a great time together—even now in the worst of times!

Generally, she favored sentimental compositions. In her hands "If You Were in My Place," "There's a Lull in My Life," "Isn't Love the Strangest Thing," and "A Lonely Co-ed" became memorable, haunting ballads, brimming over with loneliness and melancholia as well as with technical virtuosity. Her renditions of Ellington's "Mood Indigo" and "Solitude" remain definitive. When she is inevitably compared to Billie Holiday, about all that can be said is that she never gave in totally to emotion as Lady Day did. (Nobody else did either.) Ivie Anderson had an objective correlative in her work. She gave Depression audiences the emotional content, yet always held herself and the listener at a distance so they might not only hear but understand too.

Years later when commenting on the Ellington Orchestra of the sixties, music critic Ralph Gleason wrote: "In only one respect has this band lost with the years: There never was, nor will there ever be again, a vocalist of the caliber of Ivie Anderson. She was unique and irreplaceable. There have been other good singers with the band, but only Ivie sounded as if she was born to sing to this music."

And in his autobiography *Black and White Baby*, entertainer Bobby Short said:

Like Gertrude Lawrence, she could sing the worst songs in the grandest way. And she had a rare gift. She was a popular singer who listened to the lyrics

Billie Holiday with musicians during a rehearsal in New York.

and stayed within the character of the song. She was into the words and music at a time when most girl singers flounced out and warbled lyrics about heartbreak and despair with bright smiles on their faces.

He added that she was his favorite singer "for all time."

In the early forties Ivie Anderson left Ellington's orchestra, much to his great regret and hers. It is doubtful if there was ever another girl-singer he liked as much. But for most of her life, the quiet, shy, young woman reared in a convent had suffered terrifying attacks of asthma. In time, the wear of the road, the tension of the performances, the anxieties, left their mark. Advised by her physician to give up traveling, she returned to California, performed for a spell as a solo attraction, and later opened her Chicken Shack restaurant, a favorite wateringhole for musicians in the West. In 1949, Ivie Anderson died.

Billie began her career in tiny Harlem clubs.

BILLIE HOLIDAY: THE ESSENCE OF BLACK COOL

Of all the era's girl singers, Billie Holiday became the most famous. Even in the early days of her career, everyone knew something about her past. She was born Eleanora Fagan in Baltimore in 1915, the illegitimate child of a domestic, Sadie Fagan, and a musician, Clarence Holiday, who abandoned mother and child to resume his career on the road. His attitude about the daughter who would worship him for years was that she was simply an accident, "something I stole when I was fifteen."

While her mother worked in New York, young Eleanora lived with relatives. Sensitive, mistreated, unhappy, she often hung out at the local brothel because that was the only place in the neighborhood with a Victrola. There she would sit for hours and listen to her idols, Louis Armstrong and Bessie Smith. Little Eleanora had quite a childhood. She ran errands for the prostitutes, was almost raped at age ten, and was then sent to a Catholic institution because it was assumed she had "enticed" the man. She sat silent when her grandmother died with her arms wrapped around her. By thirteen, she quit school, having gone only to the fifth grade, and by fifteen she was working as a maid in New York with her mother. For a short time she worked as a prostitute and was thrown into jail when she shunned the attentions of a Harlem dude, who had connections all over town.

Billie Holiday's early experiences and humiliations were so terrifying that they stuck with her for the rest of her life, spilling over into her personal relationships and often making her suspicious of everyone. The experiences obviously had a bearing on Billie, the artist, for in her songs she was determined to explore the emotional territory of a woman smothered by feeling, who had to sing the things she could not say.

She began to sing in tiny Harlem clubs, where she acquired a reputation among musicians as a remarkable jazz vocalist who used her voice the way Armstrong played his horn. In 1933 at age eighteen, she made her first records for Columbia. Record producer John Hammond, who signed her up, said that "she sang popular songs in a manner that made them completely her own....She was absolutely beautiful, with a look and bearing that were, indeed ladylike, and never deserted her, even in the degraded final years....She was the best jazz singer I had ever heard." Her first records (with Benny Goodman), "Riffin' the Scotch" and "Your

A glamorous Billie Holiday in the mid-thirties: lush, sensual, romantic.

Holiday went all the way with a song, turning the lyrics inside out.

Mother's Son-In-Law," were fast moving, lively numbers, a far cry from the sometimes sentimental romantic ballads or the torch songs she later became famous for. Her high spirits gave no indication of the somber, relentless brooding quality that would permeate her late work.

In 1935 she was booked at the Apollo, then the most talked about showplace in the world for black entertainers. Throughout the thirties Ivie Anderson and the Duke performed there as did the up-and-coming Moms Mabley. And in time the Apollo's famous amateur nights would see the likes of Sarah Vaughan, Billy Eckstine, La Vern Baker, and the Isley Brothers. Even Ella Fitzgerald had her big break there. With Holiday, everyone seemed caught up in the excitement of seeing a major talent coming into her own. According to Holiday biographer John Chilton, Apollo emcee Ralph Cooper saw that she was so nervous that he went out and bought her clothes for the appearance and even rehearsed her numbers for the band. The night she opened comedian Pigmeat Markham had to push her onto the stage.

Her initial shyness and vulnerability, not at all lost on the audience, simply added to the intensity of her performance. There she stood, an awkward, good-natured country girl, weighing almost two hundred pounds, scared out of her wits. She was neatly dressed and nicely coiffed. All she had to do was smile—and she was perfect. But when she sang—"Them There Eyes" and "If the Moon Turns Green"—the enthusiastic black audience screamed for an encore that brought the house down. She sang "The Man I Love." Billie Holiday was booked for a return engagement and was now on her way.

Throughout the thirties Holiday hopped from one club to another, worked with the prominent musicians of her day (Teddy Wilson, Fletcher Henderson, Count Basie), reached a far wider audience than her predecessors, received good press, and, upon agreeing to appear with Artie Shaw's band, became the first black woman to travel through the South with a white group.

She was a remarkable performer, able to turn the trite lyrics of pop tunes inside out, coming up with individualized phrasings/interpretations that made an audience think twice about a number it might have heard for years. Then, too, there was the unexpected emotional depth. The direction of her career (and life-style) was unheard of for a black entertainer. For Holiday eventually integrated the chic, glittering supper clubs, paving the way for women like Lena Horne, Carmen McRae, Sarah Vaughan, and Ella Fitzgerald. The darling of sophisticated café society of the late thirties and forties, she represented for Black America the modern, sometimes feisty and foulmouthed, black woman who had made it into the system without losing her roots. Even as she went from job to job, band to band, she was part of a progressive dream.

In terms of the professional black woman's image, she introduced a new kind of glamour. She was hardly your run-of-the-mill girl-singer. Already she was known as Lady. (In time her good buddy Lester Young would tag her Lady Day.) And while still young, she had the look of a well-decked matron with expensive full-skirted, low-cut dresses, plenty of jewelry, and lots of makeup. Later she luxuriated in furs. And, of course, there was her trademark, the gardenia pinned to her hair. Although viewed as a working girl, Billie Holiday would never have thought of doing the stricken-Depression-child bit. Throughout her career, like all the other great divas, she refused to look tacky, poor, or ordinary. Clothes always had a significance for these women, assuring them that their childhood fantasies of escape had indeed come true.

But when she sang—"Them There Eyes" and "If the Moon Turns Green"—the enthusiastic black audience screamed for an encore that brought the house down.

But what with all her success, something else was happening to Billie Holiday in the thirties. The personal myth was emerging from behind troubled shadows, gradually pushing aside the thirties' popular myth that her public was so taken with. Her lucky breaks had made it look as if the American system was holding up. But Holiday lived the problems her public didn't care to see. No other diva was ever as disoriented by success. And for no other did personal and professional deterioration set in as quickly.

Of course, often enough she created problems for herself. When appearing at a Philadelphia theatre, she was informed by the theatre owner's wife that the song she planned to sing ("Underneath the Harlem Moon") was the same one headliner Ethel Waters had intended to perform. By all rights, Holiday should have deferred to the older established star, but she wouldn't budge! A terrible row followed, in which Billie spared not a word, letting the theatre owner's wife know exactly how she felt. (Nobody knows what she said to Ethel or what Ethel said to her. Later Waters did comment on Billie's style: "She sounds like her feet hurt.") Holiday was shown the door. She should have learned, but she didn't. Later when successfully traveling with Count Basie's band, she was asked to change some of her material, to sing more blues rather than pop tunes. She flatly refused, and soon she and the Count parted ways.

Other times, Holiday was hassled by club bookers insensitive to her originality. According to Holiday biographer Chilton, at Chicago's Grand Terrace, owner Ed Fox, infuriated by a performance he thought too slow and too somber, yelled at her, "Why the fuck should I pay you $250 (actually, it was $75) a week to stink my goddamn show up. Get out!" She left, but not before speaking her mind and throwing furniture at him.

On other occasions Billie Holiday fell victim to the blatant racism of her period. In 1935, when she appeared at the Famous Door in New York City, she was told not to mingle with the patrons, not to sit at a table or the bar. Before going on, she waited upstairs outside the toilets. The atmosphere was so tense that it affected her performance. Finally, she was let go from the club. Afterward, when traveling with Basie, she was repeatedly turned away from hotels and restaurants. Her worst experiences were with Shaw, who was considered "daring" for hiring a black girl-singer. But in time this extraordinary career boost proved an emotionally debilitating experience, with the familiar problems simply intensified. It was still a hassle finding a place to sleep or eat. In Boston there were complaints about her style. The bookers wanted her to speed things up. In St. Louis a promoter insisted she be replaced with a white singer. Helen Forrest was brought in. By far, the most depressing business was that of the radio broadcasts, which became fewer and fewer because music publishers griped that she did not stick closely enough to the written melody and lyrics. When she appeared with Shaw at New York's Lincoln Hotel, she was not permitted to visit the bar or the dining room and was told always to use the kitchen entrance. It was getting to the regal Lady Day and the tension showed.

Black America watched the drama of Billie Holiday, connecting to this troubled, restless girl as it did with no other diva. For whatever problems this young woman had in such "high" places were no different from their own.

By 1938 Billie Holiday had left Shaw. She had left Basie. She had left Teddy Wilson. She had left innumerable clubs. She probably had been fired more frequently than any other major star of the time. And she was rapidly becoming even more of an introspective, withdrawn, difficult woman. Her love affairs weren't going right. Her eating habits were erratic. Her reputation as a hell-raiser and carouser had grown. She was always being hassled

by men. And she was drinking. Clearly, she was headed for a tragic decline that she seemed to invite. In conversation, she started painting herself as the victim: of a terrible childhood, of men, of callous club managers, of racism, of you-name-it. She loved to dramatize her woes and tribulations. In the beginning all her talk may have been nothing more than a public pose she felt comfortable with. One of her tenderest songs, "God Bless the Child," became her anthem, touching on her feelings of isolation and alienation. Unfortunately, Holiday later became trapped in the persona she had at first played with. What eventually took over was the other Billie, the drug-ridden, self-pitying, magnetic star who could be unbearably temperamental and impossible to deal with.

As an artist, the thirties may well have been Billie Holiday's musical high point, the period of intense creativity when her voice was clearest, strongest, and most vibrant. Her most stabilizing experience was at Cafe Society, one of the first New York white niteries to integrate not only its performers but its audiences too. There she introduced "Strange Fruit," the moody dirge about a southern lynching. For years it played on jukeboxes throughout the country, particularly in tiny hidden black bars and restaurants. And so paradoxical as it may seem now, in the days of the Great Depression audiences saw in Billie Holiday a hopeful sign for the future, a representative of the basically decent young black woman, who, having survived the toughest of times, was bound to get through anything else without any pain. As Duke Ellington said, she was the essence of black cool.

Billie's childhood fantasies come true—furs, jewels, and escape from poverty.

Hattie McDaniel, Shirley Temple, and Evelyn Venable in *The Little Colonel*.

LOUISE BEAVERS AND HATTIE MCDANIEL: THE DIVA GOES WEST

Nowhere in American popular culture of the thirties was the black-woman-as-pop-myth more prominently displayed than in Hollywood. During the Depression era more black women worked in important American movies than ever before. The hitch was that the place the film industry found for the black actress was in the kitchen or pantry or servants' quarters. The divas of the stages and clubs, the girl-singers and actresses, may not have had control over the way the American public chose to view them, but at least they had shaped their own personas and exerted control over their material.

The Hollywood diva was dressed by the studio in gingham and rags and made to speak a "dem and dose" dialect. Audiences saw black movie heroines playing servants—and rigidly stereotyped ones at that. Yet the history of American cinema has always been infused by contradictions, unexpected complexities, and oddball triumphs. And demeaning as Hollywood's casting system was, some remarkable black women were able to inject their cheap, trashy roles with some much needed vigor and pizzazz. Interestingly enough, the black woman of the thirties films came—on her own terms—to represent beneath the stereotype the idea of energy, drive, spunk, that good old American virtue of self-sufficiency too: the ability to get through, no matter what. Throughout the thirties and into the forties, certain women presented distinct personas, giving in the long run intensely interesting idiosyncratic performances. In *Flying Down to Rio* and *Gold Diggers of 1933*, Etta Moten held onto her grand dame hauteur. Theresa Harris emerged as the intelligent pretty brown black girl. Gertrude Howard, Libby Taylor, Marietta Canty, Lillian Yarbo, and Ruby Dandridge (the mother of Dorothy) were the giddy happy-go-lucky numbers. The Randolph sisters, Lillian and Amanda (who would later work in the fifties television series "Amos and Andy"), could so easily push people around that no one would have wanted to tangle with them offscreen. And there was the cold-eyed, mean-looking Madame Sul-Te-Wan, one of Hollywood's strangest characters, rumored to be the mistress of D. W. Griffith. And the high-pitched voiced, diminutive Butterfly McQueen always had the gift of operating in a world entirely her own, set apart from the culture of the film. In the black community no one ever disliked these women, for everyone understood role playing. What was despised was their movies' lopsided sensibilities.

Out of this insane stereotype system, there appeared two powerful forces, Louise Beavers and Hattie McDaniel, who managed to come up with workable pop myths that reached huge audiences. Sometimes the myths were so entangled with the stereotypes and misconceptions of the movies' scripts that the actresses had trouble making personal statements through their characters. Much of the way in which America was to conventionally view the black woman grew out of these women's performances.

Cincinnati-born Louise Beavers came to prominence portraying overweight mammy figures ready to take on the troubles of the world. Beavers was a big-boned woman, dark, full-faced, wide-hipped. She perfected the optimistic, sentimental black woman whose sweet, sunny disposition and kindheartedness almost always saved the day. In such features as *Rainbow on the River, She Done Him Wrong, Bombshell, Big Street, Bullets or Ballots*, and the classic tearjerker of 1934 *Imitation of Life*, she emerged as the Depression era's embodiment of Christian stoicism and goodness, lending a friendly ear and hand to down-on-their-luck heroines, who knew that when the rest of the world failed them, Louise would always be there. In *Made for Each Other*, when Carole Lombard and James Stewart are down to their last penny, who shows up with food for the hungry, but their former servant Louise! In *Big Street* when Lucille Ball lies ill and lonely in the hospital, who suggests to Henry Fonda that by pawning Ball's jewelry, there will be money for medical expenses? Why good old Louise. And in *Bombshell*, when platinum blonde Harlow, as a movie star surrounded by greedy sycophants, finally has had it, who is the one person she screams has ever really done anything for her? None other than her friendly maid, Loretta, played by Beavers. Her roles, of course, were absurdities, white myths about black lives. But Beavers approached them with the seriousness and integrity of a true trouper. She also appeared in independently produced movies made outside the studio system. Because of her skill as well as her own awareness of what the scripts neglected to say about her characters, she herself said much, with a look or a gesture, and was a more subversive presence than any movie mogul might have thought.

In *Imitation of Life* she played her most famous character, Aunt Delilah, a domestic who, because of the hard times, shares a house with a white woman who becomes a friend. The movie prided itself on its theme of

In *Judge Priest*, Hattie had a chance to strut and dress up.

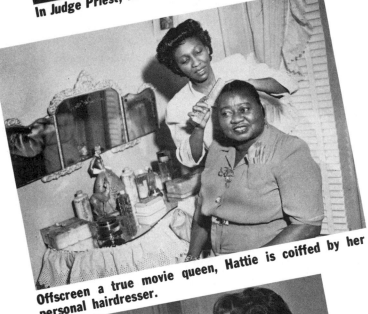

Offscreen a true movie queen, Hattie is coiffed by her personal hairdresser.

In 1939 McDaniel (here with Fay Bainter) walked off with an Oscar.

racial harmony. White and black could unite and make a go of things during these hard times. But no one who has seen the film could fail to be haunted by the image of the tender, sensitive Beavers, still living with the white woman once they have both struck it rich, descending the stairs late at night to return to her quarters in the basement. And in another scene when Beavers' heart is breaking because her only daughter has decided to pass for white, American movie audiences, for a few minutes, were no longer in a Hollywood fantasy world, but were confronted by a complex social situation disturbingly real.

While Beavers was relaxed and easygoing, Hattie McDaniel was anything but. Also a large, dark black woman typed as the mammy, McDaniel was as well one of the most charismatic performers, black or white, to work in American motion pictures. In scores of movies McDaniel kept her own with some of the most famous stars of the decade: Gable, Hepburn, Harlow, Vivien Leigh, Shirley Temple, Olivia de Havilland, and Barbara Stanwyck. Boldly, she looked her white costars directly in the eye, never backing off from anyone. Her extraordinary sonic boom of a voice delivered perfectly timed one-line zingers with the greatest of ease. Sometimes McDaniel seemed angry. Although the movies never explained it, her undercover hostility, even when coated with humor, was never lost on the audience. She set her own standards and sailed through many films with an astonishing sense of self and personal dignity. For her work as the cantankerous character Mammy in *Gone With the Wind*, Hattie McDaniel became the first black performer to win an Academy Award for Best Supporting Actress of 1939.

The characters McDaniel and Beavers created were given full-blown treatment by Ethel Waters in the late forties and fifties. And in the late fifties Lorraine Hansberry created a character, the mother, Lena, in *A Raisin in the Sun*, who finally had a chance onstage and in film to say all the things about a black matriarch that McDaniel and Beavers had fought to bring to the forefront of their shallow films.

With these actresses, though, we see the importance in American pop culture of the black matriarch myth. The myth turns her sexless, has her more caught up in someone else's life than her own, makes her entirely faultless, the essence of Christian goodness, and teaches us that she is noble for adjusting to a trying situation without complaining. Looking at the life of Hattie McDaniel, one can see what nonsense the popular myth was. Hattie had three husbands, lived in a plush

Hollywood home, loved entertaining, and, if pushed, she pushed back. But the matriarch has become one of the staples of the culture: the dark, all-knowing, all-seeing, all-understanding spiritual force that we can go to when all else fails us. In the seventies gifted actresses Cicely Tyson and Olivia Cole would get caught up in just such a dazzling conception, one-part true, one-part national wish fulfillment. Brilliant as these actresses' characterizations were, here again were acceptable matriarchs out to heal and soothe everybody's wounds, never to open them up.

Louise Beavers and Hattie McDaniel had long careers that spanned some four decades. At the time of her death in 1952, McDaniel was starring on radio and television as Beulah. Ethel Waters, then Louise Beavers, took over the lead role in the series. Beavers' last movie performance was in *The Facts of Life* in 1961.

Other actresses did a few films, then left Hollywood. Butterfly McQueen might have had an ongoing movie career playing helpless hysterical maids. But even by the early fifties, when she joined the cast of television's "Beulah" to play the daffy neighbor Oriole, she was ready to leave the film capital because the industry failed to give her a chance to grow as an artist. In 1929 Ethel Waters sang "Am I Blue" in *On with the Show*, then did not appear in a major movie for almost ten years. The delightful Edna Mae Harris appeared in *Green Pastures*, then left Hollywood. But she continued working in independently produced all-black movies made in the East. So did such actresses as Bee Freeman and Ethel Moses. Ivie Anderson appeared in *A Day at the Races* (along with the young Dandridge sisters, Vivian and Dorothy) and with the Duke in *The Hit Parade*. Billie Holiday appeared in the musical short *Symphony in Black*, and later worked with Louis Armstrong in *New Orleans*. (The shocker of this last film was seeing Holiday playing a maid.) Eventually, Lena Horne, Hazel Scott, and Katherine Dunham had a chance to carry their stage personas intact to films. None stayed in Hollywood, but they all realized that film exposure added to their glamorous aura. Nightclub customers were anxious to see the movie star in person.

All the divas, though, had a passionate hope that the movies would eventually find a place for a sensitive, serious black woman. That place was a long time in coming. But on no other thirties figure did the dream seem to have so great a chance of being fulfilled as with Fredi Washington, who emerged as one of Black America's most compelling, electrically charged pop myths of the era.

Louise Beavers (left) with Fredi Washington in the 1934 *Imitation of Life*.

Beavers as the stoic Mother Barton in the all-black movie *Reform School*.

In *Bullets or Ballots*, with Joan Blondell (left) and Edna Mae Harris, Beavers played a Harlem numbers' racket queen.

THE WASHINGTON SISTERS: ORPHANS OF THE STORM

You would never know she was Negro or considered herself such to look at her. She can "pass" whenever it is necessary or convenient, but she makes no attempt to pass: in fact, she feels herself to be entirely identified with the Negro group. Yet Fredi, in a white environment, would be considered white.
Earl Conrad, The Chicago Defender.

Fredi Washington, well known on New York stages . . . [is] not seen on them so frequently as she would be if skin color were not of such surpassing importance . . . . Fredi is one of those people who find color a special problem in this country for the odd reason that she has little of it. You could describe her in two ways. She is a white girl who could pass as a Negro girl or a Negro girl who could pass as white. Elsewhere there might be no question of being either, but here in this democracy Americans are supposed to be one or another and they have to make a choice. Fredi Washington made it when she was a kid.
Arthur Pollock, The Daily Compass

Today the words of these newspaper columnists aptly touch on some of the peculiar racial dynamics of American life during the Depression and World War II years. What happens to the black woman who does not look black? What kind of career can she have if she refuses to pass? How is she viewed by her society? These were questions that confronted the legendary Washington sisters, Fredi and Isabel. In theatre and social circles, the two were among the most talked about black beauties of their age. And whenever their names came up, so too did their color.

They were light-skinned with straight hair and Caucasian features. Slender and green-eyed, Fredi (her full name was Fredricka) looked like a fiercely intellectual young career girl on the move. She was something of a mystery, a lovely, quiet woman seemingly given to melancholy. Isabel was less intense: an extroverted, happy-go-lucky young woman ready for a good time. For a number of very prominent people, perhaps most particularly white men, they represented the ultimate taboo: miscegenated beauties "cursed" by that drop of "negra" blood, which somehow, so the myth said, made

them more exciting and passionate than your ordinary white lady. No doubt in the popular imagination they were viewed as objects that should not freely mingle in society. Instead, they had to be kept locked away, pampered, and glorified. The sisters never saw themselves in this way. If they had, they would have been able to clean up, to run New York City dry. (Years later Eartha Kitt, aware that whites saw her as a classy exotique, would play up the exoticism bit to the hilt.)

For the black community the two sisters, who spoke without dialects, who understood the social codes and manners of both cultures, and who gave no indication whatsoever of having come from a harsh urban ghetto experience, were considered highborn, upper-class beauties, representatives of the old southern Negro aristocracy. This was what the popular imagination assumed the women to be. Actually, their background was not so much privileged, or moneyed, as simply different.

Born in Savannah, Georgia, they had been sent to a northern convent for orphaned black and Indian children after the death of their mother. Once teen-agers, they left. Isabel returned South, married at sixteen, and had a son. Fredi journeyed to New York to live with her grandmother and to finish school. At sixteen she dropped out and worked in a dress company stockroom, making seventeen dollars a week. Later as a bookkeeper at W. C. Handy's Black Swan Record Company, she heard of auditions for *Shuffle Along*. Never having danced professionally before, she decided to take a chance anyway. After all, the pay was thirty-five dollars a week. When she told her grandmother of her plans, the older woman simply looked at her and said: "If you do it, make something of it." Fredi replied: "Don't worry." With the help of black choreographer Elida Webb, she landed a spot in the chorus.

So began a career that had many high points, many disappointments, and which was often enough governed by the response of theatregoers to Fredi Washington's looks. After *Shuffle Along* she appeared as a dancer at New York's Club Alabam', and was spotted by Lee Shubert. Obviously dazzled, he suggested she audition for a new play *Black Boy*, starring Paul Robeson as a prizefighter. Opening in the play on Broadway, she had what remains for her an archetypal role: a fair-skinned black beauty who decides to pass for white. With good reviews she was soon one of Broadway's most talked about ingenues. Inside the theatres some came simply to see if the girl they had heard of looked that white. Outside theatres, stage-door Johnnies, black and white, pursued, chased, and harassed Fredi Washington like mad.

Relaxing on a movie set *(from left to right)*: Bill Robinson, Fredi Washington, Adam Clayton Powell, Jr., Isabel Washington, and Fannie Robinson.

Green-eyed Fredi Washington was often urged to pass for white.

Millionaire Otto Kahn, who told her she looked French and could easily be French, was so convinced of her potential to become a major star, if freed of the "burden of her race," that, according to printed theatre gossip of the day, he even offered to pay for her dramatic education if she changed her name to a French one. "But I want to be what I am," Washington told him, "nothing else."

During the twenties Washington toured the smart night spots of Paris, London, Berlin, and Monte Carlo with Charles Moore, billed as the dancers Moiret and Fredi. Mingling with European royalty, she even taught the black bottom to the Prince of Wales.

The late twenties found her back in the States in *Hot Chocolates*. Later she appeared in such plays as *Sweet Chariot* and *Run, Little Chillun* and in short musical films with Cab Calloway and Duke Ellington. For a time she was married to Lawrence Brown, trombonist with the Duke's orchestra.

But during the thirties she emerged as one of Black America's most exciting dramatic actresses. There had not been many. Rose McClendon's dramatic career had been cut short by her premature death. Edna Thomas was a spectacular Lady Macbeth in the Orson Welles/John Houseman New Negro Theater's production of voodoo *Macbeth*, but she had few opportunities to sustain her dramatic career. Washington, however, had strong roles in such movies as *Emperor Jones, Imitation of Life, One Mile from Heaven*, and the play *Mamba's Daughters*. For a spell it looked as if Hollywood had a serious young black actress it would have to reckon with. But, ironically, Fredi's greatest success almost did her in.

Her big triumph was as Peola, the light-skinned black girl who passes for white in the original version of *Imitation of Life*. Seen today, the movie is a classic cornball weeper, but compellingly watchable. The movie told the story of two women, one white (Claudette Colbert), one black (Louise Beavers), each a widow with a young daughter to raise, who meet and decide to live together. The white woman goes out to work everyday. The black woman takes care of the house. One morning the black woman is fixing breakfast for the white woman, who is so taken by her friend's pancakes that she wants to know the recipe. It is a family secret, the black woman explains, passed down from generation to generation. Eventually, the white woman strikes it rich with the black woman's pancake mix, and has everything money can buy—furs, jewels, beaux. Everything is going so well that she offers her black friend a twenty percent interest in the company! The black woman, submissive and kind, refuses.

Heartache follows when the black woman's mulatto daughter, Peola, having grown up in a household with whites no lighter than herself, but for whom there is now a world of opportunities, rejects her mother's submissiveness and crosses the color line, going so far as to tell her that if they should ever meet by chance they must act as if they are strangers. The movie ends with Peola returning home for the funeral of her mother, who has died of a broken heart, falling onto the casket, crying, "I killed my mother." There was not a dry eye in the movie house.

A runaway box-office success, *Imitation of Life*, no matter how corny its story might seem today, had an uncanny impact on both Black and White America in 1934, for it was one of the few films to even remotely suggest there was such a thing as a race problem. In the black community a nerve cord had been hit, and emotions and sentiments flew high. Ministers preached sermons about it. Intellectuals wrote articles about it. Everyone seemed caught up in its fever, the focal point of which was daughter Peola. On one occasion, as Fredi

For a spell it looked as if Hollywood had a serious young black actress it would have to reckon with. But, ironically, Fredi's greatest success almost did her in.

Washington sat in a beauty parlor, she overheard another woman telling a beautician that she knew Fredi Washington and that that high-yellar so-and-so was, in real life, just the way she had been on screen. Of course, the woman did not know Washington at all, and when Fredi introduced herself, the lady promptly shut up. On another occasion, as Washington was leaving a Chicago theatre that had shown the picture, she was grateful not to be recognized because all the conversation centered on the ingrate daughter. "I bet that Fredi Washington is just like that too" was a comment the actress heard too often.

The feelings about Washington were ambivalent. In one sense, she was a classy woman audiences loved to hate, the kind of villain contemporary soap opera viewers endlessly criticize, but whose every move they are sure to watch. Peola's dilemma, whether to pass or not, in essence whether to submit or rebel, was a far more serious issue than the moviemakers had realized. Black audiences could understand how a woman felt when denied such an ideal as personal freedom. Aware of the girl's frustration, many responded to her determination to break the rules of a trumped-up, exploitative, decadent capitalistic society with a *why not?* Then, too, Fredi Washington, because of what the black community thought it knew about her personal life-style of privilege, sometimes was viewed as a princess entitled to all she could get.

There were other reactions. The movie had been so manipulative that no one could forgive the girl's treatment of her mother. Here another issue arose, that of identification and loyalty to one's racial heritage. Peola seemed to have broken not only the white world's rules, but those of the black community too.

Of course, much of the ambivalence was due to the slipshod way the character had been written. *Imitation of Life* had failed to deal squarely with a woman who does not want to be white as much as she wants white opportunities. Regardless, the movie made Fredi Washington a household name throughout Black America, and what with the frequent reissuing of the film, Washington was associated with the character for the duration of her career. That may partly explain why afterward her roles were few and far between. For the mass audience, under the power of film and the print media that had established

---

The tragic side to Washington's dilemma was that she never had the opportunities for strong new roles that might have wiped away the Peola myth.

---

a Washington persona, Fredi and Peola were one and the same. As such, Washington emerged a gorgeous oddity, no longer an actress, but one of the most dazzling myths of the period. The popular imagination always simplifies complex experiences. And for Depression audiences, white as well as black, anxious to point the finger at someone or something responsible for the loss of order, she would remain an ideal target: the guilt-ridden, troubled, anguished mulatto in whom were embodied the best and worst of the races.

The tragic side to Washington's dilemma was that she never had the opportunities for strong new roles that might have wiped away the Peola myth. In 1939 she made a triumphant Broadway appearance as Ethel Waters' lovely daughter Lissa in *Mamba's Daughters*. Fresh, alive, energetic, her character was a symbol of a new day, the well-brought-up child who would have all the advantages denied her mother. This role, however, was an exception, and impressive as Washington's Lissa was, the type did not take hold. Fredi Washington has said that had she remained in Hollywood, she would have had to play the standard black maid bit that Beavers and McDaniel perfected. But even the coarsest movie moguls were not

that nearsighted. Far too sleek and sophisticated in even their eyes to ever be cast as a "realistic" black woman on film, she was a scary problem they chose to do without. (Even earlier in her career, during the shooting of *Emperor Jones* opposite Robeson, Fredi learned one afternoon that all their love scenes had to be reshot. It was thought she looked too white and that there might be an uproar throughout the country if movie audiences saw Robeson holding a white girl in his arms. So Fredi was darkened for new sequences.) Unfortunately, neither the movie moguls nor audiences nor even sophisticated theatre producers had enough imagination to see Washington as an actress able to do any part. White actresses had played black women in plays and films. In fact, even when *Imitation of Life* was remade in 1959, a white actress, Susan Kohner, was cast in the part originated by Washington. But no black actress was given this kind of freedom.

Around this time, Washington's professional frustrations may have started getting to her. She threw herself into politically oriented activities. She was a founding member and Executive Secretary of the Negro Actors Guild, which aided the black performer in fighting discrimination in show business. Later her articles and reviews appeared in *The People's Voice*, published by her onetime brother-in-law, Adam Clayton Powell, Jr.

As the years moved on, she appeared in such plays as *A Long Way from Home* and the all-black version of *Lysistrata*. In the fifties she married a Connecticut dentist and retired from show business.

Shortly after Fredi's unexpected success in *Shuffle Along*, her sister Isabel (spelled Isabell for a time), captivated by the costumes, the bright lights, the glamorous atmosphere of Harlem nightlife, hit New York, determined to have a crack at showbiz herself. She debuted in *Runnin' Wild*, later danced at Connie's Inn and the Cotton Club, and appeared in the stage shows *Bamboola*, the extraordinary *Harlem*, and *Singin' the Blues*. In the latter she worked with Fredi, a fact the press was quick to pick up on. When the *New York Herald Tribune's* critic reviewed it, he seemed more caught up in the sisters' celebrity (and in getting off some swipes at one of their admirers, Walter Winchell) than in the play. He wrote:

It was interesting last night to learn from the all-knowing Mr. Winchell that the two most startling Negroid players in the play (the Misses Washington, Fredi and Isabell) are sisters, that they live in

Fredi Washington (*right*) and Ethel Waters in the Broadway hit *Mamba's Daughters.*

exclusive hotels and that they take themselves and their art with a smiling and a cunning semi-seriousness. Miss Fredi Washington acted the evil intrigante with all the poise of a declasse, pale patrician; and Miss Isabell equipped the heroine with many of the noble qualities known to weak, though sacrificial, womanhood, blonde or brunet.

Like other reviewers, this one may not have done much for the play, but he certainly helped in further establishing the celebrity personas of the sisters. As for Walter Winchell, then America's most influential theatre columnist, he remained an ardent fan, almost fawning over Isabel when he wrote of her as an "irresistible siren," as pretty a "high-yellar as they come"! *Singin' the Blues* also gave Isabel her typical kind of role, that of the good-natured, sweet, soft ingenue falling victim to a trying situation. In time, this was a role her public believed she played in her private life too.

Like Fredi, Isabel also had her share of admirers, and her marriage ended during this New York period. At the Cotton Club she was almost run ragged by the attentions of a well-to-do white clothing manufacturer who sat ringside, staring her down, three nights a week. Today the fact that Isabel and Fredi were pursued by white men may not mean much. But in the twenties and thirties this was a startling social phenomenon that had never before been engaged in openly.

Isabel, however, spurned the attentions of the clothing manufacturer and an array of others, waiting no doubt for Mr. Right to come along. He did too, during the run of her play *Harlem* in 1929. A student on spring break from

Washington as the distraught heroine of *One Mile from Heaven*.

Colgate College, he was more than just Mr. Right. He was the black community's darling crown prince, Adam Clayton Powell, Jr. In no time he was courting her. Once Isabel had fallen, then the hassles began.

As the minister of one of Black America's most prominent religious institutions, the Abyssinian Baptist Church in Harlem, Adam Clayton Powell, Sr., assumed, as did the church deacons, that his son would one day take over the ministry. Now with talk of his son's romance with a previously married entertainer six years his senior, Harlem's social world was thrown into a tizzy. Isabel was viewed as the typical woman of the theatre—wild, frivolous, and callous. But Powell, never a man to back down from anything he really wanted, had a confrontation with the church deacons in 1933. He announced that he was determined to have Isabel. Finally, the two married.

Isabel gave up her career, immersing herself in church affairs, working with youth clubs, including the Abyssinian's Tiny Tots Choir. (One little girl in the choir everyone predicted would go far was Diahann Carroll.) For eleven years Isabel Washington Powell remained in the news and limelight as the gracious, attractive young wife of a very assured, aggressive young man, and won the respect of Adam's family, the churchgoers, and the black community. Then Powell's political hungers grew more intense. Isabel once said she had no idea just how ambitious he was. After Powell's election to Congress, she was prepared for a new life until Powell informed her one evening that she would not be going to Washington with him. The marriage was over. Shortly afterward, in 1945, he married another diva, Hazel Scott. For Isabel Washington the breakup and divorce were the toughest experiences of her life. The man for whom she had reshaped most of her life had walked away. She admitted later she fell into shock and lost fourteen pounds in two weeks. Her anxieties and sorrow were not helped by her status as a celebrity. The black press seemed to know as much about her private life as she did. The story had the makings of a wonderful romantic melodrama. Attractive people. Money. Power. Position. Another woman. The wife who never knew. Earlier Fredi Washington had starred in a glorious, gaudy Hollywood soap opera. Now Isabel was the star of a real life one. Publicly humiliated, Isabel found her greatest friend was sister Fredi, who stepped in and helped her put the pieces of her life back together. After considering a return to show business, Isabel finally decided she wanted no more of the footlights. She remained in Harlem, continued sponsoring youth groups, and contentedly worked as a barber.

Ethel Waters's rendition of "Stormy Weather" marked a turning point in her career.

ETHEL WATERS: SWEET MAMA GOES LEGIT

The diva who brought the thirties to a much needed, roaring crescendo, who remains one of the Depression era's quintessential creations, was Ethel Waters. During her sixty-year career, Waters underwent a series of startling image changes, greater than that of any other star, black or white. In the thirties audiences saw Sweet Mama Stringbean undergo a distinct transformation right before their very eyes: from the high-kicking figure given to flash, who popped up at the start of the decade, to the been-through-hell-but-still-holding-on matriarchal figure at the era's end. Both were types Waters, the woman, was more than familiar with.

By the thirties Ethel Waters had had even a stormier personal life than the young Billie Holiday. She had survived a terrifying childhood and the exhausting backbreaking and backbiting road tours. She had been cheated out of money and kicked around by a steady stream of men. In her autobiography she related a nightmarish experience that took place on an early road tour. Outside Birmingham, she had been seriously injured in a car crash, which had left her lying on the road pinned under a car for hours. Shattered glass from the window shield had cut her badly. Boiling water from the damaged radiator scalded her breasts and stomach. A tendon had snapped. And her left leg was ripped open from the knee to hip. Whites passing by at first had refused to help. Only after her desperate pleas was Waters taken to a hospital where, as her leg wounds were being dressed, she had screamed out in agony, only to be told by the attending white physician: "You needn't holler, gal. This is what all you niggers should get when you wreck...cars." Afterward she was promptly deposited in the "nigger" quarters, there left unwashed, uncared for, unattended by a doctor.

Later, out of the hospital, recuperating at the home of friends, Ethel Waters learned that hundreds of blacks in the Birmingham area, upon hearing of her accident, had contributed pennies, nickels, dimes, to help pay her medical bills. The soft, sentimental side of Waters never forgot the kindness of the poor "little" people who had helped a stranger.

But the other side of Waters never forgot the cruelty. To her, this all seemed but one more in a long line of experiences of deprivation, humiliation, and terror that had hounded her for years. Today she is remembered as one of America's warmest dramatic actresses. But most who worked with her have agreed that, like the charming Bill "Bojangles" Robinson, this model of sobriety onstage was a raging holy terror off.

During the thirties her paranoia grew as she became increasingly more restless and difficult. Few got close to her. Whenever there was a dispute, she saw only one side of an issue: hers. Often she was dead right about the wrongs done her. But often, too, her fierce suspicions caused her unneeded problems. Her repeated bickerings with club managers, her associates, producers, and fellow entertainers not only rattled them but drained her too.

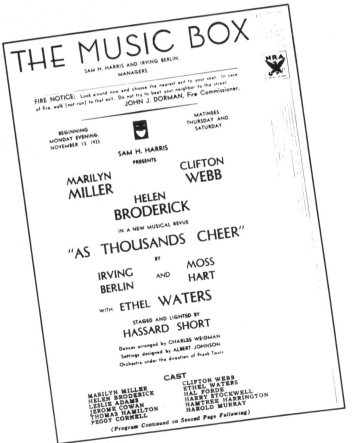

As Thousands Cheer **launched Ethel Waters as a Broadway star.**

Despite the problems, Ethel Waters was able to reach full artistic maturity in the thirties, although at the start of the era, growth hardly looked promising. She had hoped to become a Broadway star, but when her shows *Vaudeville, Blackbirds of 1930,* and *Rhapsody in Black* had failed to become bona fide hits on the Great White Way, she just gave up and returned to singing in clubs.

As a singer, many had thought she had already peaked. Waters herself, however, felt she had not yet fulfilled herself artistically as a singer. When she performed, everything was refined and distilled. But unlike the singers she admired (Ma and Bessie), who went all the way with a gut response to their material, Waters seemed to hold her feelings in. All her life she had had few emotional supports. Ma had a husband to protect her. Bessie had an unreal toughness and the love of the battle itself. But all Waters had was her sense of self, and that was pretty shaky. In song, it seemed as if she were afraid to pull out all the stops for fear that if she went too far emotionally she would end up right back in hell with too many bad memories. Ethel Waters was always in need of controls and structures to keep herself together. In time, she would find the one lasting thing that could sustain her—religion, her private sense of God. During the Depression era Waters got a new taste of emotional freedom. And her first liberator was the Harold Arlen song "Stormy Weather."

Today the legend persists of her splendid live rendition of the song. Standing on the floor of the Cotton Club—a big-boned woman who looked like a black madonna—she transformed a tale of love gone sour into one of a life gone wrong. Waters admitted that she had introduced the song at a time in her life when she was feeling particularly low, and had used it as self-therapy to sum up "the things I couldn't frame in words." It marked a turning point in her life. "I was singing the story of my misery and confusion," she said, "of the misunderstandings in my life I couldn't straighten out, the story of the wrongs and outrages done to me by people I had loved and trusted."

Irving Berlin heard her perform the song at the Cotton Club and soon afterward offered her a part in his Broadway-bound show *As Thousands Cheer,* a revue written by Moss Hart and Sam Harris and starring Clifton Webb, Marilyn Miller, and Helen Broderick. Waters leaped at the chance, although she had her doubts. After all, she would only be "local color material" in an essentially white-oriented show. She would not have top billing and she had only four numbers to perform. But she took the dare, opening in the show on Broadway in 1933.

Ethel Waters was the highest paid Broadway star of her time.

Ethel Waters singing "Heat Wave" in *As Thousands Cheer.*

For her number "Heat Wave," she strutted onstage dressed in colorful rags with an elaborate headdress of bananas and apples and other fruit, openly parodying Josephine Baker, the rival who had taken her chance and gone off to Europe. The audience went wild. Then she delivered "Supper Time," a mournful song about a black woman preparing her family's dinner, aware that her husband will not be returning home because he has been lynched. Waters had not known how a white theatre crowd coming to see a lighthearted revue would respond to this number. (At one time the producers had thought of dropping it altogether because it might be too much of a downer.) But as she performed it, she kept in mind that this song touched on "the whole tragic history of a race." "In singing it," she later said in her autobiography, "I was telling my comfortable, well-fed, well-dressed listener about my people." "Supper Time" moved Broadway audiences in a way never before experienced. And here Waters emerged as the first diva to deal explicitly with racial matters in a very popular song. (Holiday's "Strange Fruit" came a few years later.)

As Thousands Cheer firmly established Ethel Waters in the legitimate theatre and marked the beginning of her peak years when she became the highest paid woman on Broadway. Later elevated to star billing, she toured with the show, becoming the first black personality to costar with white performers below the Mason-Dixon line. While on Broadway, she also doubled at a nearby nightclub, earning $2,500 a week. And her radio broadcasts with the Jack Denny Orchestra on Sunday nights were considered major breakthroughs for a black entertainer. During this time she also lived in style, ensconced in a ten-room apartment (with one room given over entirely to religious artifacts and objects). When asked about her luxurious life-style—fur coats, jewelry, big cars—she explained: "The main reason I have for buying such extravagant objects is because a Broadway star cannot dress like a waif or ride in the subway. People will talk and you can say, 'The hell with them!' but they are my customers and I gotta live and appear in public as they expect me to."

In 1935 she was back on Broadway in *At Home Abroad* and finally, by the era's end, Waters had what she longed for most, the starring role in Broadway's *Mamba's Daughters*. This new melodrama by DuBose and Dorothy Heyward, the husband and wife team who had written the book for *Porgy*, told the story of three generations of black women, focusing mainly on the character Hagar, a large, half-crazed mother with a singular passion: seeing that her beautiful child, Lissa, has all the things in life the mother missed out on. During the emotionally charged climax of *Mamba's Daughters*, Hagar, in a fit of uncontrollable rage, strangles a "sporting man," who has raped her child.

Originally, the backers had doubts about a musical comedy star carrying a heavy dramatic play. But in January 1939, with a cast that included Georgette Harvey, Canada Lee, Jose Ferrer, Alberta Hunter, and Fredi Washington, Waters' performance in *Mamba's Daughters* won her seventeen curtain calls, made her the most talked about dramatic actress on Broadway, and garnered the following praise from Carl Van Vechten:

> *Whatever may be said for or against the play, the performance of Ethel Waters in the role of Hagar calls only for superlatives and has received them from all the critics. Rarely have I encountered such unanimity of opinion, such consistent enthusiasm. Seldom have I seen a first night audience so excited, so moved, so carried away by "make-believe." The*

As *Thousands Cheer* firmly established Ethel Waters in the legitimate theatre and marked the beginning of her peak years when she became the highest paid woman on Broadway.

> *fact is the audience and the critics were enjoying what is known as "great" acting, a phenomenon so rare that any generation is permitted only a few examples of it, a phenomenon almost unheard of on our contemporary stage. A great actress should not be confused with a celebrated actress....In the final scene Miss Waters, so far as the effect she makes is concerned, might be playing the Love-Death of Isolde, or Juliet in the potion scene....I have only admiration for the rest of the cast....The fact remains that in the presence of a star of such magnitude as Ethel Waters these matters sink into secondary importance.*
>
> *What is to become of Ethel Waters in the theatre? Few roles immediately suggest themselves as appropriate. Perhaps some playwright...will be inspired by her genius to create a new part worthy of her... but I cannot help feeling confident that in a Greek play, particularly in "Medea," Ethel Waters would more securely establish herself as the world actress of the first rank she indubitably is.*

Inflated as some might now find Van Vechten's praise, it captures the extraordinary impact Waters had on the

Waters's radio broadcasts were a major breakthrough for black entertainers.

theatrical community of the day. When Brooks Atkinson of the *New York Times* wrote an unenthusiastic review of her work in *Mamba's Daughters*, an advertisement was taken out in the following Sunday *Times* by a group of theatre people (including Tallulah Bankhead, Norman Bel Geddes, Dorothy Gish, Aline MacMahon, and Burgess Meredith), who, in essence, announced that the very influential *Times* critic was wrong, that Waters' performance was indeed an altogether remarkable one. Atkinson went back to see the play, re-reviewed it, and admitted he had made a mistake. *Vogue* did a photo layout on Waters and *Life* ran a splashy spread on the play. Even Eleanor Roosevelt mentioned the production in her "My Day" newspaper column, saying: "Ethel Waters really achieved a remarkable dramatic success in the character of Hagar. For me, it was an unforgettable evening, so real that I could hardly believe that I was not actually on the plantation. . . . It is to me an extraordinary success." And indeed it was of significance because Waters had shattered the longstanding myth that black women could perform only as singers, dancers, or comediennes. Here she brought to fruition what actresses

Rose McClendon and Edna Thomas had worked so hard for: the establishment of a black woman as a major American dramatic actress. Waters never had the chance for a classic role. But she did give other fine dramatic performances.

Her future dramatic roles often seemed elaborations on the character Hagar, in time taking on a solitary mythic structure so etched in the public consciousness that she would be thought of only as that pop myth come true: the ever-endurable black woman, a figure of rage and anger, ready to fight if wronged, yet a woman of towering heroic compassion. What distinguished Waters' heroines was her personal "evil" side, which showed itself during her powerful scenes of righteous moral indignation. Finally, Waters had been able to do in theatre what her idols Bessie and Ma had done in song, to go all the way emotionally with a work of art.

For years after *Mamba's Daughters*, Ethel Waters, the woman, remained something of a mythic heroine and she may have felt trapped. Part of the price she paid was relinquishing her sexuality, becoming matronly, far too early in her career. Rival Baker never gave hers up. She also seemed so superhumanly strong that it was thought by her public that she could handle anything. Later, too, the religious fervor and conviction that had inspired one era would become a bore for another. And the Ethel Waters myth would be considered obsolete by a public in search of new entertainers to distract and delight them. Yet for a long time, there was no black star like Ethel Waters, held in affectionate high regard by white and black audiences.

By 1939 the divas seemed well situated. Waters was on Broadway as was Fredi Washington. Ivie Anderson was still touring with the Duke. Holiday was at Cafe Society. And the young Lena Horne was debuting on Broadway in *Blackbirds of 1939.*

All in all, the divas had made remarkable inroads in the mainstream of American cultural life. Broadway, the clubs, radio, and movies had been integrated. There was even an optimistic sign in the world of serious music when a round-faced, wide-eyed, baby doll of a woman named Dorothy Maynor had suddenly shown up at the era's end, glowing with a gold mine of publicity. For years the friends of this Virginia-born soprano had tried arranging an audition for her with the conductor of the Boston Symphony Orchestra, Serge Koussevitzky. Once the maestro had finally heard her, he exclaimed, "Marvelous. Marvelous. The whole world must hear her." The next day, at Koussevitzky's request, she sang German leider and spirituals at an informal picnic outside Boston. The *New York Times* music critic Noel Strauss happened to be present and the following day startled the music world with a full column devoted to this new discovery. The story was picked up by the Associated Press and ran throughout the country. Three months later, Dorothy Maynor had a sold-out debut at Town Hall. Olin Downes wrote in the *New York Times* that she had a "voice of a golden quality," adding that she was "one of the most remarkable soprano voices of the rising generation." Maynor's success made it look as if a dark diva would soon crack the world of grand opera. It didn't happen until 1955, but for late Depression audiences Maynor embodied the lopsided notion that now progress might be in store for everybody.

There was also Marian Anderson, whose legendary People's Concert in 1939 was another symbol of progress. Curiously, though, Anderson herself would remain a thorny problem for many Americans until the forties. Throughout the great slump, the various personas and moods of the divas—be it the mellowness of Ivie and Billie or the humor and energy of Hollywood actresses Louise Beavers and Hattie McDaniel—as well as the popular myths some had embodied, all had had a part in making the era endurable, perhaps even a bit more comprehensible.

June Richmond was a vocalist with Jimmy Dorsey's band.

· THE 1940S ·
SOCIAL SYMBOLS

The forties opened with a roar. But not from the divas. It came from Europe instead.

From the moment the Japanese invaded Pearl Harbor in 1941, American society underwent another series of dramatic changes. In the early forties a call rang out for patriotism and national unity. By the second half of the decade, a triumphant America-as-Giant World-Power basked in its new national prosperity and the international prestige the war had brought.

During this period the divas, like everyone else, also witnessed a great awakening within the black community, which was becoming increasingly more vocal. Black America was invigorated by protests, demonstrations, arguments, many directed by black leaders toward the gut of wartime America, the military, still segregated and blatantly racist. Race riots shot up in the early forties in Detroit, Harlem, Atlanta, Philadelphia, and parts of Tennessee and

Texas. And before the forties ended, Black America had an array of new-style political heroes—A. Philip Randolph, Walter White, Ralph Bunche, Adam Clayton Powell, Jr., Paul Robeson, and those sports figures, Jackie Robinson and Joe Louis. At the same time, as the NAACP rose to the height of its power, the idea of full racial integration was slowly taking root in the mainstream of American political and social thought.

What with Black America's determination to make it into the system and what with White America's determination to show that the system still worked for everybody, the forties gave way to a figure both White and Black America saw as positive: the bourgeois diva as social symbol. Such forties women as Lena Horne, Hazel Scott, Katherine Dunham, and Marian Anderson emerged not only as performers of skill, but symbols of the new black who could easily fit into the dominant culture. The idea was that the ordinary hardworking black

Lena Horne: a pinup girl for black GI's and a social symbol for Black America.

90

youth could grow up to be like these heroines, who, as seemingly educated, articulate, poised citizens, had seized the golden opportunities the nation offered.

As a figure everyone felt comfortable with, the bourgeois-black-beauty-as-social-symbol soon fully crossed over, finally "making it" into mainstream American culture. As she did so, often performing for white audiences more than black ones, her "rough" ethnic edges were almost completely wiped away. Forties audiences accepted only those black beauties whose color could, when so desired, be overlooked. White audiences could watch a Horne or a Dunham without feeling uncomfortable, without being reminded of ghettos or poverty or social ills and inequities. Gradually, audiences became more and more fixated on color, or again the absence of it. Now the most successful black beauties would be those with mulatto looks (best exemplified by Horne) or high mulatto style of dress or manner (like Eartha Kitt and

Diana Ross later). Now for years to come, Ethel Waters would remain the last of the big-time brown ethnic stars.

And this was the period when the diva's interracial romances became of national interest.

But most importantly, in the forties, America's black beauties realized they could talk—in print. Newspaper accounts—interviews, reviews, news stories, feature stories—all trace the diva's metamorphosis. Comments flew all over the place. And more often than not, the comments were on America's racial situation. For a spell, the divas got by with their talk. Only after the war may they have wondered if they had said the wrong thing at the wrong time.

But in the beginning, none of that mattered. All anyone knew or cared about was that the black beauties who came to prominence during the war years were the right dreams at the right time. And none was dreamier or more right than Lena Horne.

Lena Horne and Hazel Scott (*at the piano*) sing a duet in *I Dood It*. In movies, they performed their songs, then disappeared.

LENA HORNE: THE GIRL BEAUTY COMES OF AGE

For many, the young Lena Horne represented bourgeois haughtiness. She was the pampered black girl/woman never required to do anything. Who cared what she said or thought when it was more than enough just to stare at her. In the history of American popular entertainment, no woman had ever looked like Lena Horne. Nor had any other black woman had looks considered as "safe" and nonthreatening. Past mulatto types like Fredi Washington and Nina Mae McKinney had been so close to the white ideal that troubling questions had arisen. What indeed were notions of white superiority based on? Skin color? Features? Hair texture? What kind of insane system was it that denied opportunities to these women who met the culture's beauty standards far more closely than even Joan Crawford and Bette Davis? Lena's looks, however, were far more manageable for she was something of an invisible black woman, a perfect balance who presented no problems. Most importantly, she had color, a rich, glowing coppertone. She wasn't too dark or too light. Her hair was straight. She was labeled the café-au-lait Hedy Lamarr, and when she first started to perform, she was even urged to change her name and pass as a Latin. But looking back on the period now, it is obvious that nobody would ever have wanted Lena to be anything but Lena.

At the same time the Horne demeanor—distant and aloof—suggested she was the girl off somewhere in a world of her own. Of course, it was unheard of to find a black woman who became a star without doing anything (where was the aggression all the fabled past divas had?), who appeared as if all her life she had been placed on a pedestal and everything had come easily to her.

She was born Lena Calhoun Horne into a respectable middle-class Brooklyn family in 1917. Her grandfather liked Verdi and fine cigars. Her grandmother, a suffragette and an early member of the NAACP, was an ardent fighter for equality on all fronts. Shortly after her birth, Lena Horne's parents separated. For years, as her mother, Edna, struggled to become an actress, the young Lena, separated from the father she adored, was shifted and shuttled throughout the South, staying in one home or another of friends and relatives.

Her career took off in 1933 when sixteen-year-old Lena appeared in the chorus line at the Cotton Club. Later she was the girl-singer with Noble Sissle's Orchestra, and then appeared on Broadway in the short-lived *Blackbirds of 1939*. A year later she appeared with Charlie Barnett's Orchestra, then went on to satisfying engagements at Barney Josephson's Cafe Society Downtown, which put her on the showbiz map. (For a while she was known as Helena Horne.) In between all these activities, she married Louis Jones, the son of a middle-class black family in Pittsburgh, had two children, then divorced him. In the early forties she went to Los Angeles and quickly became the West Coast's latest "in" sensation.

MGM spotted her, signed her up, and afterward Lena Horne, no longer simply a cabaret singer, was transformed almost overnight into a national social symbol. Civil Rights groups took a keen interest in her budding movie career. NAACP Executive Secretary Walter White felt that as the first black woman with a long-term contract at a major Hollywood studio, she could do much to alter the image of black women in American motion pictures. Everyone was determined not to let the movie capital turn her into the conventional clownish black maid.

Well, Hollywood didn't turn her into a housekeeper, but it didn't turn her into another Harlow either. At heart, Lena Horne knew she was simply a celebrated token who could be picked up and dropped or used however MGM saw fit. And with the exceptions of *Cabin in the Sky* and *Stormy Weather*, her eleven movies of the forties represented case studies in Hollywood duplicity. Usually, she didn't play characters. She just came on as herself (her

At age sixteen Brooklyn-born Lena appeared in the chorus at the Cotton Club. At one time she was billed as Helena Horne.

Some Hollywood razzmatazz, sepia style: leggy Katherine Dunham *(above left)* in *Stormy Weather;* Lillian Randolph *(center, sitting)* in *Happy Go Lucky;* Nina Mae McKinney *(bottom left)* ready to sing and dance up a storm in *Hallelujah;* and a young cowgirl named Dorothy Dandridge *(above)* enlivening a local saloon in *Moo Cow Boogie.*

glamorous nightclub persona intact), looking terrific, singing her number, then disappearing from the picture. Because she seldom appeared with the white stars of the features, such as Mickey Rooney or Judy Garland, in sequences integral to the movies' plots, her scenes, should they ever "offend" southern audiences, could easily be scissored out. Still her movies took her fully into the mainstream of American popular culture, making her one of the most famous black personalities in the country.

Whether in movies or out or back in nightclubs, Lena Horne's style and presence remained fresh and exciting. For a black star, her material was different, never the blues, spirituals, or jazz. Instead she performed the kind of sophisticated Cole Porter or Gershwin ballads her audiences in the classy cabarets favored. The voice was smooth and vibrant and, as the years moved on, it seemed filled with tensions. But what distinguished her was her intelligence and sophistication. She had a total understanding of a lyric situation. Then there was her inimitable style. The diction was impeccable. She almost spat each word out. The eyes were anxious and afire. The teeth gleamed. And the mouth was magnificent.

There was also the Horne aloofness, which never unnoticed, became the hallmark of her style. Sometimes as she sang, her face went vacant. Other times she seemed condescending. But always she held something back. In the middle of her career, *The New Yorker* commented on her unusual detachment: "Curiously, as her style has developed, she seems to have withdrawn further and further from her audience and into herself. She never addresses her listeners directly, and her eyes are

closed, or nearly closed, a good part of the time. In acknowledging applause, she tilts her head, eyes cast down, and bends and turns with...self-effacement."

But no one was more aware of the withdrawal than Lena Horne herself, who clearly used it for therapeutic reasons. More than any other diva before her, Lena Horne had grown up in front of white audiences, repeatedly encountering the same slights and indignities every other black female star knew of.

"Even as a performer I sensed that the white people in the audience saw nothing but my flesh and its color onstage. I was not ready for this," she once said. "I didn't know anything about white people."

She also sensed an extraordinary loneliness onstage, feeling she was being fully exposed. "I don't know how to say it," she once explained, "it's so physical, it's all body. There's whiskey, there's sex, there's something that is experienced when people are drinking in a nightclub and having a good time. There are so many ways they look at you, their emotions aren't disciplined....It's you and you are at the mercy of their thoughts." It was a rough experience that got to her as much as it did to Holiday. Horne was every bit as disoriented by her white audiences. In time, she remembered Noble Sissle's advice: "Remember, you are a lady, and you are not a whore— don't let them treat you like one." So she learned always to pull back from her white audiences, developing a guile and toughness, using her remoteness, her high-flung inaccessibility as an aggressive protective shield. She developed also a hostility and an edge that often she felt her audiences overlooked because "they were too busy

Lena was called the café-au-lait Hedy Lamarr.

Lena and Fats Waller in Stormy Weather.

96

seeing their own preconceived image of a Negro woman. The image that I chose to give them was of a woman who they could not reach. I think this is why I rarely speak to an audience. I am too proud to let them think they can have any personal contact with me. They get the singer, but they are not going to get the woman. I think many Negro performers feel much the same way and they find their own methods of letting people know it. In other words, we all find our own means of rebellion."

Lena Horne summed up the feelings most divas had when appearing in clubs. Different ones used different techniques, and the techniques had different effects. In Lena's case, she was telling her audiences that she was one black woman who could not be had.

The irony is that during the war years, her withdrawal, which alternately puzzled or put audiences off, was accepted nonetheless, perhaps as a by-product of the war itself. She became a symbol of the melancholy girl back home, ill at ease and sad because her man was off somewhere in combat.

For black GI's who viewed *Stormy Weather* and *Cabin in the Sky* on army bases around the world, she was, as Hayworth and Grable were for whites, a luscious pinup girl, a dream for those long nights away from home.

Even the military brass was not blind to Lena's special appeal. Like other glamour girls pitching in to help at USO shows and Stage Door Canteens, she was asked to entertain at army camps. She was shocked to find segregated audiences. Often she did not see the black soldiers until the next day after her big appearance. When at a performance in Fort Riley, Kansas, she spotted German prisoners of war sitting in the best seats in the front of the house, she stepped from the stage, whisked past them, then sang to the black soldiers in the back.

By the late forties Lena had career problems. MGM, having sunk money into an all-black Broadway show (*St. Louis Woman*), in which it hoped to star her, was hardly pleased when she turned the lead role down. Matters were not helped either when, in 1947, she married Lennie Hayton, a white composer/arranger at Metro. This was the postwar era's first big interracial romance, and it did not sit too well with anyone. In the fifties when the studio remade *Show Boat*, it cast Ava Gardner in a role Horne had her heart set on, that of the mulatto Julie. Finally, there was the business of the Horne politics. By the end of the era the Communist hunts had started, leading to numerous investigations, subpoenas, and hearings. Once newspapers attacked Cafe Society Downtown as a "red" hangout, many of the artists who had worked there could not find work anywhere else. Lena Horne had also remained friendly with Paul Robeson, even when he was so hotly denounced. Eventually listed in Red Channels, a compilation (put out by rightist group Counter Attack) of entertainers said to be either Communists or Communist sympathizers, she was blacklisted from television work. In the sixties, when so many old-time black stars were viewed by the new generation as being "politically obsolete," Lena still held on, her style becoming both looser and gutsier. In the long run she was not only the war years' most glorious siren, but also its most durable.

On the set during the filming of *Cabin in the Sky*: Lena with *(from left to right)* columnist Billy Rowe, Vincente Minelli, and Melvyn Douglas.

KATHERINE DUNHAM: UNDERCOVER SEX GODDESS

Dancer/choreographer Katherine Dunham was another major forties black social symbol. Dunham was known in and out of dance circles as a brainy, scholarly young woman with degrees in anthropology and ethnology. But sex appeal may have had as much to do with her uncanny success as the books or her great artistry.

Dunham grew up in Joliet, Illinois, where her father ran a dry cleaning business. She studied at the University of Chicago. Then one evening during a public performance she gave in an abandoned Chicago loft, she was spotted by the daughters of philanthropist Julius Rosenwald, who promptly suggested she apply for a Rosenwald Foundation grant. For almost two years she used her fellowship to travel, study, and take notes on primitive dance and customs of various island peoples. In Jamaica she lived with the Maroon peoples of the high country, who taught her the Koromantee dances remembered from Africa. In Martinique she saw for the first time the wrestling dance L'Ag'ya, from which she later drew inspiration for a number in her famous *Bal Nègre* revue. In Haiti she studied voodoo. In 1930 she returned to the States armed with enough material for a master's thesis as well as for a full-length book on the Maroons. Her account of her experiences, *Journey to Accompong*, published in 1946, reveals a perceptive young woman with a lush, romantic sensibility.

Once back in the States, Dunham soon put her field studies to work. She came to New York, and by the forties she formed her own dance company. In a short time the city was awash with stories of this innovative and highly dramatic dancer/choreographer whose series of ballet recitals titled "Tropics and Le Jazz Hot" introduced audiences to "Primitive Rhythms," "Rumbas" (Cuban and Mexican), "Island Songs," "Plantation and Minstrel Dances" (including "The Ballet Bre'r Rabbit"), and "Le Jazz Hot" (with everything from boogie-woogie to honky-tonk numbers). Almost single-handedly, Katherine Dunham saw to it that Negro dance was taken seriously. Critic John Martin wrote in the *New York Times*:

> With the arrival of Katherine Dunham on the scene, the prospects for the development of a substantial Negro dance art begin to look decidedly bright. Her performance with her group . . . may very well become a historic occasion, for certainly never

before in all the efforts of recent years to establish the Negro dance as a serious medium has there been so convincing and authoritative an approach.

> Miss Dunham has apparently based her theory on the obvious fact so often overlooked that if the Negro is to develop an art of his own he can begin only with the seeds of that art that lie within him. These seeds are abundant and unique. Indeed, it would be difficult to think of any people with a richer heritage of dance begging to be made use of. Yet in the past . . . there have been those who have started out by denying this heritage and smoothing it over with the gloss of another alien racial culture that deceives no one. The potential greatness of the Negro dance lies in its discovery of its own roots and the crucial nursing of them into growth and flower.
>
> . . . It is because she has showed herself to have both the objective quality of the student and the natural instinct of the artist that she has done such a truly important job.

In 1940 she appeared on Broadway in *Cabin in the Sky*, the all-black musical extravaganza starring Ethel Waters and Dooley Wilson, directed and choreographed by George Balanchine. *Times* dance critic John Martin had his say again, summing up the attitudes many theatregoers would have about Dunham for the duration of the decade:

> Throughout the evening it is Miss Dunham's chief business to sizzle, and that is one of the things that will seem most extraordinary to those who have followed her work in its previous phases. In her personal programs she has frequently represented women of distinctly torrid temperament, but never before has there been one at all like Georgia. . . . In her own creations she is never without comment, presenting the character and telling a wealth of secrets about it at the same time; as Georgia, however, she has no chance for comment, no chance for the very quality that gave her art its charm and its validity. She is a hundred percent seductress.

Following *Cabin in the Sky*, Dunham and her company were able to reach a far wider audience with *Tropical Revue*, *Carib Song*, and *Bal Nègre*. Yet serious artist that Dunham was, audiences often seemed to focus on her as the kind of sultry, sexy vixen she had played in *Cabin in the Sky*. In time, Katherine Dunham, the dancer, was an ideal undercover sepia sex symbol. American audiences of the period still were not ready to officially parade or accept a black woman as any kind of feminine ideal, not even a sexual one. But there were always covert ways in

Katherine Dunham: dancer, choreographer, anthropologist—and sex symbol. Her innovations changed black dance.

Sophisticated lady: Hazel Scott, who became a nightclub star at age twenty by giving the classics a boogie-woogie sound.

which such a woman was discovered nonetheless. So while audiences congratulated themselves on appreciating Dunham's skillful renderings of island ritual dances, what they actually responded to most was the healthy sexual ambience Dunham and her troupe exuded. Excerpts from reviews of the company's work simply spotlight the era's fascination with Dunham's sexuality. Of *Tropical Revue*, the *New York Mirror*'s critic wrote: "A tropical revue that is likely to send thermometers soaring to the bursting point.... Tempestuous and torrid, raffish and revealing." The *New York Sun* said: "Shoulders, midsections and posteriors went round and round. Particularly when the cynosure was Miss Dunham, the vista was full of pulchritude." The *New York Daily News* wrote: "The program notes read: 'The fertility ritual, here associated with marriage or mating.' Amen, brother!" The *Times* added: "Sex in the Caribbean is doing all right." And *Life* had its say: "Wows Broadway with a Sizzling show!"

None of this sexuality business was lost on Hollywood, which, seldom known for spotlighting a serious dance company, soon imported Dunham's troupe West for appearances in *Star Spangled Rhythm*, *Stormy Weather*, and *Casbah*. Movie audiences around the nation often viewed them as colorful, exotic, erotic black entertainers with plenty of rhythm and pizzazz. Interestingly, when MGM filmed *Cabin in the Sky*, it chose the mild-mannered, less exotically sexy Lena to play Georgia. For a movie industry that both enjoyed and feared the idea of black sexuality, Katherine Dunham may have well been considered too brazen to be cast in a proper role in a film that cut her off from the cultural veneer that generally made her sex acceptable.

During a 120-city tour of her *Tropical Revue* in 1944, Dunham made newspaper headlines following an incident at a Cincinnati hotel. Arriving at the hotel with reservations made for her by her white secretary, only to be told by the management that there was no room and that she would have to leave, Dunham flatly refused to budge, informing the hotel, "You'll have to carry me out!" Later she sued. Then in Louisville, Kentucky, when she discovered that, except for six blacks on the lower floor, the rest of the black population at her performance in the Municipal Auditorium was made to sit in a "special section" in the balcony, she interrupted the applause at the conclusion of her show to make an announcement to the audience. "Friends," she was quoted as saying, "we are glad we have made you happy. We hope you have enjoyed us. This is the last time I shall play Louisville because the management refuses to let people like us sit by people like you. Maybe after the war we shall have democracy and I can return. Until then," and at this point it was said in newspapers that she shook her finger at the audience, "God bless you, for you will need it!" Needless to say, the white audience was in an uproar. But afterward the management did announce that there would be no more segregated audiences if Miss Dunham chose to play the house again. Of course, the management neglected to say whether or not there would be segregated audiences for other Negro performers. Dunham had made her point.

Later when she played the army camps, she again took a strong stand against the military's segregated policies.

No one can say for sure what effect Dunham's outspokenness had on her career. But it is now obvious that the forties were her peak years. She kept her company alive for three decades although there were always financial difficulties. In the fifties she was back in Hollywood for *Mambo* and segments of *Green Mansions*, which she choreographed. In 1962 she launched a spectacular production, *Bamboche*.

By the end of the forties Dunham's use as a symbol had

"Friends, this is the last time I shall play Louisville because the management refuses to let people like us sit by people like you," announced Katharine Dunham.

had its day. For White America, she had been at first an agreeable social symbol, simply the Negro making progress in a free society. But once she took that symbol business seriously and spoke out, she was no longer needed. Then, too, who is to say what effect her marriage to white costume designer John Pratt had? In the fifties Dunham, no doubt feeling the stings of bias against her company, publicly asked why the State Department had not backed a group that had already performed in over thirty-eight countries. The familiar fighting spirit was still there. But by the mid-fifties, the serious black-beauty social symbols were anachronisms. And at the same time, when sepia sirens Eartha Kitt and Dorothy Dandridge emerged as open, aboveground sex symbols and were publicized as such, Dunham's reign as underground sex goddess came to an end. Katherine Dunham's career—her position in popular American culture—was never a relaxed affair. Yet Dunham, like Horne, introduced the idea that the black entertainer indeed did have a specific responsibility to his/her community. And, perhaps most importantly as an artist, her striking dance innovations were to remain a source of inspiration for generations of black dancers and choreographers to follow.

102

Ladies' night out: a cigar-smoking Katherine Dunham *(left)* proving that a little flamboyance never hurts; an extravagantly overdressed Ethel Waters *(bottom center)* singing "Heat Wave"; a hepped-up, Latinized Etta Moten *(top center)* singing about flying down to Rio; and the three Peters Sisters *(above)*, huge stars in Europe, dressed as tropical sirens, doing their version of a Hawaiian luau.

HAZEL SCOTT: SWINGING THE CLASSICS

Jazz pianist Hazel Scott was another diva whose career indicated such a shift in political consciousness. She, too, was something of a covert sex symbol. During the forward-looking forties most chose to view her as an example of a Black American woman who had made it into the system.

Scott was born in Trinidad in 1920, the only child of R. Thomas Scott, a black scholar, and Alma Long Worrell, a ranking debutante in local black society as well as a talented music student. When her parents migrated to the United States in 1924, little Hazel was the family's pride and joy, in every conceivable sense, a remarkable child. She read at three, was discovered to have perfect pitch at three and a half, played the piano at four, and was improvising at the piano at five. A Juilliard professor who heard her play, proclaimed her a "genius," then began teaching her privately because she was too young to study at the school. By age thirteen, having mastered the classics—Bach, Chopin, Rachmaninoff—she was also growing impatient with them and soon jazzing the classics up with a contemporary beat. Then a year later when her father suddenly died, Hazel and her mother were left on their own. Mrs. Scott joined Lil Hardin Armstrong's all-girl band, then organized her own women's orchestra, The

American Creolians, with Hazel playing the piano and doubling on brass. In 1938 Hazel appeared on Broadway —at eighteen—in *Sing Out the News*, stopping the show cold with her number "Franklin D. Roosevelt Jones."

Two years later, when she opened at Cafe Society Downtown, Hazel Scott took New York by storm—and in an unprecedented way. She played the classics. Had anyone before ever come to a New York nightclub to hear a pianist perform Chopin or Liszt? Scott, however, had so perfected her unique way of transforming the classics into swing ballads that audiences couldn't resist her. She began her classical numbers in a conventional way, then gradually changed the rhythm, letting boogie-woogie notes creep in, until, finally, Hazel Scott just gave in to the sounds within her and pounded the keyboard as if any minute might be her last. And the entire nightclub swayed and jumped to her original sounds. Initially brought into Cafe Society as a three-week replacement for ailing blues singer Ida Cox, she was such a knockout success that the club became her home. When Cafe Society Downtown moved uptown to Fifty-eighth Street, Hazel Scott went with it.

Her album *Swinging the Classics* nearly broke sales records. Her nonclassical discs "Mighty Like Blues," "Calling All Bars," and "Boogie Woogie" sold well too, and remain definitive period pieces. Throughout the era she had class bookings: the swanky Ritz Carlton Hotel in

Hazel Scott takes a bow in *Broadway Rhythm*. In the South her scenes were often cut from the films.

The most outspoken diva in the forties, Scott married Adam Clayton Powell, Jr., in 1945. She refused to appear before segregated audiences.

Boston; the huge Paramount and Roxy theatres in New York; and the prestigious Carnegie Hall, where in 1940 she played Liszt's Second Hungarian Rhapsody to rave reviews. Of the latter performance, a critic wrote: "It was the most impudent musical criticism since George Bernard Shaw stopped writing on the subject. It was witty, daring, modern but never irreverent. I think Liszt would have been delighted." And the stories run on her in the leading mass publications of the day verified her complete crossover entry into the cultural mainstream.

Not long afterward, Hazel Scott found herself in the movies: *Something to Shout About, I Dood It* (with Horne), *The Heat's On, Broadway Rhythm*, and most memorably in *Rhapsody in Blue*. In this last film, in a brief interlude where she was seen playing Gershwin's "The Man I Love" in a Paris nightclub, Scott was about as elegant and sophisticated as they come, a blazing symbol of the contemporary black woman completely at home in the most continental of settings. Striking as Scott's movie appearances were, her scenes were cut

When a restaurant in Pasco, Washington, refused to serve her, she not only raised a stink but sued for $50,000. She married Adam Clayton Powell, Jr., amid much to-do.

when the films were shown in the South. Still she reached a large audience, appearing always as herself, beautifully dressed and coiffed.

As a social symbol, her classical bent placed her in a rarefied atmosphere. Yet anxious to promote and publicize herself, she was aware that while white patrons came to hear new renditions of classics, it never hurt to give them something to look at at the same time. On occasion, she was criticized for exploiting her sexuality. Usually, she wore low-cut dresses that exposed her sensuous round shoulders and gave a fair amount of attention to her breasts. Her eyes were flirtatious. And sometimes she had an insolent smile that was a bit suggestive, part come-on and part pull-back so that she still remained a lady. When she went into her swing music, her sexy body movements snapped the audience to attention.

She was also the most outspoken of all the forties divas. Like Horne, she refused to appear before segregated audiences. When a restaurant in Pasco, Washington, refused to serve her, she not only raised a stink but sued for $50,000. In 1945 political momentum was added to Scott's public image when she married Adam Clayton Powell, Jr., amid much to-do from the press. But Scott,

whose West Indian background may explain her haughty demeanor, seemed oblivious to criticism as she went from one dazzling concert performance to another, never giving up her career, and remaining for years more famous than her husband. The two had a son and were seen as the modern black couple: educated, well traveled, attractive go-getters and doers.

Following the war years, Hazel Scott's career was not as glowing. In this era of blacklisting, when Paul Robeson and Canada Lee could not find work, Hazel Scott was listed in Red Channels and her engagements fell off too. Her open criticism of America's racial problems may have been looked upon as anti-American comments; so, too, was the fact that in 1943 she had performed at a rally for Benjamin Davis, an avowed Communist running for the New York City Council, which, of course, in the minds of some meant she had to be a Communist too. No one seemed interested that Scott might have gone to the rally because Davis was the only black running for the council.

Hazel Scott spoke up, going before the House Un-American Activities Committee in 1950. In an impressive fourteen-page statement, she denounced Red Channels as "guilt by listing," "a lie," and "a vile and un-American act." Going a step further, she later proposed that, in the future, musicians' and artists' unions should boycott those very radio networks and sponsors that had suspended entertainers listed in the book without proof of disloyalty. She was one of the few performers, black or white, determined to fight it out.

Following these troubles, her career was never the same. In 1950, despite good ratings, her television show was not renewed. That same year she was back in the newspapers when she refused to perform before a segregated audience at the University of North Carolina. Although she was respected as a fine pianist in serious music circles, the new mass audience came to think of her musical innovations as relics from the past. Even Scott may have felt she rode to fame on a classy gimmick because later she stopped jazzing up the classics. In the late fifties she left the States. After her divorce from Powell in 1961, she had a short-lived marriage to a European, Enzio Bedin. That same year she appeared in the film *Night Affair*. And she was back in the papers once more when Powell was accused of having falsified her 1951 income tax returns. During Powell's tragic decline in the sixties, Hazel Scott took on yet another new admirable dimension when she refused to publicly criticize him. In the seventies, after a long absence, Scott successfully returned to the world of New York nightclubs.

MARIAN ANDERSON: THE PEOPLE'S WOMAN

Of all the forties social symbols, the greatest surely was Marian Anderson. Even as a child, growing up in Philadelphia, Anderson was something of a legend. Her father, who had sold ice and coal, died in 1914 when she was twelve. Her widowed mother, formerly a Virginia school-teacher, reared Marian and her other two daughters amid great hardships. There was always something both extraordinary and sad about the young Anderson. She was large and awkward for her age. For as long as anyone could remember, the girl had sung in the Union Baptist Church choir, demonstrating her vocal skills early by singing soprano, alto, tenor, and bass. ("Come and hear the baby contralto, ten years old," an early church handbill read.)

During these early years Philadelphia's black community, keenly interested in her future and determined that her voice be heard, took up a special fund at church so she could have money for singing lessons. Even then, Marian Anderson must have realized the special responsibility she was saddled with. No success (or failure) she ever had would be simply hers alone. Already she was a social symbol for an entire community that felt its destiny tied to hers. Soon Negro America pinned its hopes on Marian Anderson, convinced that she would crack the walls of prejudice and become the first Negro concert hall performer in American history to appear in the big showplaces of the world.

In 1921 at age nineteen Anderson studied with Giuseppe Boghetti. He groomed her for a big musical competition, which came at New York's Lewisohn Stadium in 1926. Anderson won first prize over three hundred other singers. Afterward she had a short engagement with the Philadelphia Orchestra, performed at Carnegie Hall, and won a Julius Rosenwald scholarship. She continued studying intensely, vigorously, with astounding reserves of discipline and stamina.

Throughout the thirties she toured Europe, singing German leider and spirituals. The reactions to this contralto were overwhelming. The roof of his house was too low for her, composer Sibelius told her. In Salzburg, Arturo Toscanini made the pronouncement that has never died: "A voice like yours is heard only once in a hundred years." None understood her triumph abroad better than La Baker, who, upon meeting Anderson, bowed and curtsied, one diva in homage to another.

Finally, impresario Sol Hurok brought her to Town Hall in 1935. The next year her Carnegie Hall appearance was packed. Then she returned to Europe. Then back to the States, where in 1938 alone she performed seventy recitals, hitting cities all over the country, including the South, giving the longest, most intense tours in concert history. In time, Anderson probably also made more celebrated international tours than any other performer, traveling throughout Scandinavia, performing in all the great European capitals, as well as in Japan,

Mexico, South America, Africa, and the West Indies.

Throughout the long exhausting European tours of her early years, Marian Anderson may have struck many as a woman on the run, without a home. For the truth of the matter was that Marian Anderson, the greatest contralto of the twentieth century, was neither fully recognized nor wanted in her own country.

The great hurricane blew in at the tail end of the thirties. Anderson was scheduled to appear in Constitution Hall, which was owned by the Daughters of the American Revolution. Playing on a hunch, a shrewd newspaper woman, Mary Johnson, called the DAR's president and asked what the organization's position on the matter was. The position was clear: neither Marian Anderson nor any other Negro was going to appear in Constitution Hall.

Suddenly, through no design of her own, Marian Anderson was back in newspaper headlines, this time around as the star of the biggest racial flap of the decade. Across the nation, blacks and liberal whites were enraged by the incident. Walter White, Executive Secretary of the

---

For the truth of the matter was that Marian Anderson, the greatest contralto of the twentieth century, was neither fully recognized nor wanted in her own country.

NAACP, stepped in to suggest a way to best focus on the racism of the DAR: by staging a large outdoor free concert in the nation's capital. Anderson agreed to the concert, although at the time of the fracas she was so busy touring that the full impact of the situation had not hit her.

A surge of publicity arose as Eleanor Roosevelt and Secretary of the Interior Harold Ickes agreed to sponsor the concert. Mrs. Roosevelt even resigned from the DAR in protest. Supreme Court justices, senators, congressmen, Cabinet members, and other distinguished men and women announced their support of the event too. On Easter Sunday, 1939, the concert was held at the Lincoln Memorial. Seventy-five thousand people attended. Marian Anderson opened with "America" and closed with "Nobody Knows the Trouble I've Seen." Afterward the enthusiastic crowd went wild, trying its best to get to the singer. For a few scary moments it threatened to be a stampede. In the end, though, the event signaled a new era in the history of the fight for civil rights in America. And Marian Anderson became one of the most famous women in the world.

Throughout the event and afterward, she remained a gracious, quietly commanding but shadowy figure. No one can ever say exactly how she felt about any of the commotion. Even years later, when she did write of the concert in her autobiography *My Lord What a Morning*, her account was moving, but her gut feelings seemed politely veiled. "What were my own feelings?" she wrote of her response to the news of her rejection by the DAR.

I was saddened and ashamed. I was sorry for the people who had precipitated the affair. I felt the behavior stemmed from lack of understanding. They were not persecuting me personally or as a representative of my people so much as they were doing something that was neither sensible nor good. Could I have erased the bitterness, I would have done so gladly. I do not mean that I would have been prepared to say that I was not entitled to appear in Constitution Hall as might any other performer. But the unpleasantness disturbed me, and if it had been up to me alone I would have sought a way to wipe it out. . . . I have been in this world long enough to know that there are all kinds of people, all suited by their own natures for different tasks. It would be fooling myself to think that I was meant to be a fearless fighter.

What did emerge from Anderson's comments was an almost queenly air. She felt sorry for them. They had a lack of understanding. The unpleasantness disturbed her.

Of the plans for the outdoor concert, she said: "In principle the idea was sound, but it could not be comfortable to me as an individual. As I thought further, I could see that my significance as an individual was small in the affair. I had become, whether I liked it or not, a symbol, representing my people. I had to appear." The night before her concert, Marian Anderson could not find a hotel in Washington in which to stay. Yet throughout the entire affair and for the duration of her career, she functioned by somehow miraculously detaching herself, stoically accepting a symbolic role thrust on her because of her formidable talent and her color.

During the Roosevelt/Truman years, Anderson continued her record-breaking tours. She also became one of the most decorated women in the world, winning countless awards and citations from groups black and white. Finally, even Constitution Hall was opened to her. But even with the new honors, her position as a black artist in America had not been greatly altered. Doors were still closed to her because of her color. It would be more than a decade before she would finally sing at the Metropolitan Opera House.

Marian Anderson: Toscanini said hers was a voice heard once in a century, but great concert halls were often closed to her.

When she commented on her country's racial attitudes (or her own situation), Anderson was often gentler than other divas and never defiantly critical. One wonders now what her place in history, as well as her significance as a social symbol, might have been had she, like Billie Holiday, ever lashed out at American society. Surely, she would have been the most threatening lady around. Often much of White America seemed to value this sensitive, private woman because of her reticence.

By the end of the forties, as well as throughout the fifties and sixties, Anderson became a textbook commodity, written up as a model Negro for elementary and high school students, who often found the simplified version of her that was presented (like the simplified versions of the lives and triumphs of George Washington Carver and Joe Louis) a bit tiresome. The world had heard Marian Anderson sing. Young Black Americans longed to hear Marian Anderson talk. And so for years among younger blacks there was a terrible ambivalence toward her. In the late sixties her name was seldom mentioned. Only in the seventies did some idea of the complexities enveloping her come to light.

If there is a tragic aspect to Marian Anderson's career, it is simply that later generations, black and white, would view her as something of a tattered social symbol rather than as the greatest contralto of the twentieth century. Her position, with its layers of meaning and the relentless flow of myth, legend, symbol, image, and dream that swirled about it, was a complex one. Yet she handled her situation with unending reserves of intelligence and poise.

During World War II, Anderson recorded and toured extensively.

Pearl Bailey: famous not only as a singer but also as a comedienne.

POSTWAR OPTIMISM

For the most part, the postwar audience seemed anxious for new faces and dreams or modified old ones. When it was revealed that Josephine Baker had worked during the war with the French Resistance, she again was a news item. As photographs circled around the world of Baker entertaining troupes after the liberation, many Americans accepted her no doubt as a local gal who had gone off and made good, after all.

Other familiar faces prospered. Never a great social symbol, Ella Fitzgerald, the perennial girl-singer in search of her place in the scheme of things, continued to work in clubs, becoming so popular a singer's singer that for a brief spell she gave even Holiday a scare. Shy pianist Mary Lou Williams, as private a person as Ella, remained a musician's musician too. She had her own band for a short time. (Her second husband, Shorty Baker, played trumpet with the group.) Her arrangement *The Zodiac Suite*, which she introduced in 1945 at Town Hall, was played by the New York Philharmonic in 1946. Singer Ada Brown remained popular throughout the period. And Dorothy Maynor, yet in the shadow of Marian Anderson after some ten years, remained an active concert hall favorite and was still a viable social symbol. And Anne Brown, the dazzling singer who originated the character Bess in *Porgy and Bess,* also gave impressive concert performances.

New faces popped up: actress Hilda Simms, a dramatic knockout in the black version of the play *Anna Lucasta*; pianist Dorothy Donegan, who shook and grimaced while jazzing up the classics as Scott had done; singers Joya Sherrill, Betty Carter, Sarah Vaughan, and Dinah Washington; comedienne Pearl Bailey; dancers Marie Bryant and Pearl Primus (each was also a talented choreographer); the ravishing Dorothy Dandridge, who teamed with sister Vivian and singer Etta Jones to perform as the Dandridge Sisters with the Jimmie Lunceford Orchestra; and the rambunctious gospel singer, Sister Rosetta Tharpe, who strutted with a guitar as she performed. In 1938 Tharpe had come to prominence when she appeared in revues with Cab Calloway at the Cotton Club. By 1940 she took her gospel music around the country and also recorded for Decca, sometimes teaming with Marie Knight. In 1949 the rousing Sister Rosetta also recorded a duet with her mother, Katie Bell Nubin. Now that the war was finally over, Americans were anxious for the good times to begin. And all in all, these new stars were seemingly less troublesome figures than some of their predecessors.

POSTWAR MANIA

As the forties swept to their close, however, the nation's most talked about divas, Ethel Waters and Billie Holiday, were hardly malleable types. One shakily symbolized endurance. The other presented woman-on-the-edge. But both were somewhat out of whack with the era's rhythm and pace. Each, too, was the star of her own disturbingly significant soap opera, which Americans viewed with open fascination.

At the start of the era, Billie Holiday, the artist, was

Billie Holiday performing at the chic, smart supper clubs.

Ella Fitzgerald scat-singing on national radio.

Lady Day: despite the problems, Billie wears her trademark gardenia.

maturing beautifully, more poised and assured than ever, with no excess gestures or emotions. But Billie Holiday, the woman, was still headed for trouble. In 1941 she married Jimmy Monroe (the former husband of Nina Mae McKinney). For years she had smoked marijuana, and she had been able to drink even hard-nosed musicians under the table. But now, she started using heroin. She left Monroe and took up with musician Joe Guy, whom no one seemed to think was good for her. She formed her own band and it failed. When her mother died in 1945, it was a great loss from which she never fully recovered. There were incidents at the clubs too. One evening when a rowdy naval officer called her a nigger, she just about turned the place inside out, smashing a beer bottle on a table, then heading for the man. She was held back, but that was one of the few times.

For now Billie Holiday went public with her manic madness. She was uncomfortable, restless, angry, and she didn't care if the whole goddamn world knew it. In fact, she seemed to relish her growing notoriety as the

One evening when a rowdy naval officer called her a nigger, she just about turned the place inside out, smashing a beer bottle on a table, then heading for the man.

beautiful, talented woman verging on a breakdown.

Word also spread that dope was getting the best of her. Living with it was hell enough, she once said; working with it, worse. Sometimes she clutched the mike with both hands to prop herself up. Sometimes she fell behind on the beat, was inaudible, forgot lyrics, or seemed completely withdrawn. On other occasions she miraculously caught hold of herself in the middle of a disastrous performance and came back strong. Nightly, there was a disturbing figure hanging around the clubs: her pusher, silently waiting to be summoned. In time, the whiskey, the reefer, the heroin, took their toll. Yet the supreme testament to her artistry is that when the voice started to go, there was a new emotional intensity and depth, so perfectly controlled that today there is no such thing as a bad Billie Holiday recording. All her work still holds up.

In 1946 Holiday gave her first major solo at Town Hall. The next year she wisely took time off for a "cure" treatment, managed to kick the habit, then rose like a phoenix ready for action all over again, only to discover that while no one had bothered her when she had been on the stuff, they were anxious to catch up with her now that she was off.

In 1947 Billie Holiday became a tabloid queen, the star of a drug-ridden nightmarish saga as far as the press was concerned. Her Philadelphia hotel room was raided by drug agents. She fled the scene, later turned herself in, and was sentenced to a prison term in a Virginia institution. Newspapers informed their readers that the very talented, innovative colored singing star was a dope fiend. Released from prison in 1948, she gave a triumphant comeback concert at Carnegie Hall. But her career was in shambles. Because New York clubs could not issue a cabaret card to any performer convicted of a felony, she could get no work. She did perform illegally, however, at some small clubs and also was able to work in the big theatres where the law did not apply. All this simply intensified the interest of a public anxious to see the legend in the flesh. New incidents and arrests fed the legend: a brawl in a Hollywood hotel in 1948; another drug incident a month later in San Francisco. The press ran countless stories on her goings and comings, her fights, her arrests, her hassles, her never-ending round of difficulties.

Billie Holiday learned the power of the image. "They come to see me get all fouled up," she once said of her performances. "They want to see me fall flat on my can." Now so caught up was the public in her self-destructive mythos that it soon lost sight of Billie, the very fine creative artist.

Ethel Waters was also having problems, but in a far different and far less public way. In the early forties she had great success on stage and screen in such productions as *Cabin in the Sky*, *Tales of Manhattan*, and *Cairo*. For wartime audiences, she remained a glowing symbol, the noble, bighearted Christian woman who kept the home-fires burning in times of trouble. But offstage and screen, Waters was as difficult as ever.

Throughout the filming of MGM's *Cabin in the Sky*, she fussed and fumed, just about drove everybody batty, particularly the young Lena Horne, whom Waters feared was getting better treatment from the studio. One day there was a terrible blowup at the studio when Waters was to parody a song sung by Horne. How, she wanted to know, did they expect her to imitate a style that was an imitation of a style she had originated years before! (Later, one of her best moments in the picture occurred when, after having looked over rival Horne, Waters simply put her hands on her full hips and announced that she had everything Lena had—only a whole lot more of it!) Waters won all her battles with MGM. But as she later

Billed as the Dandridge Sisters, Etta Jones (*left*) and Vivian (*top*) and Dorothy Dandridge sang with Jimmie Lunceford.

Billie Holiday appeared with her girlhood idol Louis Armstrong in New Orleans.

Jackie "Moms" Mabley: the Apollo's undisputed queen.

Ethel Waters (seated) in Cabin in the Sky. (Butterfly McQueen is next to her.)

said: "Like many other performers, I was to discover that winning arguments in Hollywood is costly. Six years were to pass before I could get another job."

During those six years, much else went wrong in her life. The Internal Revenue Service closed in for payment of back taxes from 1938 to 1939. In Hollywood, a young man she had befriended robbed her of over $10,000 in cash and $35,000 worth of jewelry, and the newspapers picked up on the story. To some, it looked as if Ethel Waters were a lonely star fallen prey to a young gigolo. Her nightclub and theatre bookings dwindled. She blamed bad agents for her decline, but her fiery temperament contributed too. Her money was running out. She had an ulcer and was on a half-cream, half-milk diet. She couldn't sleep and was on pills. She moved to the homes of various friends in Harlem and sat daily with time on her hands, while word spread throughout the community that one of America's greatest Negro stars was down to her last penny. Ethel Waters didn't see or talk to anyone. To be down and out was one thing. To have everyone know it was more than she cared to bear.

Somehow Ethel Waters held on. In early 1949 she was asked to test for a new film (an unusual request for a star of her magnitude), in which she would play the grandmother of a light-skinned black girl who passes for white. Waters made the test and ended up giving one of her finest performances in *Pinky*. She won an Academy Award nomination for Best Supporting Actress. Ethel Waters' career was back on solid ground. But emotionally, she was hardly at ease. Like Holiday, she remained restless and edgy.

Despite the personal problems of Waters and Holiday and the professional troubles of Lena Horne and Hazel Scott, the forties still closed on an optimistic note. Nothing could have daunted the professional hopes of the new black goddesses coming on the scene at the tail end of the period. Such upcoming stars as Pearl Bailey and Dorothy Dandridge knew, after all, that a war had been won, that the nation was more prosperous than ever before, and that black women had played a significant part in the past era's cultural history. Then, too, the ambitious new beauties, eyeing the success of Horne and Scott, knew there was a place in movies now for glamorous, dignified black women. And so, with her optimism intact, the emerging goddess of the postwar years rightly anticipated that there would be even more recognition and fanfare for the black beauty in the next era.

In movies, black maids and cooks were expected not only to do their chores but also to spread some sunshine around too. *Above left:* Louise Beavers providing service with a smile in *Imitation of Life* and *(bottom left)* giving some cooking tips to a

rather cold-eyed Madame Sul-Te-Wan, while Butterfly McQueen (*right*) takes a break from her household duties to give some friendly advice to hero Gregory Peck in *Duel in the Sun.*

· THE 1950S ·
SEX SYMBOLS

The fifties in America are now rightly remembered as a period of national conformity and apathy. What with the Cold War and McCarthy's Communist hunts, when dissent of any kind was discouraged, America had turned quiet and sullen. America was soon bored with itself too. And throughout the era there were subtle signs everywhere of that boredom as well as of a brewing unrest. If anything, the period's various fads and trends simply revealed a great secret national desire to break through the period's lethargy. The new movie heroes—Marlon Brando, James Dean, Montgomery Clift—were all rebels who tapped the undercover dissent and dissatisfaction of America's Lonely Crowd.

The new heroines also had rebellious streaks. Marilyn Monroe shocked Americans when her nude photo ran in *Playboy*. Elizabeth Taylor's marriages kept her in the news. Often Americans thought they preferred the wholesome stars—Doris Day, Debbie Reynolds, and Grace Kelly. But Monroe and Taylor, the Light and Dark of the era, were the fifties' most famous females, touching on the nation's avid interest in sexy rebelliousness. With Taylor, too, we saw the first dark white goddess to become a major American star. Before her such women as Gene Tierney, Hedy Lamarr, and Dolores Del Rio were successful, but none were mythic like Garbo. Taylor became a legendary heroine, although Americans accepted her only as the Scarlet Woman, the Other Side of Womanhood to be feared, even rejected.

Sex opened new doors for the fifties'

"The Bronze Blond Bombshell": Joyce Bryant.

black beauty. New stars—Joyce Bryant, Dorothy Dandridge, and Eartha Kitt—often played with or dramatized sex to mock or defy traditional middle-class values, taboos, and hang-ups. None, however, seemed comfortable with her sexy image.

Aside from sex, the fifties diva also found this bland new age surprisingly receptive to the cult of personality. Kitt and Pearl Bailey had huge egos and striking public personalities, far more idiosyncratic (and at times more neurotic) than Lena Horne and Hazel Scott.

PEARL BAILEY: THE SEXY GIRL NEXT DOOR

In this new gamy atmosphere of sex and personality, Pearl Bailey, the first black beauty to make waves, was hardly anyone's idea of a woman who might use sex to stalk a man down or to lash out at society. Instead Pearlie Mae personified the lively down-home diva, the ordinary, chatty, wisecracking neighborly lady who was telling a generation scared of its own shadow to just cool it, honey, sit back, relax, and have some fun. She became a star by often laughing at and joking about the birds and bees, romance and men.

Pearl Bailey had been around since the forties, stumbling here and there, trying to find her niche. Born in Newport News, Virginia, the daughter of a minister, she had gone to live with her mother in Washington, D.C., after the divorce of her parents. She began her career at amateur night shows in Philadelphia and Washington. At first she was known as the kid sister of dancer Bill Bailey, who was then a far bigger star.

In the forties Bailey performed at New York clubs, did USO tours, had a hit record called "Tired" (a woman's lament about the way her life and her man have been treating her), and dazzled Broadway audiences in 1946 in *St. Louis Woman*. In a cast that included Ruby Hill, June Hawkins, the Nicholas Brothers, Rex Ingram, and Juanita Hall, Pearlie Mae, with only two numbers, stole the show. "Pearl Bailey was a special favorite on opening night," wrote the *New York Morning Telegraph's* critic George Freedley, "and . . . stopped the show twice which is

A wisecracking, ribald Pearlie Mae singing up a storm in the lavish all-black musical *Carmen Jones*.

Pearl Bailey started her career at amateur-night contests, working her way to Broadway.

as unusual as anything I can think of now....Pearl Bailey positively triumphed." Later Freedley saw the show again and was as enthusiastic as ever, writing:

> The highlight is still the wonderfully comic Pearl Bailey who can take any number and make it sound better than it is....Her handling of the highly moral "Legalize My Name" is a joy to behold....The audience was eating out of her hand before she finished. When she saunters into "A Woman's Prerogative" in the last act, the spectators began to laugh before the first lyric was out of her mouth. That is how great comediennes are born and Pearl Bailey certainly has what it takes to achieve high rank among the comic singers of our stage.

For her performance, Pearl Bailey walked off with the theatre world's Donaldson Award.

Bailey was aware of her limitations as well as her assets. She wasn't much of a singer. Shrewdly, she learned to talk as she sang (or to sing a bit as she talked), providing lively, seemingly spontaneous banter in which she pushed the song aside. What really counted were the direct, personal comments. So when performing "Toot Toot Tootsie, Goodbye," Bailey would interrupt herself,

look at the audience, throw her hands forward, and say "Good Riddance!" to indicate she was glad the darn rascal was out of her life. While she performed "Ma, He's Making Eyes at Me," audiences saw a whirling delight. Pearl might be twisting and turning, fidgeting nervously but happily, her eyes widening, her face hot with romantic anticipation 'cause she was tickled pink the guy was giving her the onceover. Her hit song "Takes Two to Tango," was filled with sexual innuendos. No matter what the song, Pearl Bailey's impromptu conversations presented a portrait of a daffy romantic trapped by her own sense of realism.

Another comic selling point was her fatigue. "Why should I stand, everybody else is sittin'?" she would tell her audience, then take a seat onstage, immediately setting up a free and easy rapport with the crowd. Sometimes Bailey's act was criticized as being a throwback to prewar stereotypes. Actually, the humor was both old and new. She was influenced by the chitlin circuit stars like Moms Mabley and Redd Foxx. Like them, she set herself up as a kind of deliriously engaging community leader of sorts. "Now, looka here, honey," she might begin a routine. Bailey had also learned from Hattie McDaniel, who could be funny, charming, and downright

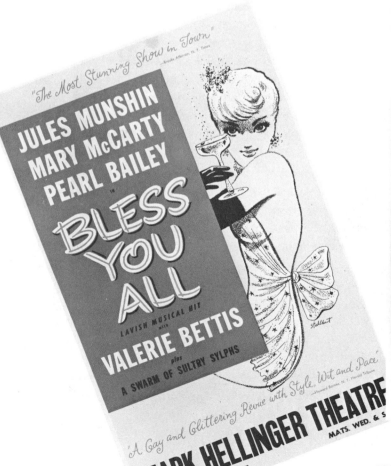

Controversy: Bailey's marriage to musician Louis Bellson.

hostile or rebellious all at the same time. Yet influenced as she was by the old-timers, Pearl never pushed her humor to the point where it might disturb an audience. Sometimes Moms or Redd and later Richard Pryor seemed bent on driving audiences up a wall with their incisive barbs. Bailey, however, was always a soothing figure. She used humor to communicate her view of the world as a joyous, harmonious place that had no great problems or tensions. (This point of view, so much admired in the fifties, often distressed younger black audiences of later periods.)

In the late forties and early fifties, Bailey, determined to make the big time, was an ambitious, competitive performer who seemed to be running in circles. She popped up on Broadway, in such disappointing shows as *Arms and the Girl*, *House of Flowers*, and *Bless You All*. In Hollywood she appeared in such films as *Variety Girl* (in which she sang "Tired"), *Isn't It Romantic?*, *Carmen Jones*, *That Certain Feeling*, *All the Fine Young Cannibals*, and *Porgy and Bess*. But neither Broadway nor Hollywood seemed to know what to do with this magnetic personality, whose timing and delivery were always letter perfect.

During the fifties Bailey finally became a national celebrity due to her nightclub appearances where, in the middle of her act, she would talk and tease her patrons, and most importantly, due to her highly successful appearances on a new phenomenon called television. She appeared on everything from Ed Sullivan's to Perry Como's shows. She was America's first black television star. She was lucky that she showed up when there was a place for her high-flung far-out broadness. Seeing television for the communal vehicle it was, Bailey was clearly at home, exchanging quips and chitchat with Ed or Perry in her casual style. She knew just how far to go too. She played more with the idea of romance than sex, and stayed clear of racial material that was then taboo. Moreover, although good looking, she played down her looks. Nothing was going to set her apart from the other gals. Television divested Pearl Bailey of her sexuality and some of her originality too. But because of her appearances, middle-class, comformist American viewers slowly grew accustomed to seeing a black face in their homes. Even at that, she did not star in her own series until the early seventies.

For the most part, Pearl Bailey was an ethnic diva who knew exactly how far to go with the whole ethnic business. She was an immensely likable woman who, as far as fifties audiences were concerned, made but one mistake. In 1952 she married white drummer Louis Bellson in London, amid a storm of controversy. His father's objection to the interracial match was picked up by the wire services, and the two were besieged by the press, making front page headlines throughout the country. Later Bailey was back in the papers after an incident at a New Jersey nightclub where she had been beaten and kicked by a group of unidentified white men.

But the good-natured, optimistic Pearlie Mae remained on the scene. A great professional triumph came in the late sixties when she starred on Broadway in the all-black version of *Hello Dolly!* As the years moved on, she seemed to enjoy her fame, posing for photographs with one American president after another. In later eras her humor was less saucy and ribald. The fifties remain her peak period when her joyous chatter about romance had taken the black beauty right into American living rooms.

EARTHA KITT: THE CAT WOMAN

The era's next important black beauty was Eartha Kitt, an energetic tiny terror of a performer. She was a sex symbol, part campy, part absurd. She purred, snarled, scratched, and acted up like crazy. Performing at the smartest supper clubs in America, she strutted out in Balmain gowns. Even before she opened her mouth, patrons sat in anxious anticipation, aware of the stories circulating about her temperament, her life-style. Men were said to have lavished gifts on her—yachts, cars, furs, diamonds. Her songs, "Monotonous" and "C'est Si Bon," touched on a life of sheer unadulterated pleasure and self-indulgence. Onstage, sex and money were what she treasured most. She was the ultimate temptress, who sometimes used her audiences, sometimes made fun of them. Her hypnotic coldness, the eyes that stared and blazed, the petulant pouty mouth, the simmering air of arrogance and indolence, the metallic quality of the voice itself, were all knowingly used to entrance her audience. She was the fifties high priestess of the cult of personality. With her, audiences witnessed briefly a blatant triumph of will, a poor backwoods colored girl who provided the silent generation with a far-flung fairy tale, a Cinderella story turned sepia.

As befitting a fairy tale, the Kitt beginnings were humble. She had been born in North, South Carolina, the daughter of a sharecropper who named her Eartha in homage to the goodness of the earth. When Eartha and

Eartha Kitt (with Robert Clary *(left)* and Paul Lynde in *New Faces of 1952*): a-backwoods-Southern-girl-turned-Cinderella.

Eartha Kitt *(right)*, **as the mean bad-girl (dressed in black), and Ruby Dee, as the sweet goody-goody (dressed in white), in** *St. Louis Blues.*

her sister were still youngsters, the father deserted their mother. Later sent to live in New York, she was a country girl dumbfounded by such big city mysteries as indoor plumbing, electricity, and radio. In 1943 she left high school to work as a seamstress in a Brooklyn factory. One day when a girl asked for directions to the Katherine Dunham dance studio, Eartha tagged along, later auditioned for Dunham, and by age twenty was a featured dancer, traveling with the troupe through Europe and Mexico. By 1950 she had left Dunham, embarking on a career as a nightclub chanteuse that carried her to Paris, London, and Turkey. A transfixed Orson Welles dubbed her "the most exciting woman in the world" and audaciously cast her in his European production of *Dr. Faustus.* She played Helen of Troy, "the face that launched a thousand ships."

During her early period abroad, Kitt, by some accounts, was a tough, ambitious, driven young woman who refused to slow down because she felt time was running out. In each country during off hours from work, she had studied the people, soaking up the sights, the cultures, the customs, and the languages. For a girl who had grown up with nothing, she seemed desperate to discover herself by means of another cultural experience, one free of American prejudices and pruderies. Throughout her career Eartha Kitt seemed to hold America in disdain, never forgiving this land of opportunity for her early sufferings. Her entire professional stance—everything from her particular kind of elegance and arrogance to the way she spoke with a strange accent—always suggested exotic Eurasian chic. Consequently, while it took Americans time to discover and appreciate her, in Europe she immediately got attention.

In America, Kitt's career did not take off until her Broadway appearance in *New Faces of 1952,* in which she cleverly mixed sex with humor. And she was rewarded by becoming an instant celebrity, hotly coveted, courted, and promoted by the press. She played the posh

126

clubs, made movies (*Mark of the Hawk, Anna Lucasta*), was a guest performer at the 1957 Newport Jazz Festival, appeared on television shows (everything from "Voice of Firestone" to "Toast of the Town" to the title role in Oscar Wilde's *Salomé*), bounced back to Broadway for lead roles (*Mrs. Patterson, Shinbone Alley, Jolly's Progress*), and had one hit record after another with songs that bristled with sex and decadence ("I Want to Be Evil" and "Santa Baby"). Her first album, *RCA Victor Presents Eartha Kitt*, sold over two million copies in little more than sixteen months, followed by another hit album called *The Bad Eartha*.

Records, shows, movies, and television spots kept her in the public eye. Her life was described as an endless round of benefits, parties, dinners, luncheons, trips to photographers, the hairdresser's, a whirl of railroad stations, international airports, studios, dressing rooms, rehearsal halls, press conferences. Well publicized as a sex kitten, she was linked by the press with such celebrities as Orson Welles, playboy Porfirio Rubirosa, and millionaire Arthur Loew, Jr. She interviewed Albert Einstein, had tea with Winston Churchill, and dinner with India's Prime Minister Nehru. In 1954 the undergraduates at Yale voted her the girl they would most like to take to the Senior Prom.

The press was infatuated not only with her grand style, but her fiery temperament too. When she performed for visiting monarchs King Paul and Queen Fredericka in Los Angeles, the city's mayor, Norris Poulson, was offended by her selection of suggestive songs. In 1955, when an illness cut short the national tour of the play *Mrs. Patterson*, rumors flew that it wasn't Eartha's kidneys that had acted up; it was her temperament. That same year newspapers reported she had been named defendant in a $200,000 damage suit by a nightclub that charged that a rude Eartha had dumped champagne onto patrons. Despite all the ballyhoo, it is safe to say she was never as great a public heroine as Baker, Horne, or Waters. Her attitude eventually antagonized not only some of the press, but some of her fans as well. As early as 1954, a columnist for the *New York Morning Telegraph* wrote:

> You idly wonder why a girl who has reached such fame and position from such a humble start allows herself to behave as rudely as she does....You remember what another actress told you about how Miss Kitt acted at the party given for her....A noted man of theatre came up and said: "Miss Kitt, you were quite wonderful," and Kitt languidly replied: "Of course."...Is this an egotist, doing her

best to alienate people, or a frightened girl who covers her panic with rudeness?

> Then you remember what Jimmy Kirkwood told you of how charming and simple she was in her early success at the Churchill Club in London and what a change he found a year later when she was in "New Faces."...."She was a simple kid working hard for success in London," he said.
> "Backstage at 'New Faces' I found a bored, languid girl in leopard skin slacks, black satin waist, footlong cigarette holder and an affected, 'Oh, hello,' said with a vague 'Now I wonder who you are' manner. People haven't got time for that kind of nonsense."...Which is something Miss Kitt should learn: people haven't got time for that kind of nonsense....There were great performers before her and there will be great ones after she has been forgotten.

Though *Ebony* seldom ran critical articles on black celebrities, it nonetheless carried a 1954 cover story with the banner: "Why Negroes Do Not Like Eartha Kitt."

One could dismiss these comments as those of a white columnist put off or threatened by Kitt's unbridled confidence. Why should her humble start stop her from behaving as rudely as she pleased? But even the black press commented on Kitt's rudeness. *Ebony*, that bastion for the values and sentiments of America's black bourgeoisie and a publication that seldom ran critical articles on black celebrities, nonetheless carried a 1954 cover story with the banner: "Why Negroes Do Not Like Eartha Kitt." The piece was hard-hitting.

> Eartha Kitt...was approached one Sunday afternoon by a...Negro who had...watch[ed] her play a ball game of "catch" with a little white girl....He interrupted to hand Miss Kitt a note. She took it, frowned slightly as she read it. "Why don't you come out...and visit some Negro places and be with other Negroes," the note read.
> Miss Kitt...said she was sorry but she would have to decline....In much less polite language she told him what he could do with his "Negro places."...
> What he apparently did not know was that...many Negroes find Eartha Kitt cold and a little hard to take. Up to now, it has seldom been mentioned that this rejection of her by other Negroes has become almost contagious and that her aloofness has become a subject of much talk.

Later questioned about her reaction to the piece, Kitt was quoted as saying: "I don't have to defend anything. I do not carry my race around on my shoulders. My work is not racial and neither am I a racial personality."

There is no reason to believe that Eartha Kitt ever regretted this statement nor any other she might have made. Had she, there might have been more sympathy for her when her career decline set in. It is hard to say exactly what went wrong. But perhaps the haughtiness, which had long been an integral part of the black beauty's style, now seemed out of control with Kitt. Her dilemma may point up the fundamental uneasiness the black sex symbol felt with her new role. Kitt pushed to extremes the idea that she could not be taken for granted, that her public had to show her respect. Every black goddess would cherish the fact that she was a sexy lady, but every black goddess also felt compelled to let everyone know she was more than simply *that*.

Finally, though, Kitt's problem may well have been that she was too much a personalized fairy-tale heroine to ever be a woman of myth. Fairy tales have been described as personal gratifications, end products of private dreams and desires, compensation fantasies for the shortcomings of cruddy real life. Eartha had lived out her dream of herself as the poor backwoods girl alone in the world, who triumphs over hostile or seemingly insurmountable forces to become a star. Her success gratified her personal wishes. But unlike every other diva on record, she did not seem to share her triumphs with the community. In the end, Kitt may have surely alienated her power base, the black community.

By the time the Eisenhower era ended, so too had much of her blazing appeal. (Her marriage in the 1960s to white businessman William McDonald did not help matters.) She toured the country in a production of *The Owl and the Pussycat* and turned up as the Cat Woman on television's "Bat Man." Then in 1968, she was back on the front pages when at a luncheon with First Lady Lady Bird Johnson, she denounced the Johnson administration's involvement in Vietnam. Kitt later announced that an angered President Johnson did all he could to wreck her career, instructing the FBI to gather a dossier on her. Club and cafe owners were pressured into canceling engagements. Almost a decade later, she returned to the spotlight with the Broadway production of *Timbuktu!*, in which, upon entering the stage, Kitt stared directly into the audience, announcing haughtily, "I am here!" It was one of her great moments. At the end of the seventies the slinky, sexy Cat Woman of the fifties was once again a star.

Eartha Kitt with Nat King Cole (left) **and Cab Calloway** (right) **in** St. Louis Blues.

JOYCE BRYANT: THE BRONZE BLOND BOMBSHELL

In the early and mid-fifties, Eartha's only real rival was Joyce Bryant. She was billed as the "Black Marilyn Monroe," the "Belter," and the "Voice You'll Always Remember." But, sadly, through her own design, she had a surprisingly short reign.

Bryant was the daughter of a San Franciscan who worked as a chef for the Southern Pacific Railroad. Her father was a carouser. Her mother was a devout Seventh-Day Adventist. Young Joyce, the oldest of eight children raised in a suffocating atmosphere of religious dos and don'ts, was a quiet, lonely child. As a teen-ager on a visit to a cousin in Los Angeles, Bryant joined a singalong with other patrons at a local club. No sooner had she opened her mouth than everyone else became silent, impressed by her four-octave miracle of a voice. She was immediately offered a job as a professional singer. She went from club to club, slowly acquiring a reputation and a following.

By the middle of the decade Joyce Bryant was a star not only because of her voice, but also because of her image as a kooky, dreamy woman. Like her contemporary, Monroe, Bryant exuded sex. Sometimes when she sang, she was cool and relaxed about sexual matters. Her tones were mellow. But other times, as she belted the tunes out, she became a steamy performer. So provocative were her big sexy hits "Love for Sale" and "Drunk with Love" that both were often banned from radio play.

But she generated most of her heat during live performances. She was known for her backless, fishtail, skintight dresses. *Life* reported that the costumes were so tight that often she could barely walk in them and had to be carried to the stage. The dresses revealed enough cleavage to make even Marilyn do a double take. Onstage, she burned up so much energy—twisting, turning, gyrating, shaking—that newspapers reported she lost as much as four pounds at each performance.

In due time, though, Joyce Bryant's great trademark was (like Marilyn again) her blond hair. She had been born a brunette. But the hair color change came about one evening when she found herself appearing on the same bill with Josephine Baker. Terrified of competing with a legend, she finally hit on a surefire gimmick. That night she arrived onstage in a tight silver dress, with silver nails, silver floor-length mink, and silver hair. She had

grabbed a bottle of silver radiator paint and poured the stuff all over her head. As she herself said, when she appeared, "I stopped everything!" (Even Baker gave a nod when the two passed each other in a hallway, as if to say "Touchez!") In no time the bronze blond bombshell was plastered all over newspapers and magazines and even started a fad among some more adventurous black women. Eventually, the silver hair became her trademark, turning her into a glorified national oddity.

With the gimmick and voice intact, Bryant picked up as much as $2,500 to $3,500 a performance, earning as much as $150,000 a year. She was called one of the most beautiful black women in the world. And now, for the first time, a dark black woman had become a certified national sex symbol. A 1953 *Life* magazine layout ran steamy photographs of her, the kind readers seldom saw of white love goddesses. In one shot she was bent over, her backside in full view. In another, she lay on her dressing-room floor with feet propped up, her midriff showing, her open blouse barely managing to cup her breasts.

Like her contemporary, Monroe, Bryant exuded sex. So provocative were "Love for Sale" and "Drunk with Love" that both were often banned from radio play.

Eventually, the image unnerved even Bryant. Just when she had hit the real big time—when Earl Wilson or Winchell was anxious for an interview or a quote, when the Copacabana, the Fontainebleau, and Miami's Algiers Hotel signed her for appearances, when no less than the queen of Hollywood social arbiters, Louella Parsons, was happy to be photographed by her side—Joyce Bryant's fairy tale was already about to come to a bad end. The silver radiator paint made her hair fall out, and everything else seemed to fall to pieces too. Because of her early religious indoctrination, she was never at ease with the sexy image. She fretted about working on the Sabbath and rebelled inwardly against "acting like a sexpot." She hated the atmosphere of the nightclubs and the men who eyed her or gave her a hard time.

"I never enjoyed my career," she later told *Essence*. "I was a pound of flesh and an object of lust in my last years, and I've no one but myself to blame."

Her private tensions became so great that before an appearance she would cry that she couldn't perform. But she discovered there was no such thing as couldn't perform. Soon the managers, agents, promoters, moved in, ready to take control. On those hard nights when her nerves, rattled and frayed, drove her up a wall, pills and drugs were often available to calm her down or pep her up. "I had no peace," she said. "Pills brought sleep or pills brought energy, but never peace. I felt so alone. There was no one to talk to. I was such a big star, but I was such a little girl." And then suddenly, she decided to leave show business. In November 1955 the headline over Earl Wilson's column read: "Joyce Bryant Ends Show Career for Church." Later a United Press article carried another headline: "Torch Singer Joyce Bryant Starting on Evangelical Tour." *Ebony* ran a lengthy feature under the banner: "The New World of Joyce Bryant: Former café singer gives up $200,000-a-year career to learn to serve God."

Joyce Bryant enrolled in Oakwood College, a Seventh-Day Adventist institution in Alabama. Here she followed a strict regime. No smoking. No drinking. No profanity. No dancing. No theatre. No sex either. While a student, she did evangelical singing tours. And for a spell, she popped back up in the papers. As the bad-woman-trying-to-go-straight, she held a new fascination for readers caught up in the idea of repentance.

Once the blond hair was back to its natural black, she looked far less exotic, also heavier, strained, and lost. No doubt she struck readers as a woman who had suffered. Oddly enough, once Bryant's conversion was accepted as the real thing and not some publicity stunt, she was virtually forgotten by the public.

As Bryant later revealed, the years away from show business were almost as bleak and hellish as those in. Disillusioned, she left her religious studies to return to performing in the sixties. She appeared with the Washington Symphony and later toured with the Italian, French, and Vienna opera companies. But work was hard to find, and at one point she found herself demonstrating beauty products at Lord & Taylor's. Only in the late seventies, after further disappointments and more personal nightmarish experiences, did she return to the New York café scene, no longer a gimmicky blond bombshell, but a magnificent earthy woman.

DOROTHY DANDRIDGE: TRAGIC VENUS

aving come of age at the same time as Kitt, Bailey, and Bryant, Dorothy Dandridge rose higher and emerged as America's first bona fide black movie star. In time, she had her share of problems, ending up, like Holiday, a tragic figure. But while Dorothy Dandridge rode the crest of success, there was no one like her.

She was a child of Hollywood, growing up with her older sister Vivian in a heady showbiz atmosphere. She was born in Cleveland in 1922. Her mother, comedienne Ruby Dandridge, separated from her husband, settled with her two daughters in sunny Los Angeles. Ruby appeared in such films as *Tish*, *Cabin in the Sky*, and *My Wild Irish Rose*, and was a regular on such radio programs as "The Judy Canova Show" and "Beulah." Under Ruby's tutelage, the sisters performed as the Wonder Kids at southern churches and schools, later did bits in movies, then, as teen-agers, popped up at the Cotton Club and eventually worked with Duke Ellington, Cab Calloway, and Jimmie Lunceford. In the forties Dandridge also played bit parts in movies never mentioned later in her career: *Lady from Louisiana*, *Sun Valley Serenade*, *Bahama Passage*, *Drums of the Congo*, and *Hit Parade of 1943*. By the mid-forties, when Vivian, the aggressive, outgoing one everyone assumed would become the big star, decided to do a solo act, Dorothy, the timid sister, had a short-lived marriage with Harold Nicholas of the popular dancing Nicholas Brothers. They parted not long after the birth of their retarded daughter. During this period of great personal depression, Dandridge, feeling she had failed as a daughter, as a wife, as a mother, as a lover, was finally determined to prove she could do something right. She set out to capture the American dream and become a star.

The idea that a black woman could become a dramatic film actress was still unthought of. Dandridge was also inordinately shy and introverted. But an extraordinary drive took over and she pushed herself beyond even her limits, channeling all her energies and frustrations into her career. She exercised daily. Whatever money she made from early singing engagements was poured into costumes. She worked hard on her voice, knowing that if she perfected her style she would have a foot in the big showbiz door.

When she was not in a rehearsal hall, she was studying—acting, singing, dancing. Or she was meeting people, off to a benefit, party, interview, or audition. "My sister worked twenty-four hours a day at being a star," Vivian once said. And it paid off.

In the late forties Dorothy worked with black

Black America's most cherished star of the fifties: Dorothy Dandridge, who once said she had everything—and nothing.

composer/arranger Phil Moore, the Svengali who had been the singing coach for Lena Horne and who later worked with Diahann Carroll and Julie Wilson. Moore played an important part in shaping their styles. Horne and Dandridge (also Carroll) had striking similarities in looks, in dress, in hairstyles, in delivery. Phil Moore carefully groomed these women, helping them smooth away the rough edges. He knew exactly what type of material they should use in order to appeal to white audiences. Not one of them sang rhythm-and-blues. They stuck to the acceptable sounds of Gershwin and Rodgers and Hart.

By 1951 Dandridge appeared at the Mocambo with Desi Arnaz's band. The breakthrough performance, however, was at Los Angeles' Club Gala, a hangout for showbiz folk. Dandridge started off disastrously, so nervous, according to her manager, Earl Mills, that she could not stand and had to be seated onstage while she feebly performed. But Phil Moore, by then so enamoured of her, joked and talked with her onstage. After her problems opening night, Moore worked with her for long hours every day before she made an appearance. He loosened her up and coaxed her out of her shell, touching on the fiery personality she became famous for. By then, Moore and Dandridge had become lovers. In a short period of time her act at the Club Gala was so talked about that Dandridge was booked back into the Mocambo and broke all existing attendance records.

The press promptly latched on to her, as it did with no other black beauty. When she reopened at the Mocambo, *Life* ran a splashy picture layout, touting her as "the most beautiful Negro singer since Lena Horne." Two years later *Life* ran another Dandridge photo layout. And the following year she became one of the first black women to ever grace a *Life* cover, and she also appeared on the cover of *Ebony*.

Soon Dandridge made major appearances at important clubs around the country. When she performed at New York's La Vie en Rose, then a popular nitery in the midst of serious financial problems, her two-week engagement was such a sellout that she stayed on for some fourteen weeks and single-handedly saved the club from bankruptcy. She was the first black performer to appear at the Waldorf Astoria's prestigious Empire Room.

As Dandridge was ushered in, Lena was eased out. No doubt the name of Dorothy Dandridge was thrown up in

Dandridge at an opening with Joe Adams.

With Stephen Boyd and Joan Collins, her *Island in the Sun* costars.

Lena's face numerous times. What she thought of her fifties rival is anyone's guess. But surely there had to be occasions when, eyeing Dorothy's triumphs, Lena felt her own day had come and gone, particularly when Dandridge won movie roles in *Tarzan's Peril*, *Bright Road*, and *The Harlem Globetrotters*.

In the mid-fifties Dandridge finally got the big prize, the black woman's movie role of the decade, the lead in Otto Preminger's all-black musical *Carmen Jones*. Initially, Preminger rejected her because she looked too sophisticated to play a *cullid* temptress. She had come to his office elegantly dressed. On her second interview with him she completely changed her style. She sexily sauntered into the office darkly made up and dressed in a tight skirt and low-cut blouse. Preminger took one look and proclaimed, "It's Carmen!" The role was hers.

In this lavish, Technicolor, Cinemascope modernization of Bizet's opera *Carmen*, Dandridge played a sexy black girl working in a parachute factory, who lures a good, clean-cut colored boy (played by Harry Belafonte) away from the army and his sweet homebody girl friend. Later she dumps him for another man, only to be strangled by the hero at the film's climax. No one thought an all-black movie would do well at the box office, but what with Dandridge's rousing performance, it was the surprise hit of 1954.

Life celebrated Dandridge as something of a grand natural wonder when it wrote: "Of all the divas of grand opera—from Emma Calvé of the 1900s to Risë Stevens—who have decorated the title role of Carmen and have in turn been made famous by it, none was ever so decorative or will reach nationwide fame so quickly as the sultry young lady . . . on *Life*'s cover this week." After a nationwide poll of film critics, *Film Daily* selected her as one of the top five performers of the year. In 1954 she became the first black woman to win an Academy Award nomination as Best Actress.

Everywhere she went, everything she said or did, was of public interest. A host of publications publicized and fawned over her with a constant whirl of attention and adulation. Newspapers ran photographs of her arriving at airports or strolling along Fifth Avenue. Formally invited by the French government to the Cannes Film Festival where *Carmen Jones* had a special screening, she arrived in France triumphantly aglow amid a horde of international photographers and reporters. The following year

With her second husband, Jack Dennison.

Sheriff's deputies remove Dandridge's body.

During her career Dorothy Dandridge often played a damsel in distress waiting to be rescued. *Left:* In *The Decks Ran Red* she looks ready to pull her hair out...until the arrival of Stuart Whitman *(center)*, who seems ready to take the situation—and Dorothy—in hand! *Right:* a poster from another Dandridge movie melodrama, *Tamango.*

she was invited to England for a celebration at Oxford. In an elaborate ceremony that lasted until dawn, thousands of students crowned her the Queen of May.

For Black America, then about to launch its massive civil rights offensive, Dorothy Dandridge was part of the new day. Athletes Jackie Robinson and Roy Campanella had integrated major league baseball. Now a dramatic black actress integrated American motion pictures.

But sadly, her decline came soon after her triumph. She realized she was but a token figure within the movie colony, her position not much different than Lena Horne's in the forties. There were no great follow-up roles to sustain her fame. Three years passed before she appeared in another film. She costarred in *Island in the Sun* with Harry Belafonte and James Mason. In this drama about politics and miscegenation in the tropics, she was cast as a lovely island girl in love with a white Britisher. In *Tamango*, *The Decks Ran Red*, and *Malaga* she was the first black woman in American films to find herself in the arms of white men—Edmund Purdom, Trevor Howard, James Mason, Stuart Whitman, and Broderick Crawford. But the films, provocative for their time, always pulled back at the crucial moment. Her manager, Earl Mills, has said the producers and studios could never decide what nationality she should be. Dialogue was repeatedly changed, softened. So were love scenes. Or any talk of romance. It was a frustrating, debilitating experience that broke her. By 1959, when she appeared in Preminger's *Porgy and Bess*, she knew that even if it were a hit, she might have to wait five more years for another decent role.

She returned to nightclub work, but hated it. The clubs made her feel like a failure, a dramatic actress unable to get dramatic parts.

Her offscreen life was in shambles too. Ugly stories circulated that she was no longer attracted to black men and now, suffering from what blacks call white fever, she could only find fulfillment with white men. She was romantically linked with Preminger, Peter Lawford, Michael Rennie, and Curt Jurgens. No doubt this kind of talk was the cruelest blow of all. Dorothy Dandridge's involvement with white men grew in large part out of her peculiar position as a love goddess in a system black men never got anywhere near. Her sister Vivian has said that Dorothy would have gladly married someone like a Harry Belafonte. But the few important black male stars of her day were already married. At the same time, the black female star, like any other kind of star, black or white, male or female, often needs someone willing to take a back seat, permitting the star to glow in the light of fame. The mate often simply has to be there when the star has no one else, and, on occasion, to be dumped on by the star. Those black males Dandridge did encounter seldom understood the world in which she operated. A female star has enough problems finding someone within the business who can cope with her stardom. [A relationship with someone outside the business, unless perhaps he himself is another kind of star (as was the case with Powell during his marriage to Hazel Scott), could be disastrous. Then, too, some black stars take on white mates as testaments to their power; the idea is that they have gone so far as to have as their very own their former oppressors.]

Dandridge, isolated, desperate, older, and aware that if the career didn't go right, at least her private life should, made a terrible mistake. She married white restaurateur Jack Dennison. For years she had been thrifty, terrified of poverty, carefully saving every penny. But once her mania had taken over, once the equilibrium had been thrown off, talk spread that she was pouring her money

---

She made a trip to Mexico, worked out at a health farm, and signed a new movie contract. But a few days after her return to Hollywood, she was found dead.

---

into Dennison's new restaurant. "They had met in Las Vegas, where he had been a maitre d'hôtel," Preminger later said of Dandridge and Dennison. "'Did you invest money in this restaurant?' I asked. She laughed. 'You know me. You know I wouldn't put money into anything.' She married that man and they spent all her money. She had to sell her house and everything of value she owned. Then he left her."

The rest of her life was a sad, tragic affair. Once her creditors closed in, she was forced to file for bankruptcy. After three years of marriage, she divorced Dennison in 1962. According to her manager, Earl Mills, she drank heavily during this time and her health was also poor. Mills has said that a new physician had given her drug prescriptions to cover a multitude of ills. There were pills for energy, for dehydration, for relaxation, for sleep. Briefly, she attempted to resurrect her career. With Mills, she made a trip to Mexico, worked out at a health farm, and optimistically signed a new movie contract. But a few days after her return to Hollywood, she was found dead in her apartment. She was forty-one. Later an autopsy attributed Dorothy Dandridge's death to an overdose of an antidepressant.

A sweet memory of better times: Dandridge, glowing after her triumph in *Carmen Jones*, appears on *The Ed Sullivan Show.*

Sarah Vaughan striking a glamor-girl pose. Known as Sassy or The Divine Sarah, she performed with the bands of Earl Hines and Billy Eckstine.

OTHER FACES, OTHER VOICES

Other sepia ladies appeared in the fifties. Some became prominent simply because there was a black audience so anxious for a magnetic black female star it could glorify or identify with that, on occasion, it would take almost anything it could get—or anything that offered some kind of promise. The fifties love goddess was also fortunate because of a new black press on the rise. Now such national black publications as *Ebony, Jet, Hue,* later *Sepia,* as well as revitalized black newspapers in major cities, all helped feed Black America's appetite for news and new faces.

In 1952 *Jet* ran a cover story on actress Mildred Smith (who appeared opposite newcomer Sidney Poitier in *No Way Out*), satisfied that it was able to come up with at least one other black film actress besides Dandridge. Had it not been for a tragic automobile accident that left her partially paralyzed, Smith might have developed into an important dramatic actress. Later in the decade, actress Juanita Moore came to national attention after she appeared in the remake of *Imitation of Life* and won an Oscar nomination as Best Supporting Actress.

Hilda Simms, who now seems to belong almost exclusively to the postwar Truman years, was often reported on by the black press, particularly after her performance in the low-budget film *The Joe Louis Story.* Dancer-choreographer Pearl Primus also received a fair amount of attention as did the striking dancer Carmen de Lavallade, newcomer Diahann Carroll, and classical pianists Natalie Hinderas and Dorothy Donegan. On the Broadway stage, spunky Juanita Hall turned up regularly. She appeared in *House of Flowers,* and also played nonblack roles in *South Pacific* (as Bloody Mary) and *The Flower Drum Song.* Opera singers Leontyne Price, Mattiwilda Dobbs, and Camilla Williams emerged on the scene, each waiting for the big break, the chance to appear at the Met. (Price got it in the next decade.) Also waiting for a big break of another sort—a serious dramatic stage role—was Jane White, the bright, Smith-educated daughter of Walter White, who appeared on Broadway in *Strange Fruit.* Pint-sized newcomer Leslie Uggams played the little girl next door on television's "Beulah." Americans watched this child star grow up. As a teen-ager, she appeared on Mitch Miller's "Sing Along with Mitch." Later she had her own network television series and eventually won solid dramatic roles in such television productions of the seventies as "Roots" and "Backstairs at the White House."

There were the glamour girl singers: Savannah Churchill, Damita Jo (appearing with or without the Red Caps), and the engaging Ruth Brown, who sang the big-selling pop singles, "Teardrops in My Eyes" and "Mama."

Performers Sarah Vaughan, Ella Fitzgerald, Carmen McRae, Della Reese, Dakota Staton, Big Maybelle, Big Mama Willie Mae Thornton, Gloria Lynn, LaVern Baker, and Dinah Washington all had faithful, adoring followers. Had these women been more flamboyant or, in keeping with the age's demands, sexier, they might have well developed into legendary public heroines. But, for the most part, whatever personal dramas, pains, or joys these women experienced, they kept under wraps. Many of Fitzgerald's fans did not even know whether she was married or not. The same was true of Vaughan. Her nickname, Sassy, however, often did lead audiences to speculating about exactly what went on after a performance. A knockout creation like Dinah Washington, known for being hellishly arrogant and demanding, did shake fifties audiences up.

During her career, Washington insisted on being called the Queen, once dyed her hair as blond as Bryant's and dared anybody to make a crack. By one account, this talented jazz/blues singer had at least eight husbands. They included her first, a seventeen-year-old fellow student of hers in Chicago; four others, all musicians; a cab driver; a youthful Dominican actor; and the last, football hero Dick (Night Train) Lane. Throughout the fifties she made scandalous newspaper headlines: "Blues Singer Escapes Death by Gift of Glass Candy" (a box of chocolates that had arrived in the mail for her, presumably from a fan, contained quarter-inch slivers of glass); "Dinah Washington Quizzed About a Gun"; "Gun Rap Deepens Singer's Blues" (she had been arrested and charged with threatening her dress designer with a gun); "Dinah Washington Will Be Tried in 3rd Degree Assault"; "Dismiss Rap in Baltimore Vs Dinah Washington"; "Charge Dinah Washington Walks Out on Concert in Winston Salem Area." Washington made for juicy reading. But once onstage, she never let anything interfere with her performance.

To the surprise of many, gospel music was finally carried into the cultural mainstream by two charismatic gospel queens: Clara Ward and Mahalia Jackson. Few could yell, cry, or talk to the Lord like these women.

Mahalia Jackson *(above)* first worked as a domestic and then turned to gospel music. The rambunctious Clara Ward *(center)* and her Singers: hand clapping and foot stomping as they carried gospel to Las Vegas.

Based in Philadelphia in the fifties, the Clara Ward Singers had been founded years before by Clara's mother, Gertrude, who was known to her fans as Mother Ward. Originally, she performed at churches, carrying her two daughters, Clara and Willa, with her. In time, Clara led the group with other women, eventually taking them in the late fifties out of the churches into the gut of American popular culture. They played Las Vegas, Disneyland, night spots like New York's Blue Angel, and turned up at jazz festivals everywhere from New York to Paris. By the sixties the group was appearing on "The Tonight Show" and "The Jack Benny Program." "Make a joyful noise unto the Lord" was what the Bible had said, and that seemed to be the Ward Singers' attitude as they performed with hands and arms flailing, feet stomping, hips bumping and thumping, hands clapping and shoulders shaking, all part of an elaborate extroverted showbiz theatricality that made gospel even more direct than before, its ties to rock 'n' roll never more apparent. Clara Ward herself was a tiny dynamo who promptly posed for photographs with any celebrity who turned up at a performance. And there were plenty: Judy Garland, Peter Lawford, Dinah Shore, Jack Benny, Liberace. She had a magnificent gold tooth right in the front of her mouth and rode in a special custom-built eight-door limousine.

Mahalia Jackson, while not as energetic, was no less theatrical. A small, heavyset woman, who had been born in New Orleans and had worked as a domestic, Jackson belted out tune after tune. Her big hit was "He's Got the Whole World in His Hands." So popular was she that in the late fifties she took her gospels and spirituals to Hollywood where she sang in *St. Louis Blues* and most movingly during the funeral sequence of the 1959 remake of *Imitation of Life*. As the guilt-ridden black girl who has passed for white returns to her mother's funeral, Mahalia's hard-driving tune kept the audience in tears.

A new kind of black beauty appeared during the end of Eisenhower era: the black fashion model. At the time, black publications, particularly *Ebony*, realized the best way for major advertisers to reach the black buyer was by using black models in advertisements pitched directly at their readers. Although most advertisers still dismissed the idea, a few took a chance, and a black model named Helen Williams appeared in ads. She was a striking woman, tall and slender, with a radiant smile and dark, penetrating eyes—she never graced the pages of *Vogue* or *Harper's Bazaar*, but certainly she led the way for those models who later did.

Dinah Washington, "the Queen".

141

Carmen McRae began her career as Carmen Clarke, an intermissions singer and part-time typist.

Finally, the late fifties marked the formal comeback of Lena Horne, who triumphantly returned to Broadway in *Jamaica*. Old-timer Adelaide Hall also appeared in the production. And in 1959 a newcomer named Cicely Tyson made her stage debut in the Harlem production of *The Dark of the Moon*.

But the fifties would have hardly been complete without some word from the classic old-time divas. Josephine Baker, now a feisty, older woman, remained as outspoken as ever. In 1951 she was asked to appear at the plush Miami nightclub, Copa City. This was a historic engagement because Baker signed her contract only after it had been agreed that blacks would be admitted to the club to see her. Like most southern cities, Miami was still openly segregated. When Baker arrived in the city, many white citizens were openly astonished to see a black woman driven in a car down the streets of Miami by a white chauffeur! The engagement was tremendously successful.

Shortly afterward Baker went to New York for an appearance at the Roxy. One evening, at the invitation of a white friend, opera singer Roger Rico, she went to dinner with him and two others at Manhattan's chic Stork Club. The theatrically regal Baker entered with all eyes glued to her. After various delays, however, it was apparent that the restaurant did not want to serve her. But Baker refused to leave politely. She demanded service. When she was finally served a "pathetic little steak," she was infuriated. She immediately called the NAACP's Executive Secretary Walter White, asking him to send over an officer to certify that the Stork Club had refused to serve her. The incident made news around the world. The NAACP and other liberal groups attacked the Stork Club. Baker's flap incurred the wrath of powerful columnist Walter Winchell, who set out to "get" her in his columns. But she laughed off even him and went about her way.

Throughout the fifties Baker spoke her mind, sometimes upsetting even prominent Black Americans by her behavior. In 1952, one of Baker's staunchest supporters, *Jet*, carried the following news item titled "Jo Baker Snubs State Dept. Official":

Singer Josephine Baker has snubbed a State Department representative seeking to ask her about her anti-U.S. statements in Argentina, Harlem's Rep. A. Clayton Powell revealed in a blast at the entertainer

Americans watched teen-ager Leslie Uggams grow up on television.

Twenties/thirties star Valaida Snow *(left)* talks with newcomer Sarah Vaughan.

143

Lena Horne sandwiched by the Peters Sisters looks like she needs some air.

for her "deliberate distortion and misrepresentation." Assailing the St. Louis-born performer who later became a French citizen, Powell said that the State Department inquiry was made at his request. An official tried three times to see Miss Baker in Buenos Aires but was refused. Powell assailed Miss Baker for "wild imagings," in which she stated she had seen "daily lynchings" and concurred in a State Department report to him which said the singer had "become the tool of foreign interests notoriously unfriendly to the U.S." Powell noted that he and his wife, pianist Hazel Scott, had been friends of Miss Baker for a long time and "we cannot allow this gross misrepresentation to go unchallenged." He then noted: "She has seen no lynchings and has been present at no electrocutions. Miss Baker seems to be a manufactured Joan of Arc."

Of course, Powell had his point. The article reveals that America remained uneasy with Baker, particularly during a period when "reds" and "pinkos" were still being hunted.

Throughout the fifties and sixties Baker was very much a part of America's civil rights movement. Because she often lived on instinct and intuition, some might have thought a serious decline had set in, that emotionally she might be headed for trouble. But Baker proved all her critics wrong. In the seventies she came back strong.

Throughout the era Marian Anderson remained regal and aloof. In 1953 news accounts reported that the Lyric Theater in Baltimore had refused to book an Anderson concert. The theatre refused to discuss its standard segregation policy. True to form, no one knew how Anderson felt about this most recent insult. But in 1955, she nervously glowed when she had one of her great triumphs as the first black performer to sing a major role, Ulrica in Verdi's *Masked Ball*, at the Metropolitan Opera House. She later said her nervousness almost overcame her. But when the curtain rose, the mere sight of Anderson onstage was enough to send the entire audience into thunderous applause. Once again when Black America needed a symbol, the glorious Anderson stepped forward.

Billie Holiday and Ethel Waters remained as wildly unpredictable as before. Holiday's 1957 autobiography *Lady Sings the Blues* was a best seller, indicating that Americans were as taken as ever with her image. For the most part, these were troubled times when she would forget lyrics onstage or miss a performance. An appearance at a festival in Monterey had gone so badly that afterward the musicians had refused to speak to her.

Della Reese began her career singing gospel with Clara Ward and Mahalia Jackson. She later became famous for belting out pop tunes.

Time was sometimes cruel, sometimes kind, to legendary divas. With subtle modifications Josephine Baker altered her style to fit a new era. She became a decorated wartime heroine and a staunch civil rights activist. The image of Billie Holiday-the-artist was replaced by Billie-the-tabloid-queen, who made headlines because of drug busts.

Holiday also had cirrhosis of the liver and was still drinking too much. She was separated from her husband, Louis McKay. In 1959 Holiday died in a New York hospital. The *New York Post* reported that she had $750 strapped to her leg and 70¢ in her bank account. Newspaper serials told the story of her life. Record sales went up again for her albums. In time, the dead Billie was to be even a greater myth than the living one.

Ethel Waters, hopped up after her great performance in the highly acclaimed stage and film productions of Carson McCullers' *Member of the Wedding* and the huge success of her best-selling autobiography *His Eye Is on the Sparrow,* seemed off on a new glorious career until the IRS closed in again. The indomitable, debt-ridden Waters soon found herself appearing before the nation on the television quiz show "Break the Bank," trying to win enough money to pay off her debts. In 1959 she appeared in her last film, *The Sound and the Fury,* as Dilsey. But the movie was disappointing and did nothing for her career. As quickly as she had re-risen, she fell again. Now, alone in a career that had always encompassed an array of ups and downs, the white-haired Ethel Waters slowly drifted in and out of show business. She later did guest appearances on several television shows. But her heart did not seem to be in her work. She looked old and disheartened.

The divas had made great professional achievements in the fifties. Not only had they continued crossing over into the mainstream culture, but they had received a new kind of official recognition. The magazine covers and the big nightclub engagements were testaments to the divas' success. What with the coming of television, they found more work and greater opportunities. This was the era when American popular culture was almost completely integrated. It may have been token integration, but most saw it as positive integration nonetheless. And any casual observer would have optimistically looked forward to the future—to the gains and rewards to be had in the next era. Yet despite the accomplishments, the fifties, in retrospect, had been a difficult period for the black beauty. As successful as were such new stars as Dorothy Dandridge, Joyce Bryant, and even Eartha Kitt, they had not been at ease with that success. The optimism and innocence that had propelled the careers of divas in the past were slowly vanishing. The troubled diva life of the fifties simply brought into focus once again America's traditional racial attitudes. The big stars had run fast and hard to make it into the system. But it was precisely the system itself that was about to be questioned.

Despite a multitude of personal problems, Ethel Waters triumphantly returned to Broadway in *The Member of the Wedding* and gave the finest performance of her career.

· THE 1960s ·
POLITICAL SYMBOLS

The sixties opened with a dazzling display of optimism. John F. Kennedy stormed into the presidency with talk of his New Frontier and his lofty dreams for a modern Camelot. Martin Luther King, Jr., led a triumphant March on Washington. Over 200,000 Black Americans, and many whites, descended on the nation's capital to peacefully demand their civil rights.

Most Americans looked on calmly, confident that the troubles—be they civil rights, poverty, or a war abroad—could be resolved. But in time it was apparent the old remedies, as well as the old confidence, would no longer work. The familiar problems had escalated and become far more complex. Suddenly, Americans witnessed incredible horrors they had thought would never happen in their country. The nation was stunned by the assassinations of John and Robert Kennedy, Medgar Evers, Malcolm X, and of the one figure most Americans, black and

white, felt might be a conciliatory force, Martin Luther King, Jr. Ghettos throughout the country—in Harlem, Watts, Detroit—shot up in flames as the disaffiliated and deprived of America finally announced their rage and anger. Soon there was the rise of the black power movement, the Black Nationalists, and the Black Panthers. New black political leaders such as Stokely Carmichael, Fannie Lou Hammer, Eldridge Cleaver, H. Rap Brown, and Huey Newton came into national prominence. From Vietnam there also came word of new corruption and atrocities, of the Tet offensive and the My Lai massacre. What with the riots, and the new demands for basic human rights as well as the war protests and demonstrations, American society was undergoing some of the most dramatic changes of the century.

During this time the old-style diva was a dying breed, so much so that by the end of

Josephine Baker continued performing when most old-style divas went out of fashion.

the era she would be supplanted by a new-style figure. For the duration of the sixties there was a restless, determined search for new images and symbols, for a fresh set of fantasies and dreams that would touch on Black America's evolving militancy. Just as in the thirties, when the harsh nature of the times demanded that Waters, Fredi Washington, Ivie Anderson, and Holiday be glamorous but still close to the experiences of everyday American life, so, too, in the sixties, there was a call for social realism in all the arts. And that call obviously again touched the divas. Slowly, political heroines came into vogue.

DIAHANN CARROLL: THE RIGHT BEAUTY AT THE WRONG TIME

Few black beauties could have been more affected by the changing attitudes of the period than Diahann Carroll. At the start of the era, it was confidently assumed that she would inherit Dandridge's crown as deluxe international siren. But, gradually, as a need developed for stars of grit and grime, the mass audience may well have found it impossible to connect to so slick and mannered a performer as Diahann Carroll.

Prior to the sixties, however, Diahann Carroll had done all the right things. She was born in the Bronx, the daughter of a transit company worker. In school she worked hard for scholarships and embarked on a modeling career by the time she was a teen-ager. In the beginning, her roots were tightly tied to the black community. Years later, old-timers at *Ebony* loved reminiscing about the young Carroll showing up at the office, portfolio in hand, hoping to be used in *Ebony* ads.

In these early days, as this slim, frail girl made a steady round of auditions, she had ferocious drive and energy. She sang and acted as much as she modeled. By her late teens she had made it to Hollywood, playing a supporting role in *Carmen Jones*. Afterward she appeared on Broadway as the ingenue in *House of Flowers* and worked in another Otto Preminger film, *Porgy and Bess*. At this time she was neither glamorous nor strikingly beautiful. In fact, in her early films she looked like a good-natured homebody—and nothing more. But she had her professional admirers nonetheless. Richard Rodgers was

Moms Mabley (with Slappy White) had worked for years on the chitlin' circuit. Throughout the sixties she continued delivering her classic line: "Ain't nothing an old man can do for me except bring me a message from a young one."

so taken with her talents that he wanted her to star in his Broadway musical comedy *Flower Drum Song*. Had she played the leading role, that of an Oriental ingenue, she might have dramatically altered the history of American musical theatre. It would have been the first time a black woman starred on Broadway in a nonblack role, proving to audiences that a talented black performer should be free to tackle any kind of part. (Already that pint-sized powerhouse Juanita Hall had brilliantly portrayed non-black heroines on Broadway. But Hall had played supporting characters and surprisingly, many people outside theatre circles were not even aware that she was black.) But the audacious plans to star Carroll in the show fell through.

In the 1960s Diahann Carroll's career really picked up momentum and her professional image was greatly altered. She emerged as a sleek sophisticate with never a hair out of place nor a false eyelash badly applied. Her makeup was perfect, shrewdly used to play up her lush coloring, her high, refined forehead, her spectacular high cheekbones, her sensuous mouth, and her sensational sweeping chin. She had magnificent shoulders, and the lines of her body were perfect. Yet with all this, there was something not quite natural about her. She wasn't loose, didn't flow. She seemed to stand still like a mannequin, unable to breathe or feel.

But the new look was on splendid display when Carroll returned to Broadway in 1962 as the star of Richard

Guess who this plain-Jane teen-ager named Carole Diahann Johnson grew up to be?

Rodgers' *No Strings*. Although *No Strings* was hardly a great show, it was still a golden opportunity. Rodgers had created the musical with Diahann Carroll in mind. She had a chance to sing a beautiful song, "The Sweetest Sounds." And in theatre circles, because she had been cast "daringly" opposite white actor Richard Kiley and because of the play's interracial theme (a black fashion model involved with a white writer in Paris), the show had an impact. In Black America, however, *No Strings* may have had good intentions, but it had come too late in the day. In this era of sit-ins, protests, and of an evolving black nationalism, the idea that a black woman might have an affair with a white man was viewed as being politically treasonous. *No Strings* was a pacifier for White America, a way for it to pat itself on the back for being above the old prejudices.

Diahann Carroll, however, emerged from *No Strings* as a star. She appeared on television shows, had successful nightclub engagements, and played important roles in the films *Paris Blues* and *Hurry Sundown*. Her great professional coup came in 1968 when she landed the title role as a widowed nurse on the television series "Julia." It marked the first time a black woman was the star of her own weekly network series. Carroll played an educated, middle-class woman unfamiliar with ghetto life, something of a cloistered Goody Two-shoes sister living off in some never-never land that many Black Americans could not connect to. Often she was hampered by scripts with patently false situations and impenetrable dialogue that captured none of the rhythmic flavor and nuances of black speech patterns. Sometimes she had a pleasant rapport with Diana Sands, who played her cousin on a few episodes. "Julia" ran three seasons, then was taken off the air because of its poor ratings. Throughout its run, however, the black community was critical of the show. And Diahann Carroll may have been a bit frazzled because suddenly she had to take a long, serious look at her career.

And the cold, hard fact was that despite the big breaks—the Broadway starring role, the big-budget films, the *Look* and *Ebony* covers—she seemed a woman out of tune with her era. At a time when Black America was adopting the political philosophy of cultural separatism and when the black community looked for entertainers who were openly political (or openly against the established social order), Diahann Carroll stood as a figure from the past: a proper bourgeois lady able and willing to integrate into White America. She herself said she had become a star because she had a look and style

Presto! Little Carole transformed into Diahann Carroll. Although done over and glamorized, Carroll was a star out of whack with the demands of the sixties.

The performances of Claudia McNeil *(top)* and Ruby Dee in Lorraine Hansberry's *A Raisin in the Sun* brought social realism to the stage.

acceptable to whites. She was a well-behaved, light-skinned beauty who, during a period of great racial turmoil, was not going to rock the boat. Carroll seemed to be a woman without ethnic flavor. In the past, the great gift of divas Baker and Waters had been that, while operating as stars in the white world, they had still known when and how to give all audiences a tantalizing glimpse of their "other" black world. Through dress, speech, behavior, and attitude, they informed everyone that they had not forgotten their roots. In fact, one of their great selling points had been the ethnic flair and flavor that always crept through. Finally, black audiences may have been turned off by Carroll's private life. She was seen dating white males, and her romance with David Frost was well publicized.

Ironically enough, in another age, Diahann Carroll's particular bourgeois image might have been tolerated or even valued as being as socially significant as Lena Horne's image had been in the 1940s. But now the times had changed. The old values and ideals were being hotly questioned and denounced. Also the typical crossover mulatto diva was just about dead and done for.

Another mulatto type affected by the changes in the social atmosphere was Barbara McNair, who assumed the lead role in *No Strings* after Carroll left the cast. Less aggressive and certainly less coy than Carroll, McNair was a wholesome looking, demure young woman with magnetic dark eyes and a warm, lush smile. Throughout the era McNair performed in clubs and films *(If He Hollers, Let Him Go*, later *They Call Me MISTER Tibbs)* and on television, eventually hosting her own syndicated variety series. As the *Jet* and *Ebony* articles of the period prove, she had a certain rapport with the black community and never offended it. But the sixties, while seeming at first to offer her promise, never fulfilled it. In the seventies, however, her career and image took an unexpected turn when newspaper headlines exploded with stories of McNair's arrest for the alleged possession of heroin. Rumors of her connections with the mob flew all over the place. It was said she would never be cleared of the charges, that her career was over anyway. In the midst of all the newspaper flap, McNair, rather courageously, appeared on Dick Cavett's talk show. She seemed in control, yet obviously troubled. The charges were later dropped. But McNair was back in the papers later in the seventies when her husband was found shot to death in their Las Vegas home. McNair, so often tense and vulnerable in her public appearances of the seventies, continued on with her career.

THE NEW SERIOUS DRAMATIC ACTRESSES

nd so while McNair and Carroll, as well as Shirley Bassey, because of their looks and stance, represented an old figure, other women appeared, introducing audiences to totally new concepts on what being a black woman was all about. Black acting companies such as the New Lafayette Theater, the Negro Ensemble Company, and The Free Southern Theater as well as a host of others provided a chance for artistic growth and exposure to a number of new actresses: Clarice Taylor, Esther Rolle, Barbara Ann Teer, Denise Nicholas, and Rosalind Cash. On stage and screen, other serious dramatic actresses— Claudia McNeil, Abbey Lincoln (in *Nothing But a Man* and *For Love of Ivy*), and Beah Richards—gave impressive, invigorating performances. Of the group of new actresses reaching maturity in this period, four stood out: Ruby Dee, Gloria Foster, Diana Sands, and Cicely Tyson. Playing anguished heroines, these women seemed as if they had touched base with life's harsher experiences and were scarred or bruised by their pasts.

Ruby Dee came to prominence first. This Cleveland-born actress grew up in New York and studied at Hunter College. In the late forties she studied and worked at Harlem's American Negro Theater. Her classmates included other newcomers—Sidney Poitier, Harry Belafonte, Lloyd Richards (who later directed her in *A Raisin in the Sun*), and Ossie Davis, whom she later married. In the fifties and sixties Dee appeared in a lineup of films: *No Way Out, The Jackie Robinson Story, Edge of the City, The Balcony, The Incident,* and *A Raisin in the Sun* (in which she re-created the role she had originated in the stage production). She also costarred with husband Davis in *Gone Are the Days* (the film version of his play *Purlie Victorious*). Later in the seventies she gave strong portrayals in the stage plays *A Wedding Band* by black playwright Alice Childress and *Boesman and Lena.*

In the sixties this performer, who often seemed timid and introverted, emerged as a master of the tiny telling detail. Her emotions were perfectly pared down until the moment when her characters' hearts simply broke—or exploded. Often she seemed to wander about quietly, unobtrusively, almost as if she were terrified of someone looking twice at her. But at her crucial moment, she was able to grab the audience by the throat and not let go. Most significantly, this small woman, almost birdlike, sensitive, and unassuming, managed (particularly with her bravura performance in Lorraine Hansberry's *A Raisin in the Sun*) to go against the stereotyped conception of the emotionally strong black woman as one who is also physically large or loud. Ruby Dee helped usher in a portrait of the contemporary troubled black woman.

The same was true of Diana Sands, who represented for many the modern, bright, educated Afro-American girl aware and proud of her roots, and confident and independent enough to speak out on any issue. In theatre, Sands seemed to want to do everything to herald the new black woman's arrival. On Broadway she starred opposite Alan Alda in *The Owl and the Pussycat*, playing a high-strung hooker who falls for a testy intellectual. Because it was the first Broadway production in which white and black costars had been cast romantically without any mention of race or color, the play drew much attention. In James Baldwin's *Blues for Mr. Charlie*, Sands played an aggressive civil rights fighter. Of her long chilling monologue at the play's climax, critic Walter Kerr wrote: "Miss Sands [performs]. . .with a pulsing hysteria that is still just within control. I know of no other single sequence as powerful in New York today." Later Kerr said that Sands "is one of the most exciting of young American actresses." Diana Sands also took on classical roles in productions of *Caesar and Cleopatra, Antony and Cleopatra, Saint Joan,* and Robert Lowell's *Phaedre.* In films, she repeated her stage role as the restless kid sister in *A Raisin in the Sun,* and later gave effective performances in *Georgia, Georgia, Willie Dynamite,* and *Doctors' Wives.* Her most successful movie performance was in *The Landlord.* Sands played a variety of challenging, complex characters until her early death in 1973.

Gloria Foster was an interior actress of great power. Foster grew up in the small farming town of South Beloit, Illinois, studied at Illinois State University, and taught school for two years. But she grew restless and soon

Diana Sands (with Lou Gossett in *The Landlord*) was determined to play any good role, be it Shakespeare, Shaw, or Baldwin.

enrolled in Chicago's Goodman School of Drama. In 1963 she opened in the New York production of *In White America*. It was a stunning debut. "Most moving of all," wrote Howard Taubman in the *New York Times*, "is Gloria Foster, a young actress with talent and intensity to burn. Three of her [vignettes]...are in themselves justification for a visit to *In White America*." Foster won the Obie and Drama Desk-Vernon Rice awards for best actress of the year in an off-Broadway production. Afterward in the stage productions of *Yerma* and *Medea*, she gave searing, defiant performances, perfectly scaled to the demands of the big stage. Foster also gave impressive performances in the films *The Cool World, Nothing But a Man*, and *The Comedians*. She seemed born for films because, unlike most theatre people, she did not need dialogue. She did everything with her eyes. And of all the new-style dramatic actresses, her presence was the most troubling. She was always ill at ease, brooding, and burning over some private hurt.

By the end of the sixties Foster's promising career had a setback when, with her husband Clarence Williams III, who was then starring in the television series "Mod Squad," she moved to Los Angeles. She appeared on several television programs, and Bill Cosby, quite impressed with her talents, had influence enough in the industry to have her signed up as his costar in some promising projects. The most satisfying was the likably disjointed film *Man and Boy*. Foster and Cosby always played well together despite the fact that they often seemed mismatched. While Cosby was skillful at articulating the basic, everyday dilemmas that perplex or trouble any ordinary man, there stood Foster, looking as if she were Medea trapped in a world that could not comprehend big emotions. Wonderful as Foster could be, television wasted her. She was one of the few actresses who should have been back on the stage, taking on one heavyweight role after another. When she finally returned to New York in the mid-seventies, Walter Kerr wrote of her performance in *Black Visions:* "Gloria Foster's work in the opening monologue is as breathtaking as anything the American theater can come up with just now." Foster also appeared in *The Cherry Orchard, Agamemnon*, and *Coriolanus* at New York's Public Theatre. But she remained one of those great actresses whom the mass audience never seemed to know enough about.

During the sixties Cicely Tyson also came to prominence. She energetically went from one television appearance to another, whether it be a guest role on "The FBI" or a continuing part on the series "East Side, West Side," or from one supporting movie role to another, in *A Man Called Adam, The Comedians, The Heart Is a Lonely Hunter*. Like Foster, she had an edge and great power. Yet her career seemed to go nowhere.

Often many of the new serious dramatic actresses found themselves in conflict with audience anticipations. On the one hand, the audience had to have typical women who, operating in the black world, were not out to integrate into the larger white culture. On the other hand, the audience yearned for some breathtaking, larger-than-life (somewhat romanticized) heroine who not only touched on the real, but soared above it too. In the game of symbol and image, these actresses did not yet have the mythic thrust and power of Waters. For the most part they emerged as art house or theatregoer favorites. Of the group, only Tyson became a real diva, and that was not until the next decade.

Finally, closely aligned to these actresses were the poets of the late sixties—Nikki Giovanni and Sonia Sanchez. They became popular on college campuses. In time, they also heralded the coming of the deeply committed and fiery, political black woman.

A big voice for a little girl: former schoolteacher Melba Moore went from *Hair* to a Tony Award-winning role as Lutiebelle in *Purlie*.

155

LEONTYNE PRICE: MAKING IT TO THE MET

In the world of classical music, operatic divas Grace Bumbry, Martina Arroyo, Reri Grist, Shirley Verrett, and Leontyne Price found that doors, even those of the hallowed Metropolitan Opera House, were finally opening for black women. True to a tradition long an integral part of the opera world, these women, before, during, and after the opening of those doors behaved like classic, temperamental stars. Indeed if haughtiness were the only requirement for divadom, these women would have been at the top of the list. Of the group, however, Leontyne Price was the only operatic diva to become a national heroine.

Price was a fascinating woman to watch. She had a special, unconventional kind of beauty: golden brown skin, high cheekbones, compelling eyes. And she carried herself as regally as Marian Anderson. Yet with Price, there was a striking mixture of high and low. One minute she was all mink and ermine; the next minute, she was a down-home unpretentious girl from Mississippi. She also had a biting sense of humor. Once upon hearing a well-known tenor remark that his "lovely, pure, full, and beautiful" voice moved her to tears, Price interrupted to say, "I hate to bring this up, but it is *my* voice so warm, full, and beautiful that moves me to tears." On another occasion when she heard a well-known soprano was about to marry and retire, she haughtily asked, "Retire from what?" And during a Christmas spent in Mississippi (where she returned as often as possible), she helped out serving at her family's dinner table, remarking, "I'm keeping my hand in. The first flat C and I'll be back here."

Price had grown up in the tiny town of Laurel, Mississippi. Her father was a carpenter. Her mother worked occasionally as a nurse and midwife. After graduating from Central College (a black school in Ohio), Leontyne (originally spelled Leontine) was set to become a schoolteacher. But when a white neighbor, who had heard the young Leontyne sing (and for whom Price's aunt had worked as a maid), offered to help finance her studies at New York's Juilliard, Price jumped at the chance.

At the music school her voice and superb musicianship won her a circle of influential followers: Florence Page Kimball, the opera star who became her teacher; composer and critic Virgil Thomson; composer Samuel Barber. In 1952 Thomson selected her to perform on Broadway in *Four Saints in Three Acts*. Later that same year she played Bess in the stunning revival of *Porgy and Bess*. She married the production's Porgy, baritone William Warfield. In 1955, in what was considered a landmark production, this young black woman appeared on American television in the title role of *Tosca*. She sang *Aida* at the San Francisco Opera, at Covent Garden, at the Vienna State Opera, and finally, at La Scala. Like Anderson, she toured extensively, traveling wherever there was a chance to perform a great role. She may well have wondered if she would ever win great recognition in her own country. Stories still circulate of the young Leontyne's romantic melancholia. At a party on New York's Riverside Drive, a dancing, barefoot, dramatic Leontyne decided she had had it with life and announced she was running out to throw herself into the Hudson River. Fortunately, a friend calmed her down.

In 1961 Leontyne Price finally—triumphantly—debuted at the Metropolitan Opera as Leonora in *Il Trovatore*. Her debut, however, was not without its political overtones. The Civil Rights Movement was spreading throughout the nation. At the Met, Rudolph Bing and his staff surely must have realized some gesture again had to be made to prove the cultured world of grand opera was without biases. By this time, Price had become too great an international name and talent to be ignored. Afterward, she briefly became something of a media sensation, appearing on the cover of *Time* and in the pages of *Look*. Later she was selected to launch the Met's next season in *The Girl from the Golden West*. And in 1966 a great honor (and tribute to her box-office clout) was bestowed on her when she opened the new Met at Lincoln Center in *Antony and Cleopatra*. Her role was especially tailored for her by composer Samuel Barber.

Leontyne Price struck many Americans as being a warm, intensely likable opera star. But the tensions and pressures of her fame must have weighed on her because after all the fanfare, she soon withdrew from the public eye. As her appearances at the Met became fewer (from 1961 to early 1969, there had been 118 performances; from late 1969 to 1973, there were but six), she was the only great opera singer who never seemed to work.

Occasionally, she spoke up about some of the tensions disturbing her. "That 1966 opening was the most grueling experience of my life. It really left me almost traumatized for two and a half years," she once said. "So much was hanging on it. A new house, a premiere of a new work. I felt that if I caught a cold and couldn't perform, it would be worldwide news. So much to do, so much to think about, so much to cope with in so short a time. It got to the point where it wasn't a matter of how well one

Leontyne Price became an international star after her Met debut in 1961.
But despite her fame, she withdrew from the public eye.

performed, but just being able to perform. Maybe that was a kind of turning point. For the next season or so I kept on doing opera and other things, and sometimes it seemed I just didn't know where I was. Pressures all the time."

For the most part, though, Price remained silent about the professional or private difficulties plaguing her. And it was precisely this insistence on privacy that prevented her from becoming a legendary figure like Maria Callas. Nor did Price become a Marian Anderson: a stoic, majestically heroic figure accepting the weight of being an international social symbol.

In a way, she was also affected by the times. For great as her triumph had been, many young Black Americans now viewed the world of opera as "irrelevant," "politically obsolete," a "decadent art form" that American blacks had no business being bothered with. An evolving black aesthetic demanded that all art forms of Western culture be seriously examined; it insisted, too, that black artists return to their roots, that their art connect directly to the political goals and aspirations of the black community. As was true of many other black artists in every period, Price

was in a complex situation. The white world demanded one thing of her. The black community expected something entirely different. And her particular art itself had its peculiar demands.

In a rare interview Leontyne Price once touched on her dilemma, saying (without self-pity): "Some people criticize me for not being 'militant' or not being 'involved' or whatever. Being black and accomplished, as I am proud to say I am, gets you invited to be with a lot of people who wouldn't pay you any attention otherwise. I don't go to cocktail parties or social meetings, where you 'get the word' and are supposed to take it back to the 'lowly ones' who look up to you. What I do for my own people, to whom I might be a token black, I do in my own way, on my own level. . . . I've been that [a token figure] for years, and I accept it as a responsibility in my own way."

By the era's end Leontyne Price was aware she would always be some kind of symbol for Black and White America. But she was determined never to let the symbol business overpower her.

JACKIE "MOMS" MABLEY: THE FUNNIEST WOMAN IN THE WORLD

With the rise of black cultural nationalism, the old standards and the old values—the dos and don'ts preached to Black America by White America for centuries—were quickly eroding. Black Americans turned away from those artists who had made it within the system, who were part of something now dubbed the establishment, and sought out those personalities who somehow had maintained an "ethnic purity." And it was primarily for this reason that finally there came aboveground a woman who seemed to have been around since the year one, an old-time hipster who called herself Moms and who in the sixties discovered herself appearing on national television. In the past, some might have thought of Jackie "Moms" Mabley as a stereotyped figure. But oddly enough, she became a cultural heroine of sorts for a new audience that saw her as feisty, resilient, and endurably tough. Never had she expressed any desire to make it in the white world. In fact, more often than not, she was a knowing satirist of the ways of white folks.

Certainly, no one could have been more surprised at the sudden sixties popularity of Jackie "Moms" Mabley than Moms herself. She was doing what she had been doing for

OPENS TUES. MARCH 10
DIRECT FROM TRIUMPHANT EUROPEAN TOUR
ACCLAIMED IN BERLIN · VIENNA · LONDON · PARIS

BLEVINS DAVIS and ROBERT BREEN
present

PORGY and BESS

Music by GEORGE GERSHWIN
Libretto by DuBOSE HEYWARD
Lyrics by DuBOSE HEYWARD and IRA GERSHWIN
(Based on the play, PORGY by Dorothy and DuBose Heyward)
Directed by ROBERT BREEN

with CAB CALLOWAY
LeVERN   LEONTYNE   URYLEE   LESLIE
HUTCHERSON   PRICE   LEONARDOS   SCOTT
GEORGIA BURKE

Musical Director ALEXANDER SMALLENS
Settings by
WOLFGANG ROTH   JED MACE
Assistant Musical Director
Samuel Matlowsky
Choral Director
Eva Jessye

"ONE OF THE MEMORABLE AND MOVING
EXPERIENCES OF THE GENERATION"
—THE TATLER, LONDON

"MOST STIMULATING EVENT OF THE THEAT-
RICAL YEAR!"
—PICTURE POST, LONDON

GERSHWIN'S GREATEST SCORE

"SUMMER TIME"

"A WOMAN IS A
SOMETIME
THING"

"MY MAN'S
GONE NOW"

"I GOT PLENTY
O' NUTTIN"

"BESS, YOU IS MY
WOMAN NOW"

"IT AIN'T
NECESSARILY SO"

ZIEGFELD THEATRE
6th Avenue at 54th Street, N. Y. 19
MATINEES WEDNESDAY & SATURDAY
Evenings: Orchestra $6.00; Mezzanine $4.80; Balcony $3.60, 3.00, 2.40,
1.80. Mats. Wednesday & Saturday: Orchestra $3.60; Mezzanine $3.60;
Balcony $3.00, 2.40, 1.80, 1.20.
Please enclose stamped self-addressed envelope with mail orders
Kindly specify several alternate dates.
Use Mail Order Blank on reverse side

You don't mess around with Moms! That's what Rosalind Cash discovers when she crosses Mabley's path in the movie *Amazing Grace*.

years, ever since that day in 1913 when, at age sixteen, she had run away from her home in Brevard, North Carolina, to pursue a career as an entertainer. She soon changed her name from Loretta Mary Aiken to Jackie Mabley. It had been the name of a boyfriend. Somehow the Moms title was picked up along the way. One story has it that she was so sympathetic to the problems of her fellow performers in black vaudeville, mothering them when they were down and out, that they dubbed her Moms.

For fifty years she toured the country, hitting the legendary black theatres such as the Regal and Monogram in Chicago and the Apollo in New York, where she was the undisputed queen. Her fans called her "the funniest woman in the world." During these early years she was aware of her place as a woman operating in a world dominated by men. In vaudeville, female stars were usually a part of a team or used as a foil for the man's jokes. For a time, Mabley herself teamed up with other legendary "chitlin circuit" performers—Dusty "Open the Door, Richard" Fletcher, Tim Moore (who became Kingfish on the "Amos and Andy" television series), and the great "Spider Bruce," John Mason. As the years passed, she influenced newcomers Redd Foxx and Slappy White, whom audiences often referred to as the sons of Moms. (There were even rumors that both men actually

were her children.) But Mabley turned the male-oriented comic world of vaudeville into her own arena, emerging as the first distinctive black female comic star able to run an act on her own, using men as her foils, developing such a strong shtik that no one was ever able to take the spotlight from her.

Mabley's early monologues were written by herself and comic Bonnie Drew Bell. Moms would amble onto the stage, wearing tattered Raggedy Ann dresses with plaids, polka dots, and checks mixed every which way. She sported outsized shoes, large drooping Argyle socks, and an old floppy hat, and she would give a broad smile to show she didn't have a tooth in her head. Her audience was wild with laughter before she even opened her mouth. When that happened, she would stand silent, giving everybody the onceover or the evil eye 'cause she was here to deliver the *word*, the gospel according to Moms. "Now lissen here, chil-run," she would announce, and the audience was prepared for a monologue that touched on current events and that always bristled with sly folk wisdom and keen insights.

She was the mistress of spicy, raucous blue humor. Unlike a white comic like Martha Raye, Moms knew sex was something on any audience's mind. She played the part of the little old lady in search of a handsome young man. The last thing she ever wanted was a man her own age. "No," her classic line informed the audience, "there ain't nothing an old man can do for me except bring me a message from a young one." Another of her better known lines was that "a woman is a woman until the day she dies, but a man's a man only as long as he can!" In comic terms, she handled men as roughly as Bessie Smith sometimes did in song.

In the fifties and sixties Moms Mabley began her slow ascent into the mainstream of American popular culture with her successful record albums *Moms Mabley—The Funniest Woman in the World*, *Moms Mabley at the UN*, *Moms Mabley at the Geneva Conference*, and *Now Hear This*. She boasted of talking to presidents and prime ministers who called for advice on the world situation. "Now what you want, *boy*?" was the way she always addressed them. She also said she and Eleanor Roosevelt were good friends who liked to get together and talk about young men.

In the seventies she poked fun at political figures, saying of Richard Nixon after Watergate: "Even old Moms couldn't do nothin' for that man, 'cept give him a few licks upside the head, that is...he was just too far gone. Only thing I got to say about him is, your sins will find you out. Like old Joe Louis says, you can run but you can't hide." Of President Gerald Ford, she added: "I hear, now mind me, I hear, he's a godly man, but Moms is keeping her eye on him."

In 1967 Moms made it to network television, appearing in the all-black tribute to Negro humor "A Time for Laughter." In one skit she played the maid of an uppity black bourgeoisie couple (Godfrey Cambridge and Diana Sands) trying to be white, living in hoity-toity Westchester (which, ironically enough, was precisely where Moms Mabley was living). Whenever Cambridge and Sands put on airs, there was down-to-earth Moms giving them a look, a grunt, or a groan to remind them of their roots. (Years later Marla Gibbs would play the maid, Florence, much in the same way on the television series "The Jeffersons.") Moms also appeared on "The Smothers Brothers Show," "The Mike Douglas Show," "The Merv Griffin Show," and "The Flip Wilson Show."

Moms Mabley's popularity continued into the next decade. She starred in the movie *Amazing Grace* as Grace, a spry old lady who decides she has had enough and is going to rid Baltimore of all the corrupt politicians exploiting the common little man. In one sequence Moms goes to the all-black campus of Morgan State College where she addresses the students. Moms at the podium was no different from Moms on the stage of the Apollo.

NEW SOUNDS:
PINT-SIZED SIRENS

But Moms was not the only underground ethnic performer to find herself surfacing into the mainstream of American culture in the sixties. Nor was she the only ethnic entertainer the young of the period could identify with. Almost at the very start of the decade, the emerging new generation was humming and hopping to the tune of pop, rock, and soul, innovative musical forms and styles growing out of the heat of the ghetto and the Black American experience. The young stars of the new world of black music became cult heroes and heroines.

In the recent past, older Americans had been able to sit back and relax to the soft and slow ballads of Nat King Cole and Billy Eckstine. These men had invigorated standards (as well as standard approaches to music) with their own sense of style and phrasing. But their material was neither jolting nor particularly fresh. Now, in the sixties, no longer was popular music those familiar soothing chords delivered in the acceptable idiom and beat of the dominant culture. The new music, influenced by gospel sounds and such black rock 'n' roll/rhythm-and-blues stars as Chuck Berry, Hank Ballard, Little Richard, and Fats Domino, used language and beat in a startling fashion. The idiom was distinctly black because the new artists were performing—at least in the beginning—for an all-black record market. In time, the new sixties music acquired a fresh sound and tone all its own, sometimes fevered and anxious.

The attitude about the music was different too. In the past, Black America's music had never been sanctioned by the dominant culture. Now, however, young Black Americans could not have cared less what the official white culture thought of its sounds. There was a new confidence and pride in the music's worth. Eventually, the white kids in the affluent suburbs didn't care what their elders thought of the music either. For they knew, too, that the music was simply good. In time, all of young America turned to black music not only as a source of pleasure, but of protest too. "Way over there," as Smokey Robinson's song had announced, were innovative artists with totally different material and points of view, with songs calling for new rites and dreams. And leading the way were groups of pint-sized, wide-eyed sirens, the pubescent, Junior League teeny-bopper divas who had no idea at first what image or persona meant. All they knew was that they wanted to perform. And perform they did. Not since the

Chicago-born rock 'n' roll, rhythm-and-blues diva La Vern Baker popularized the fishtail dress and made a hit out of "See See Ryder," a former Ma Rainey song.

Killing them softly with her song: Roberta Flack came to prominence in the late sixties with her mellow sound.

blues singers of the twenties had so many talented black women had a chance to sing their songs.

In the beginning the new groups were certainly influenced by La Vern Baker, who, during the fifties, had been a full-fledged, rock 'n' roll, rhythm-and-blues diva. At that time the popular soul group, The Platters, had a female harmonizing with the group. But Chicago-born Baker was a star attraction on her own, a knockout entertainer with a truly large confident voice. Performing her big hits "Jim Dandy," "See See Ryder" (a song Ma Rainey had recorded), and "Tweedle Dee," Baker wore skintight dresses and developed the persona of the familiar bronze mama who, like Bessie, her idol, was in control of any situation. In the fifties Baker worked the black theatres and movie houses. In the sixties she was determined to take her rock 'n' roll persona out of the black theatres into the big clubs. In 1961 she successfully appeared with Louis Armstrong at Basin Street East. But although her hefty personality was intact, she left behind her music, choosing to sing such conventional ballads as "After You're Gone" and "Yes, Sir, That's My Baby." Baker soon lost her audience because she was going establishment almost at the very point when the mass audience was ready to accept rhythm-and-blues. Still La Vern Baker's gutsy rock 'n' roll renditions helped pave the way for others.

During the fifties period of Baker's initial rise, black girl groups had also come into their own. The Chantels tapped a live nerve cord with their tune "Maybe," a pulsating, dazzling wail of a woman wanting a second chance with the man she had lost. Then there was the great group of the late fifties and early sixties, The Shirelles, who had a string of hits—"Everybody Loves a Lover," "Tonight's the Night," "Soldier Boy," "Will You Still Love Me Tomorrow." They also sang the tune that became a national anthem for lovestruck high school girls everywhere, "Dedicated to the One I Love." During a time when sex was not something kids were supposed to know anything about, The Shirelles' music served as an outlet for pent-up tensions and romantic confusions. Almost all their numbers were love statements or love warnings, all delivered with a teen intensity that today still taps the tender aches and subconscious fears of adolescents caught in the glow of first love. The Shirelles set the style for the groups, dressing alike in wigs and sexy, tight dresses. They were about the same age as their fans, which helped the young to identify with them.

Once The Shirelles' records started selling, the market opened up to other groups—Patti LaBelle and The Bluebells ("I Sold My Heart to the Junkman," "Down the Aisle") and The Crystals ("Da Doo Ron Ron"). And Ruby and The Romantics (one young woman backed up by three young men) came up with a well-stylized piece called "Our Day Will Come."

Black music was in vogue. Etta James, Carla "The Queen of Memphis" Thomas, Dee Dee Sharpe, Little Eva, Barbara Lewis, the feverish Tina Turner, and sweet-tempered Baby Washington were getting their records played on radio and going on tour. All these young women had an individual style and presence. Yet few had long careers. Some lacked drive. Others became disillusioned after having been exploited by record companies and shifty promoters. Most, unfortunately, were not encouraged to think of a future in the music business. One day a record was a hit. Next day it was dead. There still wasn't a center for the young black woman, no one to groom her or promote her, to help her develop and branch out. So many faded away into oblivion. But their sweet pop/soul tunes have lingered on.

The situation changed when Motown, a new record company out of the motor city, Detroit, realized the commercial potential of black music and urban soul artists. Through costuming, choreography, and specific tunes for specific artists, Motown's Berry Gordy, Jr., came to grips with the creation of rock/pop/soul personas that

La Vern Baker helped move rock 'n' roll into the mainstream.

Odetta played the guitar and sang folk and protest songs for sympathetic audiences.

Nina Simone: a symbol of black pride. Sixties audiences knew her as much for her political commitment as for her music. South African folk singer Miriam Makeba introduced "The Click Song." After her marriage to black activist Stokely Carmichael, bookings were sparse.

The Marvelettes: Motown's first big female group. "Please Mr. Postman" brought the company its second gold record.

the American young, male and female, black, then white, could firmly connect to. In the sixties no other single record company touched on the needs and desires of a whole nation of teen-agers as effectively as Motown.

Motown's first important female headliner was Mary Wells. For a time she was the biggest star in the stable, coming out with hit after hit. Her songs, "You Lost the Sweetest Boy" and "Bye Bye Baby," were extremely energetic. The latter, which she wrote herself, was about a girl who was jilted. But she was not feeling blue. Hell, no. He had taken her love, thrown it away, but he was gonna want her love back someday, so, bye bye baby, she wailed. She added a warning too: that he better not come back running, knock, knock, knocking on her front door! Here Mary Wells broke loose, screaming as high as Little Richard, acting like a churchgoing sister who decided she was tired of the preacher's sermon—and was determined to deliver her own. The gospel beat and drive let the listener know this song was about personal salvation. Other times, with such songs as "What's Easy for Two" and "Two Lovers," she was sweet, simple, and enduringly melodic. Her biggest hit, "My Guy," became a standard for young girls in love. With lyrics by Smokey Robinson, Wells delivered a hymn of praise to the guy of her dreams.

Mary Wells was a rambunctious bundle of energy and glee, sometimes singing so fast she didn't seem to take time to catch her breath. In personal appearances she often came across like a petulant bratty kid, the kind audiences loved to hate. She looked small, had an insolent pout, big baby eyes, and a collection of wigs that she wouldn't have been caught dead without. One day she might sport a short blond hairdo. Next day Mary would

be wailing with a blond ponytail flying all over the place. Sometimes her superconfidence about her appeal could be amusing. Why should she care a hoot whether people called her tasteless or gauche or a mess. In the long run she introduced the hip, swinging, modern girl from the other side of town who loved the brash music only she could sing. In the late fifties and early sixties she was a teen fantasy come true, for she represented the spunky kid who got to play with sex and romance, the lucky runaway no longer having to put up with parents or tenements. She was living a glamorous life on the road.

Shortly after Mary Wells' success, two hot Motown female groups came on the scene. From 1961 to 1967 The Marvelettes were a big attraction. They won a gold record for "Please, Mr. Postman," the wild wail of four girls waiting, hoping, then just pleading with the mailman to look and see if there was a letter—from the boy of their dreams. Later with their moving ballad "Don't Mess with Bill," they assumed the pose of tough little mamas, announcing that there wasn't nobody gonna do nothing to their guy Bill. And with "Forever," a slow grind about enduring love, the quartet reached its artistic peak.

Martha and The Vandellas was Motown's second big female group. With them, the company attained a new artistic maturity. The writing team of Holland, Dozier, and Holland hit its stride, became confident of its talent, and acquired an understanding of the basic pop rhythms and formulas that would sell.

As performers, Martha and The Vandellas never lost their ethnic beat and pulse. More often than not, their feverish hits ("Come and Get These Memories," "Heat Wave," and "Quick Sand") touched on a new restlessness among the American young. The lyrics explained that love was the reason for all the fuss and bother. But these ghetto girls had something else on their minds. Not yet women, they felt the constraints of a repressive culture, and their delivery indicated they were fighting hard to break loose. It was precisely such rebellious undertones that made their song "Dancing in the Streets" so controversial. Here they announced that summer had come. They wanted to know if folks were ready for a brand-new beat. This was an invitation, they sang, for people throughout the nation to meet. So, come on, they said, because it was time for dancing in the streets. On the surface, the song simply called for some communion everywhere through dance. But during the period of city ghetto riots, some radio stations, fearing the record was a call for some kind of street action, an announcement meant to incite Black Americans, banned it from air play.

Dancing in the streets—girl-groups, sporting wigs and fancy dresses, sang love songs that told American teen-agers the facts of life: the Crystals (*top*), Martha and the Vandellas (*center*), and the Shirelles.

Motown's most dazzling creation, the original Supremes—*(left to right)* Diana Ross, Mary Wilson, and Florence Ballard—sold more than 50 million records. Their story was an urban sixties-style fairy tale.

THE SUPREMES: GHETTO GODDESSES

But the greatest of Motown's female groups was the dazzling Supremes. Here audiences saw everything Motown had been experimenting with—in terms of group image, style, dynamics—fully worked out. Also important was the fact that The Supremes, in the early part of their careers, were models for every black ghetto kid in America who dreamed of getting out.

Theirs was a sixties style rags-to-riches saga for an audience that had the harsh urban experience very much on its mind. The three had grown up dirt poor in Detroit's Brewster projects. There had been twelve children in Florence Ballard's family; three in Mary Wilson's; and six in Diana Ross's. As adolescents, the three girls had met and decided to form a group. When the three went to Motown chief Berry Gordy, he turned them away, telling the girls to finish school before embarking on a career. They returned to the classroom, but spent most of their time performing at churches, hops, dances, block and basement parties, wherever and whenever possible. Then with their high school educations completed, the three went back to Motown, were signed up as The Primettes (the female counterparts of a male group, The Primes, who later became The Temptations), and used as backup vocalists for Marvin Gaye and Mary Wells. They recorded nine singles of their own that went nowhere and finally hit the jackpot with "Where Did Our Love Go." Their entire world changed. "That's when," Diana Ross said later, "we started doing the hard work—meeting disc jockeys, interviews, charm school, being nice to build ourselves up." Motown, the fairy godmother in the tale, groomed the girls to be the stars.

The Supremes' ascent began in Detroit in the early sixties. By the time it ended, they had twelve number one singles, sold over 50 million records, and were more famous than any other black performing group in American history. They played Vegas, the big supper clubs (formerly closed to rhythm-and-blues and rock 'n' roll stars), national television ("The Ed Sullivan Show," "Hullabaloo," "Shindig," "The Mike Douglas Show,") college campuses, and royal command performances.

Their early big singles, "Where Did Our Love Go," "Come See About Me," "Baby Love," and "Stop! In the Name of Love," were familiar themes on love, but presented with a new musical sophistication. The Supremes were still not adults, but they were not pubescent bubble gum kiddies either. No longer was it simply whine and pine, ache, throb, and sob. Instead, here stood young women who understood something of the teen experience.

They were also a perfect ensemble group, precisely in touch with their material, their collective and individual personas, and one another. Like so many other Motown groups, this trio genuinely seemed to enjoy entertaining, exuding self-confidence and inviting everyone to join in. They had a controlled, feverish intensity as well.

Whenever they came onstage, the three were dressed alike and to the nth degree. Their clothes were expensive and swanky. They wore lacquered wigs and sequined gowns that sparkled whenever they moved. Together the three Supremes represented one ideal girl. Mary was the sweet, sexy one; Florence, the high-hat, no-nonsense one; Diana, the lively skinny one. Onstage, between numbers, they kidded one another as only girl friends could. After Diana had made all the introductions, she would laugh about her skinniness, saying, "But you know what they say. Thin is in." "Yeah," Florence would interject, putting her hands on her full hips, "thin may be in. But fat's where it's at." Their banter kept them in touch with their audiences, and they were seen as positive figures by young black kids and their parents: for these were ghetto girls making good.

Finally, of course, The Supremes, as crossover figures, represented for young white audiences (and some older ones too) new-style black girls whose ethnicity had been made more acceptable. The Supremes set out to charm, to offer escape. Energetic as their music was, it was pure soul/pop without the tension of Bessie's disturbing, disorderly blues, without the haunt and taunt of Billie's moody style. And as their interviews in *Time* and *Look* stressed, they were not really any different from any other American girl who wanted marriage, a home, and kids, and who wanted to do something to help her family.

Everything was not perfect with the group. There were problems: They were often overworked, underpaid, and extremely tense. In 1967 the group became Diana Ross & The Supremes. Stories circulated of Diana's temperament, her flaming egotism, of Florence's outrage and bitterness because Motown reaped most of the profits from their work and Diana always reaped most of the attention. In time, the fairy tale turned sour. Florence Ballard left the group in 1967, tried to make it as a solo performer, but ended up back in Detroit, broke, working as a domestic, living on welfare. She died at the age of thirty-three in 1976. Cindy Birdsong, who had previously worked with Patti LaBelle and The Bluebells, replaced

Ballard. But soon the social temper of the period changed. Black audiences now demanded undiluted soul as well as music that touched on social issues, politics, the *system* (which The Supremes were now so much a part of). Motown altered the music some. "Love Child" and "Living in Shame" were specific ghetto-oriented songs about ills and problems of inner city black victims. But these tunes were temporary postponements in the group's demise. Finally, it was announced that Diana Ross would become a solo act, with Jean Terrell replacing her as The Supremes' lead singer. Shrewdly, Motown, even at the end, kept The Supremes legend machines working: The group's last single with Diana as lead was a sentimental tune entitled "Someday We'll Be Together."

The group's celebrated history may have been tainted by its closing chapter, but their early legend still glows. And their early music, no matter how pop or commercial, still captures much of the mid-sixties idealism and energy.

Singers Nancy Wilson, Della Reese, Roberta Flack, Nina Simone, and folk singers Odetta and Miriam Makeba also acquired followings. For Black Americans with an emerging awareness of their roots in Africa, Miriam Makeba was a triumphant symbol, bringing her African folk tunes to college campuses and theatres around the country. Her marriage to Stokely Carmichael, the hero of the black power movement, was seen as a revolutionary fairy tale, the union of a strong black warrior and his beautiful black woman. But Carmichael's politics alienated theatre managers and booking agencies, many of whom closed their doors to Makeba.

Throughout most of the sixties it looked as if Dionne Warwick (spelled Warwicke for a while) would also become a major diva. With her hit renditions of Burt Bacharach's songs "Don't Make Me Over" and "Walk on By," she represented the reflective young black woman caught in the heat of a trying emotional situation. As she struggled to get the song out, there was always a plea in Dionne's voice and a moment of desperation. She was also one of the few song stylists with enough range to sing Bacharach's intricate melodies. Warwick had hugely successful concerts and won gold records too.

Performer Nina Simone was surely a political diva if ever there were one. With her songs "Four Women" and "Mississippi Goddamn," she spoke directly—and bitterly—about America's racial situation. Simone also had a haughty, testy, hot-tempered personality. Audiences never knew what to expect during one of her concerts. Sometimes they were not even sure she would show up. Sometimes they feared she might begin a performance by telling everybody off. In retrospect, it might be safe to say that because of her irascible attitude and, surprisingly, because of her looks (the dark color), the mass audience was never fully at ease with her.

Cindy Birdsong (left) replaced Florence Ballard, and the group became Diana Ross and The Supremes. The fairy tale turned sour. Ballard tried to make it as a solo performer but failed and died penniless at the age of 32.

Aretha Franklin introduced "soul" to America. With a voice as big as Bessie Smith's, she was the brilliant distillation of several streams of black music.

ARETHA FRANKLIN: LADY SOUL BRINGS IT ALL HOME

inally, the sixties closed with the full discovery and appreciation of the era's greatest ethnic down-home diva, Lady Soul Herself, Aretha Franklin. No matter what her private feelings or sentiments, she was the perfect heroine for an age now caught up in political fervor. When she sang, Aretha was described as the brilliant distillation of several streams of Black American music. She was considered part spiritual, part gospel (like Mahalia Jackson and Clara Ward), part raunchy blues (like Bessie Smith), part moody, mellow blues (like Billie Holiday and Dinah Washington), part rhythm-and-blues (like Ruth Brown and Ray Charles), part field holler (like Ma Rainey), part work song, part jazz, part holiness shout. Aretha brought everything home, down front in the open for White and Black America to see. For a new movement of black political separatists, activists, and cultural nationalists and for an age caught up in black pride, she emerged as a splendid symbol, a woman whose soulfulness flowed out of her effortlessly and whose music at every turn was a comment on the Black American experience, a summation of its pain, joy, trials, and triumphs. *Ebony's* David Llorens proclaimed the late sixties as the period of "Retha, Rap, and Revolt." She was one of the few cultural heroines to bridge all gaps, appealing to rural blacks as much as to inner city folks, her records also being played in college dorms as well as in nighttime-is-the-righttime big city bars. In time, every imaginable cliché, every late sixties trend, almost every important black political ideology of the time, was, in some way or another, laid on Lady Soul. And like Marian Anderson, Aretha endured the weight of the symbol business because at heart none of it seemed to matter as much as her music and her art.

Like the other important divas, Franklin's personal life was an important part of the legend that enveloped her. She had had a lonely, chilly childhood. She never had the harsh ghetto experience of a Holiday (or even of a Diana Ross), but nothing had been rosy either. Born in 1942 in Memphis, she and her four brothers and sisters were raised in Detroit, where her father, C. L. Franklin, was pastor of the New Bethal Baptist Church. When Aretha was six, her mother left the family and then died four years later. And Aretha's father, a popular, dynamic evangelist, was on the road, barnstorming at churches and gatherings through the country.

As a shy, quiet child whose only refuge was music, she saw many of the greats of black music visiting her father at their home, such legendary figures as Mahalia Jackson (who eventually wanted the world to know Aretha was her prized protégée), Clara Ward, James Cleveland, Arthur Prysock, B. B. King, Dorothy Donegan, Lou Rawls, Sam Cook, and even the queen herself, Dinah Washington. Aretha silently watched and studied them all, taken by their talent, their passion for their art, their regality, and their sense of the dramatic. At the funeral of one of Aretha's aunts, Mahalia Jackson sang the gospel tune "Peace in the Valley." In her fervor, Mahalia tore off her hat and flung it to the ground. "This," Aretha said later, "was when I wanted to become a singer."

As a child, she crisscrossed the country on gospel tours. In the tiny towns and hamlets, she was often turned away from restaurants and hotels. The town streets themselves were closed to blacks after certain hours. By the age of fourteen she cut her first gospel single for Chess Records.

Then in 1960 she went to New York, taking dance and vocal lessons, then signing with Columbia Records in 1961. Here, in the legend that shaped her career, she emerged as the sensitive, bruised, brooding young artist being told what to do and be by a culture that had no idea what she or her art were all about. Columbia had her singing standards. Tense and withdrawn, she cut nine albums for Columbia (one of which was *Unforgettable*, a tribute to Dinah Washington). The sales were lackluster. She refused to renew her Columbia contract, choosing instead to sign in 1966 with Atlantic Records, the company that had handled rhythm-and-blues artists Ruth Brown, Ray Charles, and Wilson Pickett. Aretha could select her material and block out her arrangements. And here the artist finally flowered.

Her first Atlantic single, in 1967, "I Never Loved a Man," sold over a million copies, followed by two other big hits "Respect" and "Baby, I Love You." Later the sales soared on her albums *I Never Loved a Man* and *Aretha Arrives*. In 1967 she also made her first European tour and appeared at New York's Philharmonic Hall, accompanied by her backup group The Sweet Inspirations (led by her sister Carolyn). By this time she was the biggest name in the world of popular music.

With her success came stories of her unhappy private life. She had married Ted White. In its cover story on Aretha, *Time* described White as "a former dabbler in Detroit real estate and a street-corner wheeler-dealer." Soon he was managing her career. The couple had three children, but it was hardly an ideal marriage. In the popular imagination White was a man who was manipulating Aretha's career for his own ends. (Before White, many people thought Aretha's father had exploited her too.) Word spread of an incident at Atlanta's Regency Hyatt House Hotel, where White had reportedly roughed Aretha up. Even Mahalia Jackson commented, "I don't think she's happy. Somebody else is making her sing the blues." *Time*, too, described Aretha as a young woman "cloaked in a brooding sadness, all the more achingly impenetrable because she rarely talks about it." The magazine added that she often retreated into her huge Detroit home to wrestle "with her private demons. She sleeps till afternoon, then mopes in front of the tv set, chainsmoking Kools and snacking compulsively." But while *Time* and other publications said this or that about her, Aretha herself remained silent.

The troubled Aretha image was, of course, readily accepted because, in the eyes of her fans, Aretha, like Bessie, sang what she lived. Aretha's songs focused on pained women pushed and pulled here and there by love, by gut emotion, by despair, by callous men.

What also added to her particular troubled image was the way Aretha looked. She was big-boned and heavy. And at times she seemed awkward, nervous, guilty, embarrassed about the weight, about the fact that she was not a glamour girl. At one point she wore wigs and billowing dresses that camouflaged her figure. Later Aretha went natural, sporting an Afro. In the seventies she lost weight and appeared in soft, sexy diaphanous gowns. Her vulnerability—the pain in her face and eyes—coupled with her fierce, gritty determination to get through the song in spite of its emotional demands drew audiences to her. But while her fans saw all of Aretha's raging power and glory, it seemed to pass Aretha by. In a rare television interview, she was fine when at the piano, but when asked to speak, she seemed lost, her eyes liquid and frightened.

In the mass imagination, Aretha took her place in a line of dedicated, tortured artists such as Holiday, Charlie Parker, and Lester Young. Sometimes an Aretha Franklin concert was a ritual for mass audience masochism. When Aretha suffered onstage, so did her audience. She was the perfect cathartic performer, though, because Aretha took her audience down *with her* to the level of *their* despair. But she always brought them back up. Afterward many may have forgotten that the great pleasure and satisfaction of an Aretha Franklin concert was that they had left with an uncanny high.

Aretha Franklin had brought soul to America. Like Ethel Waters in the late forties and fifties, she was a glowing, full-bodied rock-of-ages matriarch (a twenty-six-year-old girl going on one hundred) who symbolized endurance. And her tribal chant helped bring the restless, culturally split sixties to their dramatic conclusion. The idea was that things could and would change in America. Although the next decade would not need her as a symbol as the sixties had, Aretha would be there nonetheless, with not a drop of magnetism or power diminished.

Aretha *(left)* with Clara Ward *(next to her)* and Della Reese *(third from right)*. Even though she was pop music's biggest star, she seldom looked happy. "Somebody else is making her sing the blues," Mahalia Jackson once said.

· THE 1970S · SURVIVORS

In the seventies all the political fervor and turmoil of the previous decade slowly vanished. And the diva discovered a nation anxious once again for pure rituals and diversions. In a short period of time the seventies shaped up as a sometimes wickedly slick, trendy, fiercely contradictory era besieged by a multitude of incongruities. The decade opened with Cambodia and Kent State, the Soledad Brothers and Angela Davis, the Pentagon Papers and Attica, Muhammed Ali and Joe Frazier, Vietnam and Watergate. Before its end, it would boast of or be haunted by other images, other fads or trends, all testaments to its eerie unpredictability.

The mood that came to dominate the era seemed to be a longing for escape and adventure, which may have simply revealed America's basic uncertainty about itself and its overriding sense of alienation. Losing oneself somewhere outside the present, blotting out the harsh realities the sixties had been so determined to confront (the war abroad; the problems of an industrial culture polluting itself to death), seemed the one great mad hope of the slick seventies. Perhaps, better than anything else, that explains the rise of the discos, where everyone could dance his problems away.

And, of course, the era's desire for escape affected the styles and images of the divas. Often the important black goddesses were women seemingly operating in deluxe fantasy lands that audiences anxiously sought. What audiences cherished most about the new black heroine was that by way of the American success ethic, by way of the treasured American status of star,

Disco queen Donna Summer started off as a sexy joke but became a superstar.

she had escaped and survived the kind of humdrum existence audiences felt they themselves were saddled with. Of course, stars had functioned in this way in the past. But now the audience need for escape was intensified. And soon mass American society seemed off on a giddy star trip unlike any it had before experienced. In a gossipy, celebrity-oriented period, the American black beauty found herself fully emerging (for the first time) as a true superstar celebrity, as famous and adored as any white goddess, sometimes even more. No matter how talented a black goddess might be, it never mattered so much what she did (politically, socially, artistically) as long as she could sustain the illusion of stardom, that of the survivor who could not be kept down. Curiously, too, the era's star fixation (and the superficial star trappings: the clothes, the money, the look, the media attention) as well as the interest in the-woman-who-had-held-on now helped bring about the formal apotheosis of the classic dark diva spirit.

Oddly enough, the first important seventies divas still had some political fall-out power from the sixties. In the early seventies audiences still searched their popular entertainment for comments on America's political system. Consequently, the two divas who launched the era were women who, while definite stars, also were political heroines too. And in them, Diana Ross and Cicely Tyson, the great dichotomy of the early seventies was best summed up. One was pure political heroine with touches of glitter in her personal style. The other was glitter goddess bathed in the waters of politics.

DIANA ROSS: THE SUPERSTAR ASCENDS

By the early seventies Diana Ross was already internationally famous and fully on her own. Having left The Supremes, she had a couple of hit records—"Ain't No Mountain High Enough" and "Reach Out and Touch." She played the big supper clubs. But something still was not

Diana Ross went from Detroit's Brewster Projects to Hollywood's Sunset and Vine. As one of the nation's most publicized stars, she often seemed enamored of her own fame. In the early seventies she was also ready for a major image change.

right. There was a national nostalgia surrounding The Supremes. If the public fully accepted Ross on her own, it meant that something else had to be accepted, namely that The Supremes, a great sixties vision touching on the idealism and dreams of the era, were now dead and gone and could never return. A kind of national innocence had died. Ross herself was often thought of as the selfish, superficial, overly ambitious sister who had stepped on everyone else. Motown and Ross's Svengali, Berry Gordy, Jr., aware of the sentiments, knew something had to be done to change the image.

Diana Ross soon underwent a metamorphosis. During this early part of a period that still saw Aretha Franklin as the undisputed queen, Ross knew intuitively that she would not be accepted as a goddess until she symbolically had gone back to the holy waters, been rebaptized, and born again. What brought about her metamorphosis was a diva from the past, Billie Holiday.

In the early seventies Billie Holiday was treasured all the more by young Black America because mass White

---

Lady Sings the Blues was a melodrama dressed up with political rhetoric to alleviate any guilt feelings audiences might have about enjoying soap opera.

Americans still had not hooked onto her legend. All that sixties worship of Holiday as a tragic victim was still around. Black America identified with all of Billie Holiday's sufferings. The bigoted system that had helped destroy her was the very same system that had denied dignity and full freedom to millions of other blacks throughout the nation. In essence, Billie Holiday's troubled story was Black America's story too. And now there was a demand that the story be told. Interestingly, had Holiday's life been dramatized in the late sixties, Diana Ross would have been totally unacceptable. That heated period would never have settled for the movie Lady Sings the Blues, which would have been dismissed as but one more symbol of a decadent capitalistic culture's exploitation of a black artist. But in the seventies, the loosening social setup as well as Motown's clout permitted Ross to take the role.

When word first spread that Ross would play Holiday, there was open astonishment. She was the least qualified of actresses for the part. Her voice didn't have the shading or depth of Lady Day's. She was skinny and small-boned; Holiday had been large and full. And the personality contrasts were astounding. Holiday had been still, remote,

moody, withdrawn, intense, the essence of quiet fire. Diana was all razzle-dazzle, all get-up-and-move-extrovertism, all show and flash and talk. In the minds of many, Motown chieftain Gordy had gone cuckoo over his protégée. But Diana Ross proved everyone wrong.

Lady Sings the Blues was a lush, romantic melodrama dressed up with some political rhetoric and social trappings to alleviate any guilt feelings audiences might have about enjoying old-fashioned soap opera. Holiday's life was transformed into a standard rags-to-riches saga with the trying, unnerving experiences (the early rape, the early jail experiences, the tension in her Baltimore household, her sense of isolation as well as the tensions she herself laid out on others) all either neatly reduced to mild comic fare or ignored altogether. Nor did the film focus on her loves. Had Lady Sings the Blues dealt explicitly with Holiday's love life, the movie might have been too disturbing. At this point in history, audiences were desperate for "positive black images." Already in such films as Shaft and Super Fly, too many black women had been seen jumping too readily in and out of bed. So for the mass audience there had to be a mass acceptable Billie, one who was a bourgeois lady. Billie Holiday herself no doubt would have loved some of the phony business of the film, but she would have seen it for what it was too: a motion picture that could be appreciated and enjoyed as an elaborate escapist romantic fantasy, but a film, in the final analysis, that simplified a very complex life.

What gave Lady Sings the Blues its driving force and charge, as well as its particular poignancy and pull, were the performances of Billy Dee Williams, Richard Pryor, and mainly Diana Ross. Life's Richard Schickel wrote that while the film did an injustice to Holiday's life by trying to "shoehorn one of the legendary tragedies of popular music into one of the most trivial and conventionalized of screen forms, the showbiz biography," it still had the Ross performance to recommend it. "Singing," he wrote, "she does a fair imitation of the Holiday style. Acting, she does even more. Billie Holiday personified the vulnerability, terror, and confusion of the performer who can't hide in a crowd or in a role. Miss Ross, in an unselfconscious, bravura performance makes us feel all of that." In The New Yorker Pauline Kael wrote: "Diana Ross, a tall skinny goblin of a girl, intensely likeable, always in motion...[is] like a beautiful bonfire: there's nothing to question—you just react with everything you've got...because she has given herself to the role with an all-out physicality, not holding anything back."

The Boss: all the superstar status symbols for a triumphant Diana Ross—a hit movie, sold-out concerts, a Hollywood home, limos, jewels, magazine covers, adoring fans.

The real Billie Holiday: Black Americans identified with her and longed for her story to be told. Her legend became more powerful than ever before.

Diana Ross in *Lady Sings the Blues:* a shrewd piece of image merchandising. Although the film was pure escapist fantasy, it reaffirmed Ross's star powers, winning her an Oscar nomination and briefly turning her into a political heroine.

And William Wolf of *Cue* added: "If there's any justice, Diana Ross should be the biggest movie superstar to come along since Barbra Streisand, and she possesses deeper acting ability." In the end, Diana Ross walked off with a Golden Globe Award for her work in the film as well as with the highly prestigious Academy Award nomination as Best Actress of 1972.

But with all this aside, the ritual inherent in *Lady Sings the Blues* was obvious: Diana, the princess of ghetto chic, a girl/woman known as plastic, goes through Billie's horrors and humiliations. By doing so, she acquires a certain depth and relevance. Thus, the queen of pop (who is loved precisely because she is that, although no one is quite ready to admit it yet) is transformed into an acceptable commodity for an age that thinks of itself as still being politically motivated. Shrewdly, the movie ended on a high note, not with Lady Day alone in her West Side apartment, but with an image of Diana standing tall and proud and triumphant at Carnegie Hall (superimposed newspaper clips tell of Holiday's death), an

When word spread that Ross would play Holiday, there was open astonishment. She was the least qualified of actresses. Her voice didn't have the depth of Lady Day's.

appropriate way, of course, to announce the death/rebirth of a major star myth for the new era. Diana Ross and *Lady Sings the Blues* ushered black pop into the seventies with great pizzazz.

Afterward Ross never looked better, her skinny body perfectly decked out in glittery but tasteful gowns. Eventually, the wigs would go, the hair pulled back severely from the forehead and tied in the back. She was becoming, a bit prematurely, an exuberant grande dame, living in the Hollywood Hills, granting interviews selectively, making rare personal appearances, always traveling in style in limos, in furs and diamonds. And she was accorded status symbols reserved only for the real big-time goddesses: a cover portrait on *Life* just before its demise; sensational covers throughout the era on *Ebony*, *People*, *Jet*, *Rolling Stone*, *Cue*, and countless others; a prestigious Blackgama mink advertisement with simply a photograph of Diana wrapped in mink and the words "What Becomes a Legend Most"; and an interview by Barbara Walters. And with all the attention and the hugely successful concert performances, it was apparent the seventies mass audience had caught up with her. But it

did not end there. In time, Ross would lead her audiences into the land of ritual glitz and glitter, where it did not matter what she said or sang. She merely had to be.

Seldom was her star power more apparent than with the arrival of her second movie *Mahogany*. Directed by Berry Gordy, Jr., this disjointed and disorienting tale of a black fashion model was met with terrible reviews. Yet the picture was a smash hit, and Diana Ross succeeded in taking her fans on a star trip. Cast as an upwardly mobile woman determined to be a success, she delighted in wearing fine, *badd* clothes, while not caring what the world had to say.

The same was true in the mid and late seventies when Diana Ross went on to play huge houses—the Palace in New York, and Radio City—where her ritual, usually carefully prepared dramatic entrances and exits and carefully programmed romps through the audience while being protected by guards—gave the impression that the queen was humble enough to mingle with the hoi polloi. During these performances, too, she was more confident than ever, aware of the basis of her appeal and so magnetized by her own celebrity and personal history that her new concerts often openly, with the use of slides and film clips and old Supremes songs, paid homage to her. She presented her fans time and again with her now legendary life story, which was turned into a sentimental, sanitized journey from Detroit to Hollywood & Vine. Her concerts also paid homage to past divas Baker, Waters, and Bessie, whom she impersonated onstage, all of whom she now knew she had a definite historical link with.

In time, these concerts became part of her new legend. And some of the critics were swept away by her astounding audience rapport. Their reactions touched on the unfathomable power she had over huge crowds. In the *New York Post*, Jan Hodenfield wrote:

> *Diana Ross, who opened at the Palace last night for a two-week run, sings as though she's standing on a mountaintop.*
>
> *Whether or not she's at the height of her career, she is a star of the classic I'm-here-you're-there-and-I'm-always-going-to-be-here school, and she has been provided a superstar act. A lot of glitz.*
>
> *...She is beautiful. She has no cavities. It's all in the hips. And she is up, but carefully so, laid back. From baby panther to the most teasing of tigers, she always appears almost sure of herself.*
>
> *...And who else but Diana Ross could sing a children's song in purple, blue and silver sequins and, sitting in a child's chair, actually make it*

poignant. She may be the only glamorous woman to come out of the 60s.

And of her 1977 Forest Hills engagement, *New York Times* critic Robert Palmer seemed so taken with her he couldn't see straight.

> *Diana Ross . . . has "it." What is "it"? The answer is not simple . . . having "it" means having not just sex appeal, but also talent, personality, and the most difficult of all performer qualities to define, charisma. Because Miss Ross has "it," she can get away with the most saccharine sort of monologues. She can talk ingenuously about turning a tennis stadium into a discotheque, sit on the edge of the stage and ask a crowd of thousands to pretend they are sitting in her living room, and finally induce the entire audience to hold hands and sway back and forth in rhythm. It takes plenty of "it" to pull this sort of thing off, and Miss Ross makes it seem easy.*
>
> *There are perfectly valid musical reasons for Miss Ross's ability to charm an audience. She has been able to move out from her base in the sweet soul sound of early Motown, without sacrificing an iota of the girlish appeal she exuded during those years, into a much broader stylist arena.*
>
> *There is no truly popular singer in America who can touch her stylistic range or her ability to put across a song's emotional charge without wallowing in either melancholy or bombast. In the light of this talent, even the most contrived stage routines seem to sparkle.*

Glowing notices aside, there were moments during her peak years when she showed signs of wear and strain. Her material was not as fresh and imaginative as it had been in the sixties. She couldn't hit the high notes as she once had, and she didn't move around the stage as she had in the past. It was difficult for her to fake spontaneity too. Yet she remained so exuberantly confident of her own powers to entertain and delight that audiences could not take their eyes off her.

Throughout the seventies Ross appeared to be having great fun. Refusing to hide any aspect of her stardom, she glorified in it all, always making great copy for the celebrity sheets. *People* reported that one evening, upon arriving at Berry Gordy's Detroit mansion for a party in her honor, Ross simply waved to the one hundred guests. Then she calmly shucked her leather boots and dove into the mansion's swimming pool, "swam a length in rust-colored pants and cowled sweater, waved goodnight to the guests, and strutted dripping to bed." Diana Ross was

doing much of what Josephine Baker had done in Europe, keeping the troops entertained offstage as well as on, and reveling in all the attention.

Diana Ross fell victim, however, to a critical backlash. Sometimes the attacks on her were fierce. Her 1978 film *The Wiz* was met with scathing reviews. This $35 million musical was a flop. But far too often, the responsibility for the film's failure was attributed to Ross rather than to the sluggish direction of Sidney Lumet. On another occasion, a *Village Voice* article labeled her as the "Last of the Black White Girls." A *Newsweek* article announced that offstage "Diana Ross is not plastic, she's steel," adding that she no longer had "soul." Worse was a *Women's Wear Daily* review, which dismissed her for giving in concert "hack ballad readings and a pimpish charade of egotistical humility better suited to female impersonators. Ross . . . is merely a grade–B actress fronting a sound-track of dismal clichés."

Interestingly, while such critics raged on, the black community silently sat back and watched, its ambivalence

---

Diana Ross fell victim to a critical backlash. Her 1978 film *The Wiz* was met with scathing reviews. This $35 million musical was a flop.

---

about Ross once again on the rise. There had been the business of her marriage to a white man, Robert Silberstein, father of her three children. What may have saved Ross here from totally alienating the community were the rumors of her romantic relationship with Gordy. In the mass imagination, the two belonged together. Yet no matter what the black community's feelings, there was never an outright attack on her in the black press. As with Muhammad Ali, Diana Ross may have unnerved part of White America because there was something unreal about her, something almost superhuman about her image and the effect she had on large audiences.

For the duration of the seventies, despite friends and foes alike, Diana Ross remained a truly dazzling creation, a woman, who, regardless of critics, controversies, and contradictions, always survived and never disappointed. She was a hip, giddy gamin of a high priestess who always had the gift of gab and energy, the sense of high-flung fun that the nostalgia-crazed, discoized seventies were anxious for. In the long run, she, like her audience, may have been a figure of profound isolation and alienation. But, if so, no one seemed to mind.

CICELY TYSON: THE INCORRUPTIBLE BLACK ARTIST

The other black goddess rising to superstardom in the early seventies was Cicely Tyson, who represented for many the incorruptible black artist. She was something sixties America had been waiting for: a symbol of black consciousness and pride. Hers was an image that worked perfectly as the period opened, but which gradually, as political images fell out of fashion, showed disturbing signs of strain. Her career also indicated that American audiences still had not risen above their familiar color hangups and biases.

Cicely Tyson was born in Harlem, the daughter of a West Indian couple who had migrated from the Nevis Islands. Her father was a carpenter; her mother, a domestic worker. At age nine Tyson was on the streets selling shopping bags. The family was dirt poor but proud, and Tyson's strict and fiercely religious mother sent her three children off to church every chance she had.

Once out of school, Tyson worked a series of jobs, her last before the start of her career as a typist for the Red Cross. One day when she had had it with the grinding routine, she announced for all in the office to hear, "God didn't intend for me to sit at a typewriter all my life." She quit the job, became a model, and soon embarked on an acting career, which did not sit well with her mother at all. But Tyson stuck to her guns, lit up with a gritty determination that showed in her work. Throughout the late fifties and sixties she worked hard, studied tenaciously, slowly learning her craft and year by year winning critical attention in off-Broadway and Broadway productions—*Talents '59, Jolly's Progress* (as an understudy for Eartha Kitt), *Moon on a Rainbow Shawl,* Langston Hughes' *Trumpets of the Lord, Tiger Tiger Burning Bright, A Hand Is on the Gate, The Cool World, Blue Boy in Black, Take Me Back to Morningside Heights,* and *To Be Young, Gifted and Black.* But of all those fifties and sixties roles, her most impressive, the part that brought her national attention, was as the prostitute Virtue in the legendary 1961 production of Genet's *The Blacks,* a rousing, revolutionary piece of theatre that introduced a startling group of young players: Raymond St. Jacques, Lou Gossett Jr., Godfrey Cambridge, Roscoe Lee Browne, James Earl Jones, and Maya Angelou. In this cast of heavyweights, Tyson walked off with her first

Drama Desk Award as outstanding off-Broadway performer of the year. The next year, 1962, she won the same award again for her performance in *Moon on a Rainbow Shawl.*

Tyson soon began working in films and on television, sometimes in bit parts, where if you blinked you missed her; other times in supporting roles, where her striking face and personality were there for all to see.

In appearances on series as diverse as "I Spy" and "East Side, West Side," what always shone through was her fierce integrity—that sense of her own worth and her rigid refusal to sell herself short. In those days she did not give out that radiant smile so readily. Often, too, she seemed withdrawn and hostile, the large luminous eyes seeming to look through, rather than at, her costars. For years, as she struggled with meaningless television parts, Cicely Tyson, like so many black beauties before her, was never at ease. There was that familiar edge, not too different from Bessie Smith's or Lena Horne's. All that pent-up anger, frustration, and disillusionment, about her own career and the fact that as a black woman it was taking her longer to get anywhere, helped make her such a compelling presence. Even then, at the time of the early television spots, the large audience watching her, those millions who did not know her name, but who could not forget the face and the attitude, knew that here was a young woman better and bigger than her parts. Cicely Tyson knew that one of the secrets of great acting is holding something back.

Tyson's main problem may well have been that she was too dark. What with her color and her features and the regal way she carried herself, she did not seem Western at all. In a period when The Supremes had donned wigs and glitter makeup, looking from a distance like tiger-limbed mulattoes, Tyson looked African. Even Diana Sands, with her full lips, had the advantage of lighter skin to help make her acceptable. Cicely Tyson would never come anywhere near a mulatto ideal. Ironically, when Tyson did become a star, in spite of her looks and her particular stance, those very things would be most treasured by her devotees. For just at the moment when Tyson appeared before the mass audience in a role just right for her talents, Black Americans were anxious for a dark heroine.

And, of course, stardom finally came. In 1972 *Sounder,* the story of a troubled black family living in Louisiana in the 1930s, was released. It focused on several characters: a father imprisoned after he steals to get food on his family's table; a mother forced to hold the family together during his absence and at the same time to

At age nine Cicely Tyson sold shopping bags on the street, later worked as a typist, then became a respected dramatic actress. But stardom did not come until the early seventies.

keep her emotions in check; a young son off on the road to maturity. Arriving amid a spate of black action films, *The Legend of Nigger Charley* and *Shaft*, *Sounder* looked at first as if it had come at the wrong time. But it became the sleeper hit of the year. The critics had a field day with it, praising Tyson left and right. *Time* announced that "no American actress since Jane Fonda in *Klute* has given a film performance of such artfully and varied texture." In *The New Yorker*, Pauline Kael wrote: "Cicely Tyson plays the first great black heroine on the screen. Her Rebecca was worth waiting for. She is visually extraordinary. Her cry as she runs down the road toward her husband is a phenomenon—something even the most fabled actresses might not have dared."

Tyson in her award-winning role as Rebecca in *Sounder*. A stellar performance followed in *The Autobiography of Miss Jane Pittman*. But afterward there was a scarcity of good solid roles for her.

Afterward Tyson won the National Board of Review's award as Best Actress of the Year and also picked up an Oscar nomination, along with Diana Ross, as Best Actress. For the first time in movie history, two black women were now vying for Hollywood's most prized possession. Although Liza Minnelli walked off with the Oscar for her performance in *Cabaret*, the whole sensation was a thoroughly optimistic experience for black moviegoers who saw this event as a striking new turn for American movies.

But following all the hoopla, even with *Sounder* under her belt, Tyson did not get the big publicity shoves in the national magazines or the plugs in the syndicated columns. The media found Diana Ross infinitely more salable because of her glamorous image. Tyson's success was seen as merited and long overdue, but many also thought it was fluky, a once-in-a-lifetime experience that would never come again. For a year or so, it almost looked as if the doubters were right. Then Tyson came back strong in another surprise hit, *The Autobiography of Miss Jane Pittman*, a film made for television. Based on a novel by black writer Ernest Gaines, it traced the life of a black woman from the days of slavery to the dawning days of the civil rights movement in the late fifties. Tyson won critical raves for a tour-de-force performance.

What Tyson had done in this early part of the era was to present ordinary women in a distinctly heroic manner. Her Rebecca and Miss Jane, neither mammies nor mulattoes, stood as symbols. They were low-keyed, sensitive creatures aware of the bonds of race and sex. They struck audiences as decent but guarded women, never fully at ease in the white world because they knew too well its basic hypocrisy and its power to destroy. Yet at the very moment when they must take a stand and grasp full control over their personal destinies, Tyson's figures did not hesitate.

After *The Autobiography of Miss Jane Pittman*, Cicely Tyson became something of a national commodity. The wheels of the big-time publicity machines finally turned. Her appearances on the covers of *Ebony*, *People*, *Ms*, and *Jet* confirmed her arrival aboveground. Her persona was now directly in tune with the distinct needs of an age still in transition. There was so much about her now that the public could connect to, offscreen as well as on. Aside from her talent and charm, there was the history of her career that had taken so long to climax. There were also the intelligent comments she made to the press about the lack of good roles for black women and of the importance of role models on the screen for black audiences. The statements also endeared her to the politically conscious. There was also a strong identification with her among black women. And in time Tyson reached another group too. For during this period when everyone seemed to be struggling to get back to basics, to abandon psychedelics, to be more in tune with the earth and nature and away from chemicals, pollutants, and corruptives of all kinds, Tyson represented Natural Woman. She was the star who was also the vegetarian, the jogger, the woman who meditated daily, who sewed her own clothes. In a way, her color also made her the familiar dark woman of mystery, closer to the spirit than most mere mortals.

This was the type of publicity a Baker would have howled over. And, of course, it was the flip side of the Ross image. Yet all these revelations about a new-style, down-to-earth diva had a certain social value at the time.

But Tyson was eventually affected by changing attitudes. In time, there were artistic disappointments: an all-black stage production of *Desire Under the Elms;* the television films "Just an Old Sweet Song" and "King"; the films *The Blue Bird, The River Niger,* and *A Hero Ain't Nothing But a Sandwich.* Even the critically successful television mini-series "A Woman Called Moses" failed to win a huge audience. Often Tyson's persona was thrown out of whack by directors who failed to understand that, like Waters, Tyson had to have that big dramatic moment. Worse, a type of backlash sprang up against her. "Why doesn't Cicely Tyson stop playing somebody's grandmother?" seemed to be the attitude in even supposedly enlightened, intellectual circles. What the gripers did not stop to think about was that Tyson herself probably longed for a different kind of role. But had she not played the noble heroic types, all she might have hoped for was a bit as a prostitute. A role that might have been ideal for her was that of the mother in *Claudine.* Here her gift for light romantic comedy might have been beautifully showcased. But one wonders if the mass audience would have accepted her in such a role. For the Tyson *dark* look demanded that she play strong black women of spirit but not much flesh.

Throughout the seventies Tyson refused to budge from her convictions to fit the fashion of the times. Her public personality itself may have become too serious and "political" for an audience insistent on art and entertainment that did not ask questions or present problems. But Tyson did not wilt and die. She worked throughout the era. And for future generations her image would blaze on as one of Black and White America's few authentic cultural icons of the seventies.

BLACK LADIES OF THE SILVER SCREEN

Briefly, following the movie success of Tyson and Ross, it looked as if other black goddesses might become major stars through film. For the early seventies saw the rise of the new-style black-oriented motion picture that fully played on the needs of the black audience for political heroes. Actresses Vonetta McGee, Sheila Frazier, Brenda Sykes, Marlene Clark, and Paula Kelly suddenly found the doors of Hollywood open to them. For the political hero naturally needed a girl friend. Mostly the actresses appeared in black action dramas, souped-up

Left to right: actresses Dwan Smith, Irene Cara, Lonette McKee appeared in *Sparkle,* a film about a group like the Supremes.

male fantasies geared to please a large black male audience. In *Shaft, Hit Man, Hammer,* and *Trouble Man,* the heroines had little to do, other than to be at the hero's side during times of need. In retrospect, it is apparent that although more black women had a chance to work, the movies of a male-oriented industry still did not care about telling a black woman's side of the story. Clearly, that was the case with the films of actress Rosalind Cash.

At the beginning of the decade Cash left New York's Negro Ensemble Company to go west to costar with Charlton Heston in the highly touted *Omega Man.* At the time, what with Angela Davis still in the headlines, many assumed Rosalind Cash, with her magnificent puffed-up, larger-than-life Afro and her compelling assertiveness, would be playing a militant, politically committed heroine. There is reason to believe that the studio producing *Omega Man* felt the same way, at least when the production was first taking off. Strangely enough in the first half of the film, Cash was glowingly aggressive. She made a dramatic appearance on a motorcycle, rescuing hero

---

Seldom was a black woman so repeatedly wasted by the industry. The roles this gifted woman played revealed Hollywood's contempt for the talented black actress.

Heston, giving him commands to jump on the darn thing if he wants to keep on living. Here she was a glorious symbol, one of those heady dreams of the beautiful black woman who comes out of nowhere and saves man from his own sad plight. Then gradually the Cash character, who looked as if she were about to run away with the picture, was softened by the script and Boris Segal's direction, to the point where all her drive and force were watered down completely. Even at that, Cash's character was never the one-dimensional black superwoman type. For the actress's obvious intelligence and genuine warmth nicely shaded the role.

The same was true of her work in *Melinda,* in which she played a brooding, troubled woman caught up with a man who has taken a fancy to another woman. In one sequence, to aid the hero, she pretended she was the other woman in order to withdraw some much needed money from the bank. When the bank clerk refused her, Cash launched into a harangue that stood outside the bounds of this cheap melodrama: Her face tight and constricted, her emotions in a blast of fury and rage, she represented the difficult, sometimes next to impossible black woman lashing out at a racist culture that repeatedly had told her

the trumped-up rules by which she must live.

In the very early years of the decade, Cash's work (notably in *Melinda*) had an extraordinary impact on young black women, who identified with her strongly. Had films such as *Melinda* and *Omega Man* turned out better, had the scripts had tension or been ambitious enough to provide her characters with some kind of dramatic consistency or clarity, Rosalind Cash would have emerged as an important film star and might well have entered the ranks of the great divas. But gradually, the opportunities for exciting, compelling moments on screen grew slimmer as she drifted from one sweet-tempered role to another in such films as *Uptown Saturday Night, Cornbread, Earl and Me,* and *The New Centurions.*

Seldom in Hollywood's history was a black woman so repeatedly wasted, so thoroughly trashed by the industry. And the roles this gifted woman found herself playing often revealed Hollywood's basic contempt for the talented, not-easily-typed black actress. In a way, though, the roles, coupled with Cash's high-strung artistry, created a persona for her. As with Gloria Foster, perceptive audiences sat watching Rosalind Cash, using her as a symbol of their own broken promises and unfulfilled dreams.

Other gifted actresses seemed to get lost in the shuffle. Lonette McKee gave a blazing performance in *Sparkle,* but was unable to find another film that properly used her talents. The same was true of Tracy Reed after her exciting work in *Car Wash.*

The new black television series ("Good Times," "The Jeffersons") offered exposure to a number of actresses: Esther Rolle, Isabel Sanford, Theresa Merritt, Ja'Net DuBois, LaWanda Page, Theresa Graves, Roxie Roker, Mabel King, and the delightful Marla Gibbs. Unfortunately, many of these talented women found themselves cast as the familiar overweight, dowdy mammy figure. Of the television personalities, surely the most interesting were the women cast in "Roots" and "Roots: The Next Generations": Madge Sinclair, Olivia Cole, Leslie Uggams, Lynne Moody, Irene Cara, Bever-Leigh Banfield, Beah Richards, and Lee Chamberlain. Cole and Sinclair were two of the best new dramatic actresses around. Sinclair also appeared in the movies *Leadbelly* and *Conrack.* Cole won an Emmy for her work in "Roots" and then went on to give a glowing, complex performance in "Backstairs at the White House." But none of these actresses emerged as big stars. The same was true of Ellen Holly, who appeared on the soap opera "One Life to Live," and Denise Nicholas, who throughout the era gave lively, engaging performances on the tube.

Vonetta McGee began her career in Italian films, then appeared in black dramas. But once the movie industry stopped turning out black films, her appearances became fewer.

Pam Grier, star of cheap, sexy, often funny comic-strip movies, worked her way up from the switchboard at American International Pictures to stardom. In her movies she shot, fought, bombed, burned, and castrated her enemies, proving she could take care of herself.

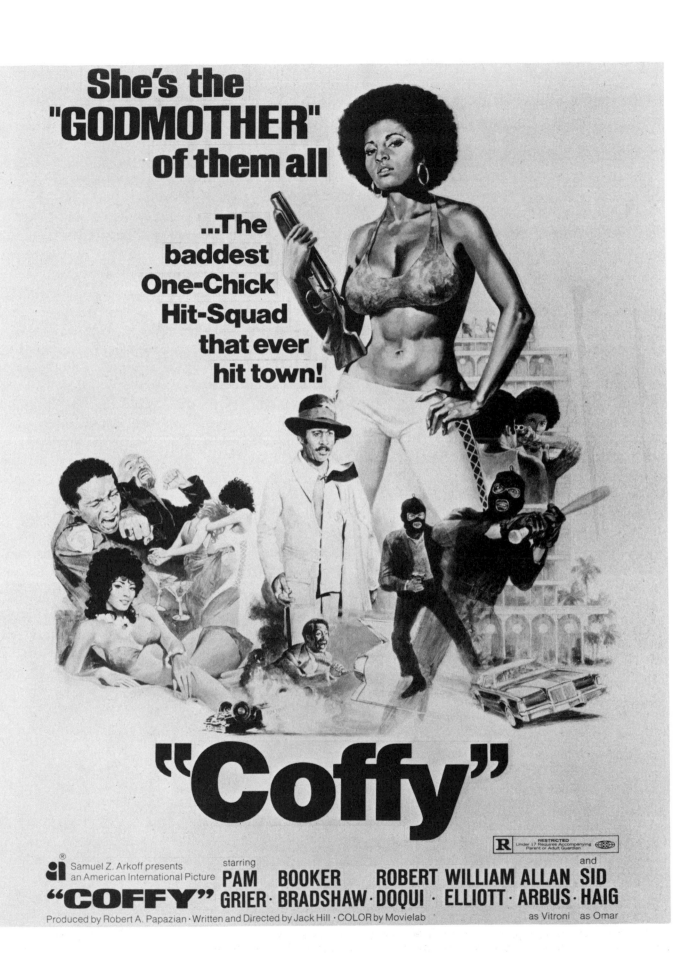

PAM GRIER &
TAMARA DOBSON:
MACHO MATRIARCHS

In the world of film, the only other names of the period (women who acquired definite followings) were Tamara Dobson and Pam Grier, each of whom was able to alternately touch on the age's shifting demands for glitter and guts.

In such films as *Cleopatra Jones, Coffy, Foxy Brown, Sheba Baby,* and *Friday Foster,* Dobson and Grier arrived on the movie scene—and nearly swept it clean. Each a tantalizing male fantasy come true, they personified the tough black mama out to avenge herself and her community on Whitey and his ills. In a way, they were matriarchal figures, beautiful mock-politicized, self-righteous versions of the Hattie McDaniel no-nonsense mammy. In a way, they were mulattoes too, gorgeous, exotic sex objects who were turning the object business inside out. They took men when they wanted. They were always in control of any situation. They had neither a penis nor penis envy. And they fought, shot, bombed, burned, castrated, and caused holy havoc, all in the name of restoring order to the black community, of ridding it of the pushers, the pimps, and the exploiters.

Of the two, Dobson was the more sedate. A former high fashion model, she struck audiences as a high class inaccessible black woman who stepped high with head held even higher. She was a living wonder to behold, but impossible to possess.

Grier's image was raunchier and livelier. And it lasted a bit longer. The star of low-budget adventure tales, Grier had originally worked her way up from a position as a switchboard operator at American International Pictures to become queen of the lot. Her ambitiousness showed too, because in her films Pam Grier always came across as a fiercely aggressive, tough, resilient, hot, and surprisingly funny black woman on the move. Her movies themselves were cheap, rowdy comic strips. But she infused them with her energy and had a following, mostly among black males. The male reactions were purely, openly chauvinistic. Grier herself seemed to play up to the chauvinism; there was nudity when hardly called for. And away from movie theatres, she struck a number of provocative bare poses for the black publication *Players.* She was the woman black college boys drooled over. It may well have been the nudity and coarseness of the Grier characters that alienated her from black women. They could respond to her funky down-home aggressiveness and they might have enjoyed the way she spoke her mind to the dumdum males populating her films. But the movies themselves were travesties, removed from the world and daily problems of most black women. At the same time, this was a period when black women, openly concerned about their image, were weary of the whole sexy-vulgar-slut image. Interestingly enough, Grier did have a following among some white women, who often saw her as a figure of liberation. She even made the cover of *Ms.*

Today both Pam Grier and Tamara Dobson seem destined to go the route of Maria Montez, emerging as camp delights for audiences anxious for old-fashioned kitsch at revival movie theatres.

Pam Grier (left) tried to change her image after blaxploitation films became unpopular. Tamara Dobson (above): a New York cover girl turned screen star.

JOSEPHINE BAKER: COMING HOME

nd who should appear precisely when needed, but the very woman who, for most, was the personification of old-time diva style —none other than La Baker herself, whose seventies return to the States was probably the best indication of all that audiences were now ready for unadulterated glitter and high style.

In 1973 Josephine Baker returned to the States for an appearance at Carnegie Hall. By this point in her life, Baker was something of a time-worn myth. She had been through much, and she had endured her traumas and terrors publicly, remaining true to the old star tradition of sharing the high and low with adoring fans. After her marriage in the forties to bandleader Jo Bouillon, Baker's great dream in the fifties and sixties had been to establish a home for her "rainbow tribe," children of every conceivable color, creed, and nationality who had been left orphaned. Hopped up with what became her mad obsession, Baker adopted a dozen orphans, moving them into Les Milandes, a sprawling three-hundred-acre estate in the Dordogne Valley in southwestern France. Here she hoped to open a resort with a hotel, restaurant, swimming pool, and theatre and golf and tennis facilities, all of which would pay the expenses for her family. It was, of course, a lavish, grandiose folly. But she believed she could pull it off, that in a world in which she, a poor girl from East St. Louis, had become an international personality, hobnobbing with some of the most important leaders and artists of the twentieth century, anything she chose to do was possible.

But reality came crashing in. The cost of the project, the upkeep of her château, and the expenses for supporting her children wiped out Baker's personal fortune, leaving her in debt. Her creditors warned her, then seized her property and belongings and later sold them at auction in 1969. Until the very end Baker held on, literally fighting off the gendarmes who had to forcibly remove her from her property, carrying her from the château out into the rain. The photograph of the evicted Josephine Baker, far from glamorous, bundled in an oversized coat, with her dark glasses hiding the angry swollen eyes, circled throughout the world. Here was a remarkable woman who had provided the world with illusion for years and who had as well lived on some illusions herself. In the past, she had been strong enough to make the illusions work for everybody. Even during the

difficult war years, one senses that much of what propelled Josephine Baker on, perhaps even contributed to her great heroism, was her gloriously romanticized view of herself and her uncanny ability to always succeed.

Reaction to the news of her eviction was curiously mixed. Like Ethel Waters during the period of her most intense personal problems, when her public knew as much about her situation as she herself, Josephine Baker had become a legendary heroine seemingly beyond human sympathy. For a brief spell, many followed her "story," content perhaps that she could still entertain them offstage. If she made it through this bad time, that would add another notch to the legend. If she did not, that might give the legend a nice finishing touch, tinging a triumphant career with pathos and tragedy. Nevertheless, it was Baker's story to work out.

Worse than these reactions to her as a legend were the reactions to her as a performer. For at this point in her history, Baker was seen by many as an over-the-hill legend without much of a career left. In photographs, she looked fat, puffy, a diva who had lost her physical appeal.

But Baker summoned up something within herself. She needed money to keep her rainbow tribe dream alive. She was not about to let go of it. Nor was she about to let go of her world-famous persona. In a way, it was a matter of self-respect. But then, too, all her life she had been an entertainer. Entertaining had kept her alive. She needed that almighty roar of the crowd. From many accounts, she was a driven, restless woman who always had to be on the move, who had to have that mass affection to keep moving and to keep her own view of self from dying. So soon she was dieting, exercising, rehearsing, working on a new act, determined to prove the cynics wrong, determined, too, to live up to the expectations of her fans as an ageless creation who could eternally please.

And all of that brought her to Carnegie Hall in 1973— back to New York City, a place that had never been home, but a place she was determined to lick this time around. The night she opened, a packed house saw a tiny redhaired lady walk out onto the stage. Private groans and whispers shot through the audience. Was this small, plainly dressed woman the legend they had heard about for decades? The groans ceased only when the woman was introduced as Bricktop, who years before had left the States and become an internationally famous club doyenne, managing the chicest night spots Europeans had seen. Her boite on Paris' Place Pigalle had been the second home of the "lost generation" in the twenties and thirties. In the fifties and sixties her dazzling nitery on

Baker back in the States for her last appearances, wooing audiences with her style and flair. She then returned to Europe and staged an amazing comeback.

Rome's Via Veneto had been the place for the Jet Set. She had taught the black bottom to the Duke of Windsor, the charleston to Cole Porter (who wrote "Miss Otis Regrets" for her), and had thrown a rowdy John Steinbeck out of her club. (Later he had returned apologetically, with a carful of roses for her.) And she had been hostess at her club to Taylor and Burton before their marriage, during the peak of their scandalous love affair while filming *Cleopatra*. Born Ada Beatrice Queen Victoria Louise Virginia Smith DuConge, she had traveled the world over, had met everybody, and had become a celebrity in her own right. And now she was introducing her friend Josephine Baker to this skeptical audience.

Bricktop's appearance—and the case of mistaken identity—simply set the stage for Baker's spectacular entrance. For suddenly, like a true goddess, she seemed to descend from out of nowhere, magnificently dressed in a skintight body suit with sequins and rhinestones covering the vital areas and a giddy, glittering campy headdress, so towering it looked as if it would kiss the ceiling. Baker let out a hoot of a laugh as her audience gaped, ooooohing and aaaaahing. She knew what they had been thinking and let them know it too, announcing, while clutching her rhinestone-laden microphone, that she was aware of their surprise. Ah, you thought I would be fat, she said, adding that no, she did not like fat. She loved thin. And the way she kept thin was by simply not eating. Then, her voice lowering a bit, as she seductively flattered and cajoled her audience as only a great star knows how, she added that she had wanted to be thin tonight for them, and so she hadn't eaten for days! Cheers, screams, and applause rang throughout the theatre. And from then on, the audience was in the palm of her hand. The Baker voice was strong, vibrant, clear. The body was in perfect shape. The old-time chorus girl strut was as defiantly sensational as ever. And that extraordinary gift—of transporting audiences into another world—was still there too.

"Forget about Liza. Never mind about Liz," wrote Fern Marja Eckman in the *New York Post*. "Josephine Baker's back in town for 27 hours, lean as a whippet, graceful as a cat ('I'm a black cat with nine lives'), 67 and no trace of bulge or slack, still the mistress of high camp, still the presence that cast a spell over Paris back in the 1920s when she sang and danced and strutted at the Folies Bergère." The years had done nothing to diminish the Baker charisma.

During the New York visit, she appeared before enthusiastic crowds in Harlem, conquering, so *Jet* reported, a whole new generation of blacks. Afterward she flew back to France, then returned to New York for an engagement at the Palace. At the time, there was a musician's strike, and during rehearsals, the tension and strain sometimes were telling. Backstage, some of the white stagehands grumbled and complained about their work and *her* demands, unaware of what a legend Baker was. It was a humiliating experience, the same kind of racism she had fled decades ago. But the indomitable star carried on. Later back in Europe at a charity benefit given by her friend Princess Grace, Baker stepped in as the last-minute star replacement for the event when Sammy Davis, Jr., was unable to appear. Shrewdly, she used this internationally important occasion to formally launch her European comeback. She was a hit all over again. Later she bought a $100,000 villa on the Riviera for her rainbow tribe. Once again she was back into the swing of things, living it up in the grand old high style. In 1975 she opened a successful new revue in Paris, celebrating her fifty years in show business. But she had pushed herself too hard. Four days after the opening, Baker suffered a massive stroke and later died in Paris. Josephine Baker had been blessed. For she was one of the few women, diva or otherwise, who saw almost all her dreams fulfilled.

Josephine Baker's great obsession—her rainbow tribe: she set up a home for war orphans of every race, creed, and nationality. The dream led her into debt, but she was determined to see it through.

THE OLD STYLE RETURNS

Baker's success lent a new air to the entire dark diva phenomenon, endowing it (for those who cared to see) with a kind of political significance. The black entertainer who had been through it all and was back to deliver the message to a new crowd now arose as a symbol of black endurance and accomplishment. Of course, the divas had always been such symbols. But it took a new generation time to discover that and to appreciate them as survivors. For years, too, black audiences had been aware that great performers such as Dietrich, Hepburn, and Davis had had star careers that spanned decades. Although even these women had sometimes been trashed or ignored by the dominant culture, an honored place was reserved still for them.

With the old black stars, however, there had been no such thing. So many of them, once they had peaked, had been forgotten. Seldom did theatre histories even cite their achievements. So it was as if they had never existed. Baker's long career proved that wrong. And her triumphant seventies return encouraged many to reexamine past popular history. What also aided in the new discovery of the old-style diva was that as the social atmosphere became increasingly more relaxed, room was being made for a return of the purely pleasurable moment. Not only did discos surge up but the smart supper clubs returned. Nightlife was in vogue once again. In New York the Cotton Club reopened, amid much fanfare. (This time around, there were no segregated audiences.) And finally women who had been on the scene for years, some working steadily, others not, found themselves called back into public service for appearances at the clubs. The very proper Hazel Scott, the extremely sophisticated Mabel Mercer (a woman who had been a mainstay in New York and European cities for years as well as an idol for an array of performers, from Holiday to Frank Sinatra, all of whom were anxious to study her impeccable diction and her sublimely cool delivery), the grimacing and giddy Dorothy Donegan, found work. Joyce Bryant, the ebullient Helen Humes, and the super-tough Maxine Sullivan all were not only working but getting publicity too, and winning younger audiences. Someone like Sullivan also appeared in the stage play *My Old Friends*, winning rave notices. Jazz vocalist Betty Carter, who had been around since the forties when she had toured with Lionel Hampton, finally received serious critical attention. The music critic of the *New York Times* lauded her as "one of the great improvisatory jazz singers." *Newsweek* reassessed her entire career. At the 1978 Newport Jazz Festival's tribute to women in jazz, Carter was honored along with Mary Lou Williams, Hazel Scott, and Maxine Sullivan.

The seventies proved receptive to other old-time divas. Lena Horne, never out of public sight, not only appeared in successful concerts with Tony Bennett, but also turned up as the star of the Los Angeles all-black production of *Pal Joey* with Clifton Davis and Josephine Premice. In 1978 she even returned to films, popping up for a cameo tour-de-force number in *The Wiz*, proving that if no one else knew what to do with this picture, she did.

In the seventies Pearl Bailey also returned to movies, appearing in *The Landlord* and *Norman...Is That You?* Butterfly McQueen whipped up a nightclub act for New York audiences. By 1978 Eartha Kitt, her purr and scratch intact, returned to Broadway in *Timbuktu!*

Diahann Carroll's turbulent career was also infused with new ironies. Now that the social order was relaxed again, she finally seemed to break through and act up. Her romance with David Frost had ended. Briefly, she married and divorced Las Vegas businessman Freddé Glusman (it lasted four months), then took as her new husband, Robert DeLeon, a black writer many years younger than she. And she did not seem to give a damn what anyone thought of it. In *Jet*, she also spoke out, indicating for the first time she was aware of some of the sentiment against her. She announced she was black and had always been so. No one was going to dictate her behavior either. At a time when she could have simply spent her time on a disco floor, she took on a feisty fervor. When her husband was killed in a car crash, she briefly emerged as one of those endurable heroines who, having finally found happiness, had it quickly snatched away by the gods. Here her career and image were touched with that most important of ingredients for a larger-than-life mythic persona: the element of fate. But refusing to exploit her personal tragedy, she kept a low profile. Most importantly, her singing style became far more dramatic (and she used more pop and soul material). She also gave her most glowing film performance, as the title character in *Claudine*, the tale of a Harlem domestic worker living on welfare with six kids and no husband. Even the way she looked in the film was refreshingly new, her face scrubbed down of the glitter makeup, the brows high and strong, the body occasionally going slack but always sensually alive. Here she stood as a good-looking black woman in her middle years somehow finding something in

Thirties big-band vocalist Helen Humes *(top)* and twenties blues star Alberta Hunter came out of retirement to become nightclub stars again.

the material of *Claudine*—perhaps simply the idea of a black woman off on a quest for personal identity—that she fully connected to. She walked off with an Oscar nomination as Best Actress of 1974.

What with this reappearance of a multitude of familiar faces, none could outclass that of Alberta Hunter, the twenties blues sister who now returned to knock audiences dead in New York club performances. Hunter became something of a media sensation. Celebrities packed her performances. *Newsweek,* the *New York Times,* and several other publications rushed to do features on her. She also appeared on talk shows, did television commercials, and scored the music for the Robert Altman film *Remember My Name.* Seventies audiences took to her in an unusual way, almost as if by giving this survivor her due, they could make up for oversights of the past.

Diva fever spread, touching even the dead. Billie Holiday, gone almost fifteen years, was now fully apotheosized as an authentic American myth with the release of *Lady Sings the Blues.* Billie-mania led to an awakening of interest in the life and legend of Bessie Smith. In the Broadway show *Me and Bessie,* tribute was paid to the blues singer by the pulsating, lively gospel star Linda Hopkins. Bessie's albums were all reissued and, for a spell, there was talk of a Bessie movie biography to star either Aretha Franklin or Roberta Flack.

Other divas were the subjects of shows and benefits. In the New Federal Theater's production of *Mahalia,* Ethel Morrow starred as gospel singer Mahalia Jackson. In 1979 a huge Carnegie Hall benefit was staged to honor Katherine Dunham. Claudia McNeil did a nightclub act centered on the songs of Ethel Waters. And off-Broadway Charles Fuller's play *Sparrow in Flight,* starring Ethel Ayler, dramatized Waters' stormy life. Sadly, though, during all this revival business, Ethel Waters was a dark diva who missed out. Throughout most of the seventies she was ignored, seen by a new generation simply as a relic from the past, no more than some tired, old gray-haired woman who now sang with Billy Graham. There was nothing campy about Waters at this period of her life,

Nostalgia fever spread: even Butterfly McQueen whipped up a nightclub act, appeared in the film *Amazing Grace* and in the road show of *The Wiz.*

196

so she could not even be embraced for that. Whatever tributes she received came after her death in 1977. Even then, American theatre circles still failed to give this extraordinary performer her due.

One of the most exciting events surely had to be the Kennedy Center's tribute to four distinguished American senior citizens: George Balanchine, Artur Rubinstein, Fred Astaire, and the most queenly of divas, Marian Anderson. At the televised benefit, a host of dignitaries and officials sat in attendance, led by President and Mrs. Carter. For the black community, the special moments were when a trio of dark divas—Grace Bumbry, Aretha Franklin, and Alberta Hunter—seemed to be performing solely for Anderson. Here the entire business of historical continuity was readily apparent.

And so the old-time diva and that old-time diva style were ushered back into vogue. Baker's influence was felt not only in the supper clubs, but on the stage too, in many of the new all-black Broadway shows—*The Wiz, Eubie, Bubbling Brown Sugar, Raisin, Ain't Misbehavin'*, the black revival of *Guys and Dolls*, perhaps even in Ntozake Shange's choreopoem *For Colored Girls Who Have Considered Suicide When the Rainbow Is Enuf*. All these shows were embued with glitter and flash. Now, as in the past, the black performers understood that style often had to transcend content, particularly on those occasions when a black entertainer appeared before a white audience. Many of the new Broadway shows may have been accepted by the typical Broadway crowd as nothing more than high-flung darky entertainments. But for the black groups—coming to Broadway from churches and schools—the shows emerged (like Baker) as emblems of pride, razzmatazz homages to the resiliency and creativity of the black community. Onstage a number of exciting female performers were blessed with the old sense of style: Clarice Taylor, Rosetta LeNoire, Ernestine Jackson, Stephanie Mills, Alaina Reed, Josephine Premice, Mary Alice, Laurie Carlos, Mabel King, Clamma Dale, Virginia Capers, Vivian Reed, Nell Carter, Charlaine Woodard, Barbara Montgomery, Trazana Beverley, Debbie Allen, and Vinnie Burrows. Behind the scenes, director Vinnette Carroll and composer Micki Grant (the creators of *Don't Bother Me, I Can't Cope*) provided the era with flash and energy. Melba Moore used Broadway as a springboard for a career as a pop vocalist. She began her career in Broadway's *Hair*, later won a Tony for her performance in *Purlie*, and returned to Broadway again in *Timbuktu!*

Striking and innovative as so many of these women were, few, however, could establish the kind of mythic

Sadly neglected and ignored during the nostalgia revival, Ethel Waters did not stage a comeback.

identities that brought personal fame and huge followings. Some were on their way. Others would always be members of the show, good solid, vibrant performers essential to American theatre and popular entertainment, and the kind of colorful background material off which the great divas would play. Occasionally, a stunning performer such as the young Seret Scott, star of the Broadway drama *My Sister, My Sister*, would find herself suddenly cast in the spotlight with critics fawning over her, with the wheels of publicity machines starting to take off. But too often the crucial follow-up role did not come. Sometimes, too, an extraordinary artist such as dancer Judith Jamison could just about turn the world of dance inside out, expressing in dance a dramatically intriguing personality. But in the final analysis, she would see her chief obstacle as the world of dance itself, still an enclosed, self-contained realm that had not yet touched base with the masses.

Many of the distinctive seventies personalities, the ones who reached and affected large audiences, came, unsurprisingly, from the world of popular music. Here, as in the past, black beauties discovered that, as singing stars, they could create their personas and exert some control over their careers. Once political messages disappeared from pop music early in the decade, such women as Marilyn McCoo and Florence LaRue (of the Fifth Dimension), Freda Payne, Valerie Simpson, Lola Falana, Gladys Knight, Natalie Cole, Letta Mbulu, The Pointer Sisters, Chaka Kahn, The Staples Singers, Minnie Riperton, and Millie Jackson soon reverted to familiar images that exuded swanky glamour.

LaBelle, formerly known as Patti Labelle and the Bluebelles, became a flashy futuristic group with soul.

Tina Turner: straight-haired wigs and scanty costumes.

TINA TURNER AND LABELLE: FUNK AND GLITTER

O f the new song stylists, LaBelle and Tina Turner were the era's most idiosyncratic performers. Turner was a true star of raunch, as earthy, upfront, foul, and funky as they come. Born Annie Mae Bullock in Brownsville, Tennessee, she and husband Ike Turner had been rhythm-and-blues stars since the late fifties when their record "A Fool in Love" had become a national hit. In the seventies Tina led Ike and their back-up group, The Ikettes, to the center of the pop music scene with new renditions of "River Deep, Mountain High," "Honky Tonk Woman," and "Proud Mary."

Eventually, Tina was out on her own, performing as the Acid Queen in the movie *Tommy*, appearing on national television, and later playing Caesar's Palace in Las Vegas. She symbolized a crazed kind of controlled abandonment and looseness. When she first attracted large audiences, disco still had not come in. But the need for disco was apparent, and Tina Turner was clearly a predecessor of the frantic, flipped-out disco queen. Her concert performances were at the height of their popularity during those anemic Nixon years when audiences were in need of a high priestess to shake them out of their own inertia and lethargy. Tina Turner did all the work for her audiences. Her arms flew and flailed. Her legs bent and split open in a provocative squat. Her head shook up and down and all over the place, her long straight-haired wigs defiantly flying up and down with her. Her costumes were brief, with lots of tassels and fringe. She turned and twirled, leaped and skittered across the stage like a whirling dervish in search of salvation. During concerts she played with her audiences, temporarily slowing the tempo, saying softly, "And we're gonna do this easy." Then she would flash a wicked smile and add, "But we don't do nothin' nice and easy. We do things nice and rough." And then she would be off and at it again, stomping, jumping, humping like mad, lost in her own feverish high. Onstage, Turner was pure ritual, one of the great instinctive performers of her age. It never mattered what the words were. It was the sounds, the movements, the crazy world away from this world, a world of incessant delirious action, that Turner offered. Janis Joplin, who was far more commercial and who often said she had been influenced by Bessie Smith, actually owed much of her style to Turner.

Other predecessors to the upcoming disco craze were the sirens Labelle, the group known in the sixties as Patti LaBelle and The Bluebells. In the seventies the group—composed of Patti LaBelle, Sarah Dash, and Nona Hendryx—changed its name and revamped its image. The three came on in flamboyantly bizarre space-age outfits, sometimes singing songs mildly tinged with social protest. But mostly they performed numbers that touched on the need for inspired madness, controlled hysteria that also could offer escape from the social and political passivity of the Nixon and Ford years. The aftermath of Vietnam and the Watergate scandal seemed the last thing Labelle's audiences had on its mind. Instead, this futuristic campy trio offered a world where no one lived by the old values, where almost anything went, where pleasure came easily and perhaps danger too. Their biggest hit, the spicy and suggestive "Lady Marmalade," asked the question—of a stranger on the street—*Voulez-vous coucher avec moi ce soir?* This was a night, an adventure, that could lead anywhere. The group's mixture of heat, flash, and all-that-trash helped set the stage for the disco divas.

The androgynous Grace Jones: model turned disco queen.

DISCO DIVAS

Once the disco scene was established, the high priestess of those head emporiums were almost all black: Gloria Gaynor, Vicki Sue Robinson, Evelyn "Champagne" King, Linda Clifford, Amii Stewart, the singing group Sister Sledge, and the sublimely androgynous Grace Jones. While the music critics ignored or dismissed disco music as simply a passing fancy, an opiate for the dull-witted, alienated masses, these women led the chants, inviting huge audiences off on a journey. The message of the disco divas was: Get away from this troubled world and into another realm, explore the past, and search for the future. Music offered perfect escape, particularly electronically frenzied music presented in an atmosphere where everyone could escape together and have a sense of community. The discos also afforded everyone the chance to be special, to take off on a ritualized quest for self-expression. Here was a place where individuality was welcomed, where the more unconventional or freakier, the better. And if, with some luck and imagination, you were flashy enough, you could become, on your own terms, the very thing the mid and late seventies seemed most in awe of: a star. Without restraints in the way you looked or behaved, everybody could be a diva.

DONNA SUMMER: THE QUEEN OF DISCO

And, of course, from all this, there arose the seventies final significant pop star, the queen of disco herself, and a bona fide diva for her age, Donna Summer. Almost single-handedly, she not only articulated what was on the disco crowd's mind, but eventually made disco respectable, legitimized it in serious pop music circles, and extended its range.

In some respects Donna Summer may also be the appropriate epilogue for the dark diva's story. In her style and her career were embodied the triumphs and tensions that had been part of past diva history. Like Baker, she was also a great success abroad before she was recognized in her own country.

In 1967 eighteen-year-old LaDonna Gaines left her home in Boston, auditioned for the Munich-based production of *Hair* and soon appeared in a major role in the play. While in Germany, she briefly married an Austrian actor, Herbert Sommer (later she Anglicized her new last name), had a daughter Mimi, then was cutting records. Two of her singles went gold abroad. Then she cut "Love to Love You, Baby," a basic rhythm track in which she seemed mostly to moan and groan, caught up in the ecstasy of sexual climax. All in all, *Time* reported, there were twenty-two orgasms on the record. No matter what the actual count, "Love to Love You, Baby" crossed the ocean and became an international hit, propelling Summer to instant fame.

She returned to the States, but no one was ready to take her seriously. For she was a sight to behold. Her puffed-out, blowy hair ballooned to the point of no return. Her eyes were always half closed. Her legs were hotly exposed. Her mouth was a ripe sexual instrument, sensually opening and closing, the tongue forever in motion across the lips. And her hands did overtime with the mike stand, so much so that *Rolling Stone* wrote that she came "damn close to copulating" with it, "writhing up and down its length with palpable shivers." There was no sex queen like this one. Dubbed the First Lady of Lust, she was part burlesque, part camp, part absurd.

The whole sex business, Summer later said, had been a gimmick, a commercial device to get her over. When some of it backfired, she was openly shaken. Even the reactions of the disco crowd, which idolized her, hurt at times because she was taken too seriously as a sexual myth. She was what she sang, the crowd assumed. Radio

LaDonna Gaines ran off to Europe to appear in *Hair*, recorded "Love to Love You, Baby," and became known as Donna Summer, "First Lady of Lust."

stations played her record at midnight, inviting listeners to have "seventeen minutes of love with Donna Summer." Stories circulated that "Love to Love You, Baby" had actually been recorded when her producers slipped into her apartment and simply placed recording devices under her bed while Donna and a partner were in it. There were other rumors. *Ebony* even ran a cover story on Summer with the headline: "Donna Summer talks about...the rumor that hurts her deeply." One story had it that Donna Summer was really a man in drag, a lusty female impersonator. Another said she was a transsexual.

Worse for Summer was the way critics repeatedly dismissed her. She fought hard to branch out and develop. When she appeared in the 1978 film *Thank God It's Friday,* the *New York Times* movie critic wrote: "Miss Summer, whose wigs are as elaborate as Diana Ross's, is competition for the superb Miss Ross in no department other than hair." Of course, simply because she was a black singer, Summer had been considered Ross's rival. Actually, the women were different types with different audiences. (Diana Ross eventually sang disco songs, but not out of any great rivalry with Summer; she simply wanted to be in tune with the latest trend in popular music.)

The pressures and tensions took their toll on Summer. The grinding tours and hassles of the music world rattled her nerves. Headaches and insomnia set in. Once she boarded an airplane gasping for breath and was given oxygen, then carried away. "Sometimes it gets to the point where you've been pushed for so long," she once said, "by those motorous, monstrous forces, this whole production of people and props that you're responsible for, by audiences and everything that trouble you, until you take it upon yourself to be a *machine.* And at some point a machine breaks down. I feel like I want to cry most of the time and just get rid of it, but sometimes I get so pent up, I can't. And that's when I get afraid."

She survived the tensions, releasing ambitious new albums, notably *Once Upon a Time,* a concept album that transformed the Cinderella story into a tale about an urban girl who does indeed find her dream prince. It marked a new artistic direction for Summer. Gradually, in television appearances, Summer's style was modified. The gowns became longer, sleeker, more sophisticated. The puffy hairdo was modified too. The moans and groans were toned down. But Summer herself seemed girlish, a bit awkward and wide-eyed, and when she talked, it was not the voice of a siren, but that of a vulnerable, slightly uneasy young woman as anxious to please as a Monroe.

By the end of the seventies her albums *Donna Summer Live* and *Bad Girls* shot to the top of the record charts. Even the critics did an about-face. In December 1977, John Rockwell wrote in the *New York Times:* "Miss

Donna Summer emerged as a polished star who extended the range of disco music and forced critics to take it *and her* seriously.

Summer has...built a real career for herself as both a singer and as someone pushing the formal boundaries of disco music even wider."

Almost exactly a year later in December 1978, Rockwell wrote of her again:

> As a disco singer, however, Miss Summer has a genuine ability to phrase with conviction. The form may seem rudimentary, but there's a gift to projecting personality on top of such a strong, structurally rigid instrumental base, and Miss Summer's success suggests that critics may have been shortsighted or premature to ignore disco as they have done.

Still later, Rockwell said of Summer's "Hot Stuff": "There hasn't been such confident all-stops-out vocalism of this sort since the best days of Aretha Franklin."

AND SO WHAT GOES AROUND COMES AROUND

onna Summer simply continued a tradition that reaches back to the days of Ma Rainey, Bessie Smith, Josephine Baker, and Ethel Waters. From the early days of the twentieth-century to the present, America's dark divas kept us dazzled with their energy, their control, their haughtiness, and their optimism. They all began their careers knowing they were thought of as the Other, the Dark Mysterious Side of Experience. And they knew too that they were considered the sexiest of forbidden fruit. Like her predecessors, Donna Summer played on such notions and used her style to become an international star. But she also used the disco sounds and the sexy image to make personal statements to her followers. She stood as one of them, basically a good-natured urban girl who had grown up with the same problems they had had. She understood their alienation and need for escape. And she was ready to lead them on a journey of fun. Having started off as a sexy joke, she ended up as a well-liked entertainer who had contributed much to the flavor of American popular culture and who had answered specific needs of her age. What Summer did in the seventies was not much different from what Josephine Baker did for the disillusioned postwar Europeans of the twenties.

Decade after decade, America's dark divas were always able to go beneath the misconceptions their culture had about them as black women. They came up with personal visions of what life could—and did—mean. Ethel Waters' early raunchy ghetto heroine said life was damn tough, but that she was determined to get through it anyway, even if it did mean she had a chip on her shoulder. Josephine Baker and Diana Ross, who had grown up on ghetto streets just as mean and hard as Ethel's, always had such unreal energy and drive that we knew immediately here were women who could never be kept in their place. We admired their guts and determination to fulfill themselves, no matter what, and to have some fun too. Cicely Tyson, in her early television roles and in films, was so rigid in her refusal to compromise or play herself cheap that we saw the beauty of having convictions and of holding on to ideals. Marian Anderson showed us that even under the most difficult situation, grace and poise could see us through. Pearl Bailey said a good laugh never hurts. Aretha Franklin let us know that life was richer and fuller if we learned to feel, to go all the way with our emotions. The talents of these women kept us entertained. Their personal styles kept us informed of who they were.

Many had troubled lives. Several ended up tragically. When we looked at their experiences—their joys as well as their heartaches—we were forced to ask fundamental questions about the society and country in which they—and we—lived. When she was not permitted to sing at Constitution Hall, Marian Anderson made us realize it was not just her problem; it concerned every one of us. Through socially troubled times, the divas were always around, ready to whisper secrets to us. No matter what their personal problems, they made us forget ours. Or they made us think all our problems could be worked out. Whether they served as pop myths, social symbols, sex symbols, political symbols, or as survivors, they enriched our lives and became cultural icons for various eras. Most important, because they were indeed black beauties, they were an uncanny source of inspiration.

All the black goddess had to say was that she was *weary* or *so tired* or *feeling so gooooood* and automatically the words meant something far different than when uttered by anyone else. Because we knew it had been harder for these black women to make themselves heard in a white world. Yet they overcame the obstacles.

And so when the houselights dimmed and it was time for the blues sister or the colored chorus girl or the girl-singer or the girl group to take her place and do her bit, the woman went forward. City, country, continent, it never mattered. We were always by her side. And as we swayed and hummed or had private dreams of our own, we were glad we were there. For through her magic, she made her story ours.

BIBLIOGRAPHY

Albertson, Chris. *Bessie.* New York: Stein and Day, 1972.

Anderson, Marian. *My Lord, What a Morning.* New York: Viking, 1956.

Bailey, Pearl. *The Raw Pearl.* New York: Harcourt, Brace & World, 1968.

Baker, Josephine, and Bouillon, Jo. *Josephine.* New York: Harper & Row, 1977.

Bogle, Donald. *Toms, Coons, Mulattoes, Mammies, & Bucks.* New York: Viking, 1973.

Calloway, Cab, and Rollins, Bryant. *Of Minnie the Moocher & Me.* New York: Thomas Y. Crowell Company, 1976.

Chilton, John. *Billie's Blues: The Billie Holiday Story 1933–1959.* New York: Stein and Day, 1975.

Cook, Bruce. *Listen to the Blues.* New York: Charles Scribner's Sons, 1973.

Dandridge, Dorothy, and Conrad, Earl. *Everything and Nothing: The Dorothy Dandridge Story.* New York: Abelard-Schuman, 1970.

Dunham, Katherine. *Journey to Accompong.* New York: Henry Holt & Company, 1946.

———. *A Touch of Innocence.* New York: Harcourt, Brace & World, 1959.

Ellington, Duke. *Music Is My Mistress.* Garden City, New York: Doubleday & Company, 1973.

Flanner, Janet, edited by Irving Drutman. *Paris Was Yesterday.* New York: Viking, 1972.

Gleason, Ralph J. *Celebrating the Duke & Louis, Bessie, Billie, Bird, Carmen, Miles, Dizzy & Other Heroes.* New York: Delta Books, 1976.

Hammond, John. *On Record.* New York: Ridge Press, 1977.

Holiday, Billie, and Dufty, William. *Lady Sings the Blues.* New York: Doubleday & Company, 1956.

Horne, Lena, and Schickel, Richard. *Lena.* Garden City, New York: Doubleday & Company, 1965.

Houseman, John. *Run-Through.* New York: Simon and Schuster, 1972.

Hughes, Langston, and Meltzer, Milton. *Black Magic: A Pictorial History of the Negro in American Entertainment.* Englewood Cliffs, New Jersey: Prentice-Hall, 1967.

Jackson, Mahalia, and Wylie, Evan McLeod. *Movin' on Up.* New York: Hawthorn Books, 1966.

Johnson, James Weldon. *Black Manhattan.* New York: Atheneum, 1968.

Jones, LeRoi. *Blues People.* New York: William Morrow and Company, 1963.

Kimball, Robert, and Bolcum, William. *Reminiscing with Sissle and Blake.* New York: Viking, 1973.

Kitt, Eartha. *Alone with Me.* Chicago: Henry Regncry Company, 1976.

———. *Thursday's Child.* New York: Ducil, Sloan & Pearce, 1956.

Mills, Earl. *Dorothy Dandridge: A Portrait in Black.* Los Angeles: Holloway Publishing Company, 1970.

Morse, David. *Motown.* New York: Collier Books, 1971.

Murray, Albert. *Stomping the Blues.* New York: McGraw-Hill Book Company, 1976.

Nicholas, A.X. *The Poetry of Soul.* New York: Bantam Books, 1971.

Shaw, Arnold. *Honkers and Shouters.* New York: Macmillan Publishing Company, 1978.

Short, Bobby. *Black and White Baby.* New York: Dodd, Mead, and Company, 1971.

Stewart-Baxter, Derrick. *Ma Rainey and the Classic Blues Singers.* New York: Stein and Day, 1970.

Waters, Ethel, and Samuels, Charles. *His Eye Is on the Sparrow.* New York: Doubleday & Company, 1950.

INDEX